Roads & Trackways

of

Wales

Richard Moore-Colyer

Above: The former Gorphwysfa Hotel, now Pen-y-Pass Youth Hostel, above Llanberis, once a famous hotel for visitors, climbers and weary travellers

Left: The former drovers road above Rowen village, descending towards the Talycafn Ferry across the River Conwy

ROADS & TRACKWAYS
of
WALES

Richard Moore-Colyer

Published by

Landmark Publishing Ltd
Ashbourne Hall, Cokayne Ave, Ashbourne, Derbyshire DE6 1EJ England
Tel: (01335) 347349 Fax: (01335) 347303
e-mail: landmark@clara.net
web site: www.landmarkpublishing.co.uk

ISBN 1 84306 019 1

British Library Cataloguing in Publication Data: a catalogue
record for this book is available from the British Library.

Print: MPG Ltd, Bodmin, Cornwall
Design: Mark Titterton
Cover by James Allsopp

Front cover: Telford's famous suspension bridge at Conwy

Back cover: The 15th Century Groes Inn, which claims to be the oldest licensed property in Wales (1573),
at the meeting of the Conwy – Llanrwst road and the road to the Talycafn ferry

Page 1: Radnorshire Arms, Presteigne, dating from 1616,
on the road to England

Title page: Pont Scethin on the old road from Harlech to London,
now the preserve of ramblers and sheep

Photograph Credits: By the author and CLM Porter

CONTENTS

PREFACE
TO THE SECOND EDITION

At the time this book was written life for a young member of staff in a British university was good. The jealously-guarded principles of academic freedom meant that within reasonable limits a lecturer could choose his own research area and pursue it at a pace commensurate with his aptitude, enthusiasm and degree of ambition. Teaching loads were light, and those being taught were by and large intelligent, highly-motivated and well-prepared by their schools. Provided the academic published regularly his findings in reputable peer-reviewed learned journals he was largely free to indulge in non-scholarly *divertissements* of which this book is a prime example. It would probably not have been written by a member of a university staff today. Academic freedom, as we knew it twenty years ago has virtually evaporated in the face of an official obsession with bureaucratically-driven accountability, limitations of funding and the alarming demands of the quinquennial Research Assessment Exercise. Concurrently, as departments have been closed, posts been frozen, and student numbers dramatically increased, many (if not most) universities have adopted a modular teaching system whose merits are, to say the least, debatable. The upshot of all this is that while the output of scholarly writing within the fields of Welsh history and historical geography has expanded impressively over the past two decades, so concentrated have minds become by the rigours of research assessment, that with a few notable exceptions academic writers have steered clear of local history issues. Happily, however, local history remains very much alive among those many amateur historians whose lively, scholarly and meticulously-researched articles grace the pages of the Welsh periodical literature. Long may they flourish!

When *Roads and Trackways of Wales* first appeared I received a number of letters from both amateur and professional historians critical of some of my observations, especially in the opening chapter dealing with aspects of the Roman road network. Some of my correspondents subsequently broke into print and I have included their works (which, in some cases, modify my own conclusions and elsewhere confirm my speculations) in the 'Further Reading' list towards the end of the book. Surprisingly enough, when I came to read through the whole volume for the first time in many years and to relate it to more recently-published material, I could find little reason for making major textual changes. Accordingly, beyond a few minor corrections and an expanded bibliography, this edition remains much as it was in 1984. The first edition, though generally favourably reviewed was, I fear, very poorly produced in terms of layout, design and clarity of print and I was delighted when Lindsey Porter of Landmark Publishing approached me over a second edition. I can only hope, as I suggested in the first edition, that readers will use the book as a travelling companion and, perhaps contribute to the local historiography on their own account. They will forgive me, I am sure, for using imperial measurements throughout, but for those too young to remember the glory days pre-metrication, the following conversions should suffice:

> 1 yard = 3 feet = 0.9144 metre
> 1 acre = 4840 square yards = 0.405 hectare
> 1 pound (£) = 20 shillings = 100 pence
> 1 shilling (s) = 5 pence
> 1 penny (d) = 0.42 pence

Richard Moore-Colyer

PREFACE

To date no book dealing exclusively with the history and development of the Welsh road network has appeared in English. The very extensive corpus of local history writing contains frequent references to the road system at various stages of its development, as do several scholarly works concerned with the social and economic history of the Principality. Yet many, if not most of these are not immediately accessible to the general reader unless he has the time and the inclination to wander along the shelves of the public library and to search among innumerable indices. One of the objectives of the present volume has been to disinter some of this material and, by studying in detail an admittedly narrow range of roads of different periods, to provide an introduction to the Welsh road network. It claims to be little more than an introduction, for in a book of this size it is quite impossible to deal with more than a very modest area of the country. The industrial south and west and the counties of the north-east are largely ignored and I have tended, unashamedly, to concentrate my attention on those parts of Wales which give me most pleasure and which offer the traveller a rich extrava-ganza of scenic delights.

The roads described are a minute fraction of the thousands of miles of highway, lane and trackway through deep valley and open mountain, linking remote villages or isolated farm-steads, running grandly along riversides, or snaking sinuously through the hills. Some have experienced moments of great drama, others have been immemorially the humble channels of local trade; the haunt of farmer's cart, brewer's dray and pedlar's footfall. Yet all repay close investigation. The farmsteads, churches, wells and houses along a particular roadline – however humble at first glance – can provide the enthusiast with hours of pleasant diversion. A rather plain Victorian farmhouse may turn out to be built on the foundations of a much earlier and grander edifice, which may itself have been preceded by a settlement of medieval date, if not earlier. To the observant traveller prepared to do a little documentary research, a journey along a road can yield valuable insight into the social and economic history of the countryside so that the drudgery of walking the dog or of easing off an ample Sunday lunch can become a mini-voyage of discovery. To schoolchildren, history and geography and the natural environment can be brought thrillingly to life if they are freed temporarily from the classroom and taken for an afternoon's walk along one of the more dramatic mountain roads. I hope, then, that my readers, be they local historians, teachers or students, will be persuaded to arm themselves with OS: 50,000 maps (or maps of larger scale), liberate themselves from the shackles of their cars and savour the pleasures of Wales on foot. If they take issue with some of the observations and conclusions in the forthcoming chapters then so much the better, since the study of the history of Welsh roads can only benefit from informed debate. I have approached the subject in a fairly conventional manner, beginning with a consideration of elements of the Roman network and working my way through to the turnpike system. However, I have not allowed myself to be altogether limited by considerations of chronology and where an interesting feature from another period occurs, say, alongside a Roman road, I have drawn attention to it. I hasten to point out, too, that I am well aware that the existence of an ancient church or field monument does not necessarily proclaim the antiquity of the road or trackway passing alongside it!

I have avoided footnotes in the text on the grounds that the 'general reader' tends to ignore them while the specialist, in any case, is normally familiar with the literature. Besides, this is an introductory book, compiled in the hope that others, working in detail on a local basis, will enlarge upon it and publish their findings, footnotes and all, in the scholarly journals. Many scholars, local historians and antiquarians will recognise their studies in the forthcoming pages and I apologise to any of these luminaries whose name fails to appear in the bibliography. Any such omission reflects my own incompetence and in no measure detracts from the importance and quality of their work. I must apologise too, to any purists who quibble with my rendering of Welsh place-names. I have been guided by Elwyn Davies' splendid *A Gazetteer of Welsh Place-Names* (Cardiff 1975) so that any orthographical inexactitudes in the text may be ascribed to my inaccurate reading of that highly authoritative volume. Throughout the book I have adhered to pre-1974 county names on the grounds of both aesthetics and convenience.

I must acknowledge the help and critical advice of numerous friends and colleagues who, at one time or another, have commented on the contents of the forthcoming chapters. I am especially grateful in this regard to Professor D.J. Bowen, Mr D.M. Browne, Dr J.L Davies, Dr C.S. Briggs, Professor R.A. Dodgshon and Dr M. Haycock, while I owe a particular debt of gratitude to Mr. J.J. Wells who has been responsible for the fine cartographic work throughout the book. To the Librarian and staff of the National Library of Wales I am particularly grateful and to the Vice-Principal of the University College of Wales I extend my thanks for financial assistance towards the cost of fieldwork and photographic materials. Finally, I must thank Mrs P. Mason, Mrs E.D. Thomas and Miss S. Jones who struggled with the desperate and depressing task of translating my handwriting into immaculate typescript. The aerial photographs on pages 27, 28 and 41 and 53 appear by courtesy of the University of Cambridge and those on pages 45, 83, 97, 108, 111, 129, 132, 133, 138, 141, 146, 153, 157, 167 and 171 by courtesy of the National Library of Wales. The remaining photographs are by the author and C.L.M Porter.

Richard Moore-Colyer

O happie princely soyle, my pen is farre to bace,
My bare invention cold, and barraine verses vaine,
When they thy glory should unfold, they do thy Countrie staine.
Thy worth some worthie may, set out in golden lines,
And blaze ye same with colours gay, whose glistring beautie shines.
My boldness was too great, to take the charge in hand,
With wasted wits the braines to beat, to write on such a Land.

Thomas Churchyard
The Worthiness of Wales, 1587

To the late Victorians civilisation flowed down the railway lines. Through the enormous expanses of sun-baked India, the massive emptiness of Canada's interior and the fabulous mysteries of Africa, Imperial rolling stock carried bicycles from Birmingham, bibles from east London and billhooks from Sheffield. Young men, too, fresh from comfortable villas in the Home Counties, their faces still pink and hands still soft, travelled hopefully down the iron roads towards unimaginable adventures . The London mandarins shouldering the heavy responsibility for Britain's embarrassingly expansive Empire genuinely believed that these youthful recruits would bring light to the Imperial darkness by promoting stable government, commerce and Christianity. Accordingly they viewed the railways as the great thoroughfares of western civilisation; of laws, of culture, of tiffin and cricket. Accompanied (often with disastrous consequences) by their starched and crinollined memsahibs, the young Victorians carried with them a system of culture and a moral code which had been many generations in the making. Neolithic farmers and their Bronze Age successors, embattled Iron Age tribesmen, lusty Saxon or Scandinavian sea-raiders and stern Normans, all contributed some minute element to the social and cultural makeup of the representative of the *Pax Britannica* who emerged from his train to blink in the harsh sunlight of India. To the native porters, if not to the French *boulevardiers* among whom he had spent his final vacation from Oxford, he was the epitome of civilised values.

It had taken the best part of ten millennia for the British to become an immensely successful Imperial power and throughout those long centuries, like the railways which they later built with such remarkable skill, roads and highways played a fundamental role in the development of the offshore island. Bronze and iron craft skills permeated southern Britain by way of sinuous tracks through the countryside, just as wine and olive oil from the Mediterranean reached the towns and villas of Roman Britain. Like the Dark Age Celtic missionaries landing on the rain-swept coastline of Wales, St Augustine would have had no difficulty in finding some sort of roadway through sixth-century Kent, even if, un-Christianlike, he cursed its poor condition. Pilgrims, pedlars, bards, thieves and civic dignitaries probably followed the same trackways (some of them along remaining stretches of the Roman road system) during the medieval and early modern periods while farmers drove their livestock along 'ways' established generations previously. Inevitably the forging of a 'way' heralded the onset of trade and the influx of external cultural influences. There was virtually no stopping them for, as we see today, only in the most remote and inaccessible regions of the world, like Amazonia and the mountains of western New Guinea, has the concept of external trade failed to develop. In Britain the ultimate expression of the road as a stimulus to trade and economic growth lay in the turnpikes whose steady gradients and 'metalled' surfaces facilitated the ready distribution of the manufactured goods of the early phases of the Industrial Revolution and the more effective movement of agricultural inputs and produce. Equally important, they allowed men to move about relatively rapidly and in comparative safety; the tradesman to his fair or market, the politician to his country weekend and the sporting gentleman to the fox-ridden Shires.

But how did it start? What was the origin of the trackways which already curved through the countryside of Britain by the Neolithic age? The short answer is that we don't really know and archaeologists and prehistorians have been distinctly reluctant to speculate upon this matter. However, where material evidence is non-existent or fragmentary, we must necessarily have recourse to intelligent speculation, in spite of the objections of those who believe that such speculation should never be made in the absence of documentary or, at the very least, artefactual evidence.

We can say with some certainty that with the recession of the third phase of the last glaciation, more or less complete by about 12,000BC, the climate gradually improved and tundra conditions gave way to scrublands of alder and hazel, and dense woodlands of birch and pine. Within this rather bleak environment, Mesolithic man, equipped with a wide range of flint implements, survived by way of hunting animals and gathering berries, roots and other natural products. Paleozoologists and archaeologists are now largely unanimous in the belief that hunting was by no means a random and haphazard operation, and that groups of Mesolithic hunters took great care in the selection of their prey so as to ensure that sufficient mature breeding animals survived to maintain stocks. In other words, they behaved in a similar manner to present-day sportsmen who will usually kill off surplus cock pheasants and avoid shooting hen birds in the latter part of the season. It seems, moreover, that our Mesolithic ancestors were able to exercise a considerable degree of control over the movements of their prey by the creation of carefully-planned fire-cleared areas in the forest. Fire clearance had the effect of stimulating new and highly digestible herbage growth to which deer, wild pigs and other grazing and rooting animals were fatally attracted. To the hunter this offered two major advantages. By positioning the cleared area close to his camp he was spared the fatiguing business of carrying his quarry over long distances, and in addition he could now be even more selective as to the animals he killed since he no longer had to wander around the forest on the off-chance of finding the odd animal, but now had an ample supply of game close to hand. Incidentally, fire clearing would have stimulated hazel growth and hence have produced a ready supply of nuts for direct human consumption. It is likely too, that the creation of fire clearings provided opportunities for cooperative hunting ventures - and, no doubt, for friction between neighbouring groups of hunters.

Previously, hunting had been merely a matter of following animals along their natural migration routes which, in view of the tendency of herbivores to graze as they move, would have become broad trackways through the forest. Anyone who has driven cattle or sheep over long distances cannot fail to he impressed by their habit of spreading out over a wide area and grabbing a bite of herbage whenever the opportunity arises. Is it possible then, that in these migration routes we see the basis of some of the earliest roadlines, with animal trackways to fire-cleared areas providing further elements in a 'road' network? To the present author at least this model seems quite plausible and it may not be stretching credibility too far to argue that by late Mesolithic times a framework of tracks, maintained by the movements of animals and men, had been established throughout much of Britain.

Although there is a school of thought which holds that the indigenous Mesolithic inhabitants were making tentative beginnings at simple animal husbandry, there can be no doubt that it was the Neolithic farmers who possessed both the technology and the will to convert large expanses of the natural wildwood into productive farming land. Indeed, recent archaeological discoveries are emphasising the remarkable extent to which Neolithic and Bronze Age

Sarn Helen above Llanfair Clydogau

communities overcame the limits imposed by the environment. The older archaeology taught us that Neolithic settlement was limited to the higher chalk and limestone uplands where people lived in rather spartan conditions overlooking the dark, impenetrable and potentially hostile forests of the plains . However, developments in archaeological techniques and dating methods, together with a series of dry summers in the 1970's wherein aerial photography revealed hitherto unidentified sites, has allowed archaeologists to elaborate a very different picture of the prehistoric landscape. With the important *caveat* that there were local and regional variations, we must now see the centuries between 4,000 and 2,000BC as a period of substantial increase in population and social organisation with large tracts of land in both the 'lowland' and 'highland' zones being cleared and intensively farmed. Heavy clayland and light sand, high plain and deep valley bottom, in fact virtually anywhere where the environment was suited to farming, all seem to have been settled at some stage and by 600-500BC farmsteads were widespread in England and Wales on all but the highest and bleakest of hills.

Careful examination of the agricultural technology available at the time has established that by the Iron Age, man was quite capable of cultivating most soil types, including the most intractable clays. Even with the prevailing 'primitive' cereal varieties, there seems to have been at least a *potential* for surplus production so that it may no longer be strictly accurate to talk of the landscape of the immediate pre-Roman period as being dominated by 'subsistence' farming. This may apply equally in some upland and marginal areas of Britain, where the remnants of prehistoric arable field systems often survive in a predominantly pastoral landscape originally of Dark Age provenance.

Between the farmsteads and hamlets, perhaps superimposed on tracks already of great antiquity, lines of communication developed so that by the Roman conquest the countryside was already served by a network of 'proto-roads'. This being so, it has become necessary to review the importance of the so-called 'Ridgeways': the 'Jurassic Way', the 'Icknield Way' and the other prehistoric hill-top thoroughfares previously regarded as the major (and by some the sole) lines of communication in pre-Roman Britain. As Christopher Taylor has pointed out, important as these were, they were merely part of a complex pattern of trackways reaching out to virtually every corner of the country.

Knowing of the existence of these trackways is one thing; recognizing them on the ground is quite another matter. Many were transient drift ways between farmsteads and field systems, occasionally highlighted today on aerial photographs, while the more important long distance ways were used by subsequent generations so that all trace of their beginnings is lost. Indeed, it may be that many of our village lanes and even some of our arterial roads had their origins in tracks along which prehistoric men, perhaps trading flint or chert axes, skins or amber, warily picked their way. As with farm hand-tools, many of them evolving their basic structure in the Bronze and Iron Ages and changing only marginally before the Industrial Revolution, the idea of continuity is central to a consideration of the evolution of roads. Once a 'way' became established, its general line would be used over the centuries, though its actual course came to vary according to the type of traffic it carried and to locally changing patterns of land occupation and ownership.

In common with the rest of Britain, continuity of use through centuries, if not millennia, is a feature of roads in Wales. The Iron Age tribesman left his well-defended hill fort on the same track used by his medieval descendants and so on down through the ages until its curves and bends were rationalised by the measuring chains and levels of the eighteenth- and nineteenth-century turnpike surveyors. It is this very continuity which makes the precise dating of the origin of a given road so difficult, and this may go some way towards explaining the sparseness of the scholarly literature on the road system for the centuries between the departure of the Romans and the development of turnpiking. For Wales, at least, there are few reliable maps before the seventeenth century, while the early literary sources, though frequently providing a valuable impressionistic view of the countryside, cast little light on the detailed courses of roads. Medieval documents relating to estate boundaries and land settlement are helpful in working out short stretches of a road as it passes through a village or township as are the later estate maps, Enclosure Awards and Tithe Apportionments, used extensively in the present volume. To the meticulous local scholar some of the content of the medieval chapter in this volume will seem highly unsatisfactory in that time limitations and the broad scope of the book have precluded detailed study of the medieval material located in the bowels of the National Library of Wales and other depositories. I can only hope that this deficiency will serve to focus the attention of antiquaries upon the need for further study of the elements of the early road network in Wales.

Place and field names, place-name elements and a strong body of local tradition provide useful clues, if not to the origin, at least to the purpose of a particular road at a given stage of its history. To the contemporary Englishman the pronunciation of Welsh words often presents prodigious difficulties. To his forbears, employed as Enclosure or Tithe commissioners, as estate agents or bailiffs, enunciation of the words was a minor problem compared to the awesome business of committing them to paper. This led inevitably to quite remarkable corruptions, necessitating a cautious approach to, for example, the interpretation of field names on a Tithe Apportionment, many of them bearing little relation to their original meaning. The pioneering work of Melville Richards showed the enormous potential of the study of place names as a means of hanging flesh on the bare bones of documentary and archaeological evidence.

Aerial photography and a laudable increase in the rate of excavation is at last beginning gradually to lift the veil from the obscurity shrouding our knowledge of the landscape and economy of immediate pre-Roman Wales. Given the nature of the evidence it is perilous to generalise, yet we can state with some confidence that a great deal of the countryside was settled by farmers, their dwellings being constructed of stone, timber, or wattle-and-daub depending upon local availability of materials. Overlooked by the local hill fort - a vital refuge in time of crisis for both men and livestock - the Celtic farmer in the lowlands cultivated permanent arable fields to provide grains and pulses for household consumption and perhaps even for the subsistence of those of his breeding livestock which he chose to maintain over winter. During the summer months he drove his cattle to graze the hills and in so doing probably passed over the remnants of the attempts of his Bronze Age ancestors to establish permanent farmsteads on the uplands. Sadly, their efforts were ultimately overwhelmed by a heartbreaking combination of acidic soils and wet climate and the remains of their settlement sites were taken over by later generations of pastoralists.

The constant struggle to farm was made more difficult by the need to be forever on guard against the avaricious attentions of the neighbours across the river or on the other side of the oak coppice, and as he applied his hand to the plough or seed basket, our farmer would have ensured that his weapons were never far away. Moreover, he would be called upon to use these same weapons from time to time in the service of his clan chief. Like the Saxons and Scandinavians of a later date then, the Iron Age tribesman was concurrently a farmer and a fighting man, loyal to his chief and subject to the will of a curious pantheon of rather nasty gods. It was against such men that the Imperial legions of Rome were obliged to try their strength as they faced the moist west wind and advanced bravely into the Welsh heartland.

1 THE ROMANS IN THE MID-WEST

I love roads:
The goddesses that dwell
Far along them invisible
Are my favourite gods.

Edward Thomas (1878-1917), *Roads*

Beyond the rich plains of England the Romans first encountered the forest and mountain peoples of Wales. Isolated, except in the borderlands, from the influence of the Belgic communities in south-east England, and out of contact with the cross-channel trade so important to cultural developments in that part of Britain, most of the Welsh tribes, in terms of material culture at least, were in a relatively primitive state on the eve of the Roman conquest. Much of Wales lay, in what has become termed the 'highland zone'. Here mountain barriers, moorland bogs and rapidly-flowing rivers combined to produce an environment which was a positive godsend to the guerilla fighter, as the Romans were to learn to their cost. Struggling against the rigours of a damp climate, and more often than not, belligerent neighbours, the tribesman wrested a living from the stony, acidic and unrewarding soil. The deeper into the mountains he lived, the greater the likelihood of his farming tools and implements being made of stone and bronze, since in some areas iron tools were even now regarded as a luxury. While he may have grown a limited quantity of corn for his household and animals our tribesman, in the upland zone at any rate, was essentially a pastoralist living in a small, strongly defended homestead, an 'open' settlement, or one of the many hill forts some of which continued to be occupied well into the Roman period. From around settlements like Tre'r Ceiri in Caernarfonshire, a hill fort densely occupied with huts, the Welsh farmed their lands and mounted sporadic campaigns against the Romans for whom they were to remain a thorn in the flesh for several decades after the initial invasion.

Of the five great Welsh tribes, perhaps the most formidable were the ruddy, curly-haired Silures who held strongholds in the Black Mountains and also occupied one of the few extensive tracts of fertile, easily-workable land in Wales: the coastal plains of Glamorgan and Monmouthshire. To the north, in the hilly terrain of mid-Wales, the powerful and warlike Ordovices held sway, keeping a watchful eye on their neighbours the Gangani who, according to Ptolemy, spent their lives on the remote Llŷn Peninsula. Further north still, in the mineral-rich countryside of Flintshire, lived the Decangli, while the vales of the Tywi and Teifi and the foothills of the Cambrian Mountains were the province of the Demetae.

During the early stages of their campaign to subdue the Welsh, the Romans do not seem to have conceived any grand overall plan, preferring instead to deal with each tribal insurrection as it occurred. They had optimistically believed that morale among the tribes would crumble following the defeat of Caractacus' armies in AD51. Despite this victory and the delivery of Caractacus himself into Roman hands by the treachery of the Queen of the Brigantes, the Ordovices (and to a lesser extent the Silures), continued to offer spirited resistance and vigorously defied Roman attempts to penetrate their territory.

This seems to have steeled Roman resolve and in AD60 Suetonius Paulinus, a seasoned African campaigner, marched against the rebellious Ordovices, taking with him the young Agricola who was to become Governor of Britain twenty years later. Paulinus' main objective was the Druidic stronghold on Anglesey. By wiping out the Druids he believed that he would at one and the same time obliterate a source of material resistance and a cult of great ritual significance. The Romans, as Gibbon tells us, generally adopted a liberal attitude towards the religious observances of their subject peoples. Their own enthusiasm for blood-letting in the interests of entertainment was well developed, yet they found the Druidic practice of using human victims for sacrifice and augury especially repulsive and were unswerving in their determination to destroy the cult. Such edifying thoughts may have passed through the minds of the legionaries as they marched towards the Menai Straits and, like Cromwell's Ironsides approaching a lovely village church, they probably relished the prospect of pulling down the Druids' sacred groves. As they began to cross the Straights in their flat-bottomed boats they were confronted by the blood-chilling sight of Druidic elders pouring terrible curses upon them and, as Tacitus explains '... the British army in dense array and lots of black-robed women brandishing torches, their hair dishevelled like Furies'. For a moment it was touch and go, the superstitious Roman troops being terrified by the appalling curses of the formidable Druids. Once they had landed on the Anglesey beaches, though, they recovered their composure and professionalism, and having launched their attack achieved an overwhelming victory . It was now merely a matter of mopping up odd pockets of resistance before establishing firm control over the island.

Before the accession of Flavius Vespasianus to the Imperial throne in AD69, the Romans seem to have lacked the determination to get on with the job and subdue Britain once and for all, their activities being characterized by protracted fighting and stop-go policies. The Flavian period, however, was in marked contrast and after they had rehabilitated those parts of Britain ravaged by the Boudiccan revolt, the military commanders took the decision to grasp the nettle and commit resources to the final conquest and subjugation of the northern island. It was within this political climate that the completion of the conquest of Wales was undertaken in AD74-78 by Julius Frontinus, Governor of Britain and his successor in that post, Julius Agricola. Druidic influence had been destroyed, yet the mountain ranges of Snowdonia and the Berwyns still offered succour to the violently anti-Roman Ordovices. Probably operating from the massive fortress of *Deva* (Chester) or even *Virconium* (Wroxeter) and making full use of the garrison facilities which he had established on the periphery of Ordovician territory, Agricola led a punitive force against the enemy in AD78. He was intent on exacting terrible revenge on the Ordovices who had virtually annihilated a Roman cavalry regiment the previous year. Ordering his men to give no quarter, he exterminated almost the whole tribe and followed up his victory by establishing a series of subsidiary military stations.

Even before Agricola's successes in North Wales, Julius Frontinus had advanced into Silurian country where he founded a system of forts based on *Isca* (Caerleon). This became the headquarters of the Second Legion and for long remained the centre of the Roman south-western command and a point of contact with the civil zone across the River Severn. In contrast to the situation in the uplands which essentially remained 'undeveloped' throughout the Roman period, the vales of Glamorgan and Monmouth offered opportunities for urban and agricultural development and in due course villas and rural estates began to mushroom under the protection of garrisons at Cardiff, Caerleon and elsewhere.

Unlike the Ordovices and the Silures, the Demetae in the south-west may grudgingly have accepted Roman rule, perhaps as a means of gaining protection from harassment by their Silurian neighbours. Certainly there are very few signs of military settlement in Demetian territory (and hence a paucity of Roman roads) while sites like Castell Gogan between the estuaries of the Tywi and Taff, and Coygan near Laugharne suggest, as do other excavated native sites, strong evidence of Romanization. It is important to appreciate, however, that the apparent lack of military fortifications does not necessarily reflect ready acceptance of the conquerors by a timid native tribe and may with equal likelihood be a manifestation of Roman military strategy. The relative sophistication of recently-discovered native sites in the lower-lying areas runs counter to Sir Mortimer Wheeler's observation back in the 1930s, that the native peasantry of this part of Wales had little real contact with the Roman world. In particular, excavation of elements of the fine Roman town of *Moridunum* (Carmarthen) with its civic amenities and well-preserved amphitheatre, has revealed beyond doubt the considerable scope and extent of Roman influence in the area. Further excavation will probably show that this remarkable cantonal capital lacked few of the facilities of towns in the civil zone to the east of the Severn.

The map of Roman Wales took on the form of a defensive quadrilateral based on the great

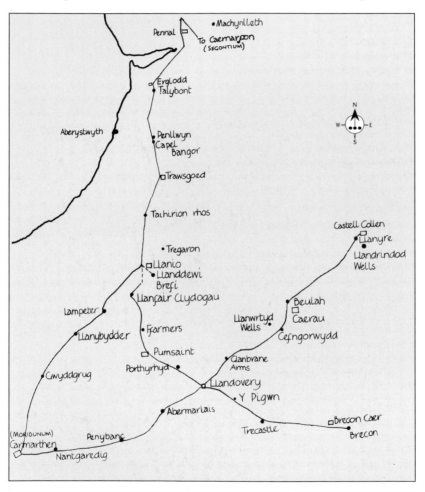

The Roman road network in southern-central and west Wales

legionary fortresses of *Deva* and *Isca* to the east and the auxiliary stations of *Segontium* (Caernarfon) and *Moridunum* to the west. Within this quadrilateral lay a series of forts centred on Caersws and Brecon. Rectangular in shape, the forts of the interior were surrounded by deep ditches and ramparts and contained granaries, workshops, barracks and administrative offices. Granaries (*horrea*) were particularly important since each station was expected to hold a full year's grain supply. Garrisoned by hardy troops and serviced by the interconnecting road system, the forts and fortlets served as a constant reminder of the danger, if not the futility, of flouting the rule of Rome. At the height of the conquest period of the late 70s some 28,000 soldiers were operational in Wales although this number had declined to around 3,500 towards the end of the first century by which time much of the countryside had been subjugated. The evidence provided by inscribed stones and stamped tiles enables us to identify at least some of the units of the Roman army involved in the conquest of Wales. Basically the job was undertaken by two legions, *Legio II Augusta* (operating out of *Isca*) and *Legio XX Valeria Victrix* which succeeded *Legio II Adiutrix* about AD86 and was stationed at *Deva*. Apart from a hundred or so cavalrymen, each legion was made up of 5,300 men, of whom all were Roman citizens and the great majority volunteers. These were the frontline troops; relatively well-paid, highly trained and severely disciplined. They were assisted by auxiliary regiments 500 or 1,000 strong, mostly comprising non- Roman citizens whose reward for 25 years of service (provided they survived it) was a grant of citizenship. From Gaul, Germany, Spain and other outposts of the Empire, these auxiliaries functioned primarily as garrison troops carrying out dreary routine patrol and police duties from the forts and fortlets along the road network. Soldiers in units like *Cohors II Asturum* and *Ala Hispanorum Vettonum* must have rued the day they left the sunny valleys of northern Spain as they cursed the dank atmosphere of Cardiganshire or shivered behind the ramparts of the fort at Brecon Gaer. They would certainly have been envious of the relative security and comfort enjoyed by their legionary colleagues in the massive structures at *Deva* and *Isca*.

In AD75, after 25 years of struggle against the Silures, the Romans began to raise the fine town of *Venta Silurum* (Caerwent) in the hope that as the town evolved the natives would be impressed as much by an example of civilised living as by the military power of their aggressors. To make sure that any necessary lessons in civilised living could be well-enforced, Julius Frontinus built the military headquarters of *Isca* several miles away. The fortress originally contained timber buildings and earth and timber defences, these being replaced with more permanent stone structures in the second century. It must have been a tremendous and awesome sight in its heyday. Twelve hundred years after the place had been abandoned, Thomas Churchyard could still write:

Now I must touch, a matter fit to knowe,
A fort and strength, that stands beyond this towne,
In which you shall behold the noblest showe.

This remarkable edifice was occupied for some 250 years before finally being abandoned when, like other deserted forts, it went steadily into decline. The removal of roofing material and stone for domestic buildings, stimulated by '.....a principle of avarice', as the eighteenth-century antiquarian Warner put it, set into motion an inevitable process of decay. The inexorable powers of the elements were complemented by the obsessive craving of travellers and antiquaries for mementos of their travels. After happily procuring Roman coins for 6d each at *Venta Silurum* in 1787, the Hon. John Byng moved to *Isca* where he wandered around the ruins and poked about among the rubble with his stick. His efforts were well-rewarded. Sitting over his wine that same evening he wrote, 'I thought it behoved me to peep about for something to carry off with me and write about, so I was lucky in stumbling on the fragment of a Roman brick on which some letters are very legible.' Against such odds, the elegantly-excavated and preserved fortress remains are with us today, serving as a reminder of the remarkable military and organisational skills of its founders.

In contrast to *Isca*, the majority of the forts, fortlets and practice camps in the Welsh military zone are now recognisable only from aerial photographs or from the remains of grassy banks, terraces and ditches which,with pottery finds or coins, provide tell-tale chronological clues for the specialist. The pattern of occupation – desertion – re-occupation of the sites mentioned in this chapter was often highly complex according to the exigencies of warfare. We find, for example, the early fortlet of Erglodd, near Talybont in Cardiganshire being re-occupied after a period of abandonment, while Caerau, Brecknockshire, was reduced in size following the slimming down of the garrison in Trajan's reign. By the time of Hadrian this process of garrison reduction, and thus alteration of the extent of fortress defences, had extended to Llandovery and Pumsaint in Carmarthenshire and Llanio and Trawsgoed in Cardiganshire, these latter two having been abandoned for good by AD125.

The visit to Britain of Hadrian himself in AD122 and his decision to build a great wall on the northern frontier of his dominions, was responsible for the abandonment or reduction in scale of some of the forts, whose occupants trudged reluctantly northwards to work on the wall. The re-occupation of southern Scotland and the construction of the Antonine Wall some years later precipitated further abandonment of Welsh forts, although by AD140 several of those remaining had been consolidated, their defences and administrative buildings being remodelled in stone. Owing largely to the absence of readily dateable pottery the subsequent history of most of the Welsh forts is rather shadowy. There seems to have been a dramatic reduction in the Roman military presence in the south after AD160-180 as the Silures and Demetae came to accept the fact of occupation, and by the later third and fourth centuries those forts still in use were apparently functioning as police posts, as opposed to military centres. In this late period the fortification of Caergybi, Holyhead, represents virtually the only major new Roman military work.

As the earthen ramparts and timber towers of the early forts were being thrown up, the locals (or, at least those of them who already regarded guerilla warfare against the Romans as a pointless exercise), naturally became curious about their overlords and it was not long before native settlements began to spring up outside the fortress walls. From these developed the *vici*, which modern excavation is uncovering in association with a number of the more important forts. These *vici*, whose fortunes tended to follow those of the fort, housed local craftsmen and traders along with the usual camp followers, and must have been the nearest thing to a Romanised township that people in the more remote regions would have seen. To them the villas and rural estates of the Vales of Glamorgan and Monmouth and the urban centre at Carmarthen, must have been rather like the city of Oxford to the medieval Cornish peasant; something to be talked of and wondered at, but never to be seen. Though they would have had access to some of the coinage and ceramic work which came with the legions, Romanization would have been very modest indeed. A little more land would have been taken into cultivation to provide for the needs of the forts while they remained occupied and there might even have been local improvements in building technology, but taken overall the Roman presence would have had very little effect on the landscape or way of life of people in the Welsh uplands. They remained for the most part in their farmsteads and maintained only sporadic and casual contact with the Roman money economy.

Military conquest and the subsequent control of a newly-conquered area through a chain of forts and fortlets required, above all, a good system of communications to enable the rapid movement of troops and the provisioning of their barracks. Apart from the numerous personnel who fed and equipped the soldiers, the force landing in south-east England in AD43 comprised 40,000 fighting men and it soon became clear to its commanders that the pre-existing trackways were quite inadequate to provide effectively for the movement of pack animals, ox-carts, cavalry and the whole paraphernalia of an invasion army. So the legions, aided by a grudging army of slaves, set out to build the extraordinary system of roads which were to remain virtually the only constructed highways prior to the proliferation of the turnpikes in the eighteenth century. Upwards of 6,000 miles of road were built throughout Britain, most of these being completed in the first hundred years of Roman occupation.

Initially the roads were of an exclusively military nature, facilitating the constant patrolling of army units in a country whose inhabitants had not yet accepted the inevitability of Roman domination . By the 50s the Romans had already extracted lead and silver from veins in the Mendips and Derbyshire and as they turned their attention towards the exploitation of other mineral deposits in their newly-acquired territory, road building became a vital component in the economic development as well as the military subjugation of the island. New roads carried iron from the Weald of Kent and the Forest of Dean, tin from Cornwall, gold from Carmarthenshire, copper from Anglesey and Montgomeryshire and lead from central and northern Wales . Moreover, as Britain as a whole became progressively Romanised, these same roads became channels for the distribution of the imported pottery, wines, fine craftwork and other luxury goods demanded by an increasingly civilised population. Concurrently there developed a complex of minor roads, many as yet undiscovered, linking the villas, farms and towns growing up in the lowland civil zone. The civil zone excluded the majority of Wales, yet it is worth emphasizing the point made elsewhere by Christopher Taylor that it was probably the minor road system which drew much of the rest of Britain into the Roman Empire and provided the means whereby Imperial thought and policy was able to influence the people in every possible social, economic and political manner.

We have virtually no written records describing the actual construction of the Roman roads in Britain so we are obliged to rely entirely on observation and excavation to elucidate the nature of the road surface, the materials used and other matters of technical detail. We do, however, have a very clear picture of how the legions went about the business of deciding on the overall alignment of their roads and how they carried out the necessary surveys before starting construction. The achievements of the *agrimensores*, the trained surveyors responsible for fixing the major road lines, were quite astonishing. Working in hostile environments under constant threat of attack from recalcitrant natives they managed remarkable feats of engineering.

Bearing in mind that his principal objective was to create a road providing the army with an opportunity for rapid movement and relative security from attack, the surveyor's first task was to carry out a general study of the area. This involved gathering local information about pre-existing trackways, the best points for fording rivers and avoiding marshy ground and other aspects of the terrain which would help him to decide where deviations in alignment or major changes in direction were likely to be needed. Having carefully noted this information our surveyor, with his assistants and servants now set out to examine the ground, to assess the difficulties posed by major obstacles, boggy terrain and excessive inclines and finally to decide upon the actual line of the road. Constantly aware of strategic objectives and the fact that the personnel laying out the road would be relatively unskilled, the surveyor sought a road line which could be laid out from point-to-point with lengths as straight as natural conditions and engineering convenience permitted. On the lowland this implied angular changes of direction to avoid natural obstacles, with short zigzag lengths to facilitate ascents of hillsides. In upland country, however, the principle of the angular change of direction was often abandoned in favour of following the contour or of securing a constant gradient, although wherever possible the zigzag method would be used to get to the top of a ridge. Indeed, ridge-top road lines with commanding views were eagerly sought by surveyors and engineers as these provided more secure travelling conditions than the wooded and boggy valley bottoms.

The surveyor's ultimate task was to fix and mark the final position of the road before construction. This was a relatively simple matter involving the use of a set of movable markers – poles or possibly fire baskets – which were visible over considerable distances from adjacent points. In hill and upland country, visibility would frequently have been possible only with hilltop markers, which may explain the frequent changes of direction of Roman roads in this sort of terrain. It is worth remembering too, that since the bulk of the earlier roads in the uplands were used almost exclusively for the package trains and foot patrols of the military, they did not need to be especially sophisticated. Indeed, there is some evidence that less than skilled engineers were employed in their construction than was the case with the great lowland roads. Also, in Wales and other 'military' zones of Britain, eventual troop withdrawal gave way to rather less sophisticated civil government than in the lowland, and this may partially account for the relative lack of development of the road system.

The quality of Roman roads and the methods of construction varied widely according to local topography and the availability of materials. Though subject to overall supervision, the engineers responsible for specific sections seem to have been left to decide details of construction for themselves so that we find a great deal of variation in material used along the length of any given road. Some were laid out with foundations of large stones surfaced with gravel, others were elaborately paved with slabs, and others still were simply tracks with little or no definite plan or surface material, this last category being particularly common among the minor roads in the highland zone. Invariably the Roman engineer sought a firm, well-drained base for his road and where this was not available he built embankments (*aggeres*) of large stones or earth often 45-50ft wide and 4-5ft high. Elsewhere the road might be laid between drainage ditches on a foundation of large stones topped with rammed gravel, clay and turf, a central rib-stone and large kerbs lending stability to the structure. The major roads through low-lying country, frequently carried on substantial *aggeres*, varied from 20 to 28ft in width. In broken and mountainous terrain, however, the *aggeres* if present at all, were usually rather modest affairs and the sophisticated structural techniques employed on the lowland gave way to simple terraced roads of as little as 10ft wide. These, like so many early roads in hill country, are now extremely difficult to trace.

Even more difficult to find, in both hill and lowland, are the points where the road crossed a river or stream. Natural fords seem to have been used wherever possible, often necessitating an alteration in the alignment of the road as it approached the watercourse. Alternatively a ford could be constructed on the original alignment or, in the case of a deep narrow stream, a culvert built to carry the water under the road. Wide and unfordable rivers were crossed by bridges of timber and stone and the few vestiges suggest that these were often of massive construction with wide embankments or ramps approaching the edge of the water.

Besides the important military and commercial roads with their bridges and milestones and heavy traffic of soldiers, imperial officials and traders, there were the thousands of miles of local trackways serving the purposes of both agriculture and trade. Of recent years aerial photography has revealed surprising numbers of these trackways in many parts of the country from the wet Welsh hills to the chalklands of the south, and from the clay vales of the Shires to the limestone ridges of the south-west. As we have come to know more about the Roman road network in Britain, there has inevitably been a tendency to link known Roman tracks and highways to existing roads, thereby fabricating a complex of routeways which relate in no way whatsoever to the original Roman pattern. There is nothing new in this beguiling temptation to connect existing roads with Roman roadlines and the quest for the detailed course of Roman routes in Wales has not been helped by the obsession of antiquaries over the past three hundred years for this subject. Virtually any trackways looking remotely straight and ancient were often, by prodigious feats of the imagination, conjured into Roman roads and duly recorded in learned articles, most of which need to be read with a highly critical eye. A parish boundary, for example, may follow a 'modern' road in a straight line across country for several miles, but this does not necessarily bespeak a Roman road. It may follow a Roman road, but in the final analysis this can only be substantiated by careful study of the relationship of the road to landscape features such as bogs, waterways and the like and by seeking uniquely Roman features including rib and kerb stones and gravel metalling. This implies excavation, of which, for one reason or other, there has been lamentably little in Wales. Thus words like 'may', 'might', 'possibly' and 'probably' will feature with tedious regularity throughout this chapter!

Essentially the Welsh road network evolved from the major military routes between Chester and Caernarfon and those from Caerleon, Cardiff and Brecon connecting with the forts, camps and mining centres of the heartland. The total complex of roads, gradually being elaborated by detailed fieldwork, covers far too large an area for a book of this size and I have chosen to concentrate on the major elements of the road network in southern-central and west Wales, an important military and mining area. The roads considered will include those connecting Carmarthen, Llandovery, Llandrindod Wells and Brecon and the *Sarn Helen*, linking Llandovery with Pennal on the Dyfi Estuary and ultimately with Caernarfon on the Menai Straits.

SARN HELEN

The Flavian auxiliary fort at Pennal on the northern bank of the River Dyfi was a vital link in the chain of military structures between Caernarfon and the Roman establishments in south Wales. Lying in part beneath the buildings of Cefngaer Farm (SN704001), the fort covered rather more than 4.4 acres and is believed to have accommodated a garrison of some 500 men. As much of the original fort is now overlain by Cefngaer Farm (itself of some antiquity) little remains to be seen apart from a few grass-grown banks marking the original earthen ramparts. Even so, the visitor can readily appreciate the strategic importance of the site lying, as it did, at the southern extreme of the great block of the Snowdonia range and at the mouth of the tidal Dyfi. Here, at the junction of land and seaways, this isolated garrison was ideally placed to supervise the *Sarn Helen* road and to keep a close eye on seafarers in Cardigan Bay. Moreover, as with the fortlet at Erglodd further south, it would have been possible, given the high probability of the river having run close to the outer walls in Roman times, to provision the fort by sea if this became necessary.

The early stages of the southerly course taken by the Roman road are as obscure as the origin of the name *Sarn Helen* itself. The existence of place and field names embodying the word *sarn* (causeway) has often been taken as indicative of the presence of a Roman road or trackway although of course, such a causeway (or assumed causeway) may equally be of medieval or even later provenance. While *Sarn* has a clear meaning in English, Helen presents difficulties. Most probably *Helen* is a corruption of *Lleng* (legion), hence *Sarn y-Lleng* (road of the legion) or rather less likely a corruption of *halen* (salt) thereby referring to the relatively close proximity

Modern fenceline running along embankments
of the Roman fort at Pennal

of the road to the coastline of Cardigan Bay. Tradition, nurtured by the writing of Geoffrey of Monmouth and the chroniclers of the Welsh epic *The Mabinogion* links the name of the road with Elen, daughter of a native chieftain married to the Roman Magnus Maximus who, in AD388, marched on Rome with his Welsh allies to lay claim to the Imperial throne. There is strong evidence to sup-

The River Dyfi near Furnace; Pennal lies in the far distance

The presumed Roman road from Furnace to Talybont

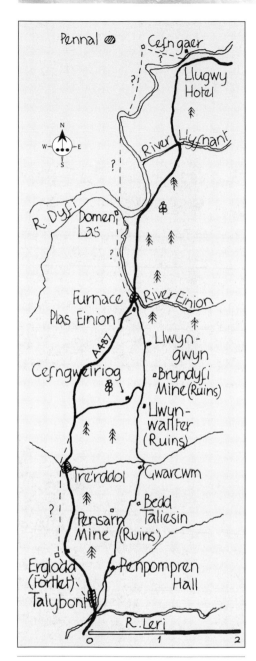

Pennal to Talybont

port the belief that Magnus (or Macsen Wledig as the Welsh chroniclers preferred to call him) did attempt to grab the crown with the assistance of troops from Wales, only to be defeated at the hands of the Emperor Theodosius. Whether he married a Welsh girl called Elen is another matter, yet it may not be without significance that his name features in the genealogies of a number of Dark Age Welsh princes.

The derivation of the name of the road is likely to remain a tantalising mystery as indeed is the point where it crossed the tidal reaches of the River Dyfi. Tracing ancient roads in estuarine areas is fraught with problems, not the least being the irritating habit of rivers to change their courses quite substantially over a short span of years. Even in non-tidal areas many rivers exhibit a high rate of channel mobility as indicated by Dr John Lewin's findings that some Welsh rivers annually shift course to the extent of between 0.1 per cent and 5.5 per cent of their areas. This being so, it is virtually certain that any remains of Roman *aggeres* in the vicinity of the Dyfi estuary were swept away centuries ago.

The very absence of material has yielded a rich harvest of speculation as to the location of the Roman ford (or even bridge) across the Dyfi. One school of thought favours a crossing point near the present Llugwy Hotel to the south-east of the fort where the river forms a narrow channel with firm ground adjoining it on either bank. Supporters of this view see the southerly course of *Sarn Helen* running either by way of one of the several old trackways across Bwlcheinion towards the Llyfnant Valley, or along the line of the modern A487 as it curves around the edge of the hills towards the village of Furnace. A crossing near the Llugwy Hotel, of course, pre-supposes that the river occupied its present position in Roman times. The second of the more plausible theories proposes that the trackway from the south-western gate of the fort may have been carried by a causeway over the mud-flats to cross the river some distance to the south-west. A few yards below the point where a trackway issues from the present farm buildings, two pre-Flavian glazed-ware vases and a red-ware *mortarium* were discovered several years ago in what some authorities believe to be the remains of a burnt-out building of Roman origin. Although the remnants of the trackway (now a farm lane) peter out in the wet land towards the river it is noteworthy that a continuation would have aligned closely with the medieval motte and bailey on the bank of the Dyfi at Domen Las (SN687969). A medieval site at this location, where the river makes a great curve around the boggy saltings, suggests not only a crossing point but that here at least, the course of the Dyfi has not changed significantly in the last millennium however much it may have changed elsewhere in the estuary. Standing on a rocky eminence amid a bird reserve, the motte commands a tremendous view of the mountains to the north and the sea to the west. From this lonely spot, where the weird cry of the curlew hangs on the wind, it is not difficult to conjure up a vivid image of a solitary Roman patrol heading across the marshes for the river crossing.

Before 1976, this suggestion would have seemed rather far-fetched. However, during the dry summer of that year aerial photography identified the turf ramparts of a Roman fortlet on the farm of Erglodd (SN653905) between the villages of Taliesin and Talybont some 8 miles to the south of the fort at Pennal. Located near the significantly-named *Cae maes y palman* (*palman, palmant* = pavement), the fortlet, whose surface features are no longer visible, occupied an area of some 0.625 acres. Dr J. L. Davies has carefully surveyed this Flavian site and has suggested that it may have formed an important element in the well-established fort-fortlet-fort system of Roman control, particularly as it lies more-or-less equidistant between the forts at Pennal and Penllwyn, near Capel Bangor (SN650806). The fortlet was clearly built to police the Leri river crossing in Talybont and to supervise traffic passing from Pennal to Penllwyn, from which one must conclude that it lay in close proximity to a Roman road. Such a road probably pursued roughly the line of the present A487 and linked with the Dyfi crossing at Domen Las or elsewhere. Following S. J. S. Hughes's discovery that certain objects from Roman sites in west Cardiganshire contain lead from mines in the Talybont area, it seems that the Erglodd fortlet also may have served as an administrative centre for lead or silver mining activities. Certainly there is strong circumstantial evidence to substantiate a claim for Roman mining in the vicinity of Erglodd and in the woods on the bank to the east of the fortlet. Indeed the name Erglodd itself might even be a corruption of *Aurglodd* (*aur* = gold, *cloaddfa* = mine, excavation) thereby hinting at the possibility even of gold mining in the vicinity of this site.

The identification of the Erglodd fortlet proves beyond reasonable doubt that there existed a Roman road (whose detailed course we can now only surmise) linking the Leri crossing at Talybont with Pennal. The question, however, arises as to whether this formed part of the *Sarn Helen* system or whether the latter took what is traditionally believed to be the Roman road running along the country lanes through the hills between Furnace and Talybont. This 'upper' road was obliged to negotiate several steep-sided valleys, yet it would have possessed the advantage of directness, besides commanding extensive views of the surrounding countryside. It tends, furthermore, to be laid out in short, straight alignments with typically angular changes of alignment at several points. Could there have been two roads? Since the Erglodd fortlet is known to have been abandoned in the mid-second century, and presumably the road with it, is it possible that the 'upper' route was subsequently developed to provide for patrols and to service mining ventures in the hills? All we really know is that this is an old and important road as the early maps indicate, and that apart from a lengthy tradition, there is at present no evidence to prove whether or not it is of Roman origin. The road traverses unspoilt countryside of quiet beauty and I make no apology for describing its course, hoping, as I do so, that people will walk and enjoy it and that some day it will be subjected to more detailed investigation.

Leaving the A487 below the old smeltery in Furnace (SN685952) the road climbs steeply along the western side of the Einion valley to pass behind Plas Einion. Here, where the present road swings eastwards, the old lane is carried straight on, its overgrown course being contained by stone walls on either side until it is crossed by another trackway towards the top of the hill (SN684946). Before long the walls sweep away from the road which is now carried along the outskirts of a patch of woodland on a raised causeway, constructed in all probability when it was used as a coach road in the eighteenth century. At Llwyngwyn (SN683941) our lane is crossed by a modern forestry road beyond which it runs south-westwards between

Victorian bridge over the Clettwr with line of earlier road in foreground

finely-constructed eighteenth-century stone walls to pass the Victorian ruins of the Bryndyfi Lead Mine (SN683934). With extensive remains of the dressing floors, ore bins, crusher house and wheelpit, Bryndyfi is a veritable feast for the industrial archaeologist. As happened so often, the speculators investing in all this high quality masonry failed fully to investigate the potential yield of the underlying lead seams and the enterprise collapsed within two years of the mine's opening in 1881. Workers engaged during the brief life of the mine enjoyed much the same exquisite views as Roman patrolmen fifteen hundred years beforehand. As they watched banks of rain sweeping from the sea through the hillside woodlands of oak, birch and alder, both may have thrilled to the curves of the estuary and to the mysterious and rather menacing Cors Fochno, source of a rich corpus of Celtic legend.

After a long, slow ascent from Llwyngwyn the old lane drops down to join the metalled road for Cefngweirog Farm at SN680933. From this junction the logical Roman alignment would have been straight across the fields to the east of the farm in the direction of the Clettwr valley. However, there have been no finds of metalling or causeway in the reseeded fields, so it must be assumed that the older road followed the present one on its course along the slightly higher ground, passing through a larch plantation and eventually aligning with Gwarcwm Farm on the south side of the deep gulch of the River Clettwr (SN674917). Here the two roads diverge, the metalled one being carried across the narrow river by a handsome single-span bridge of nineteenth-century type. The earlier road takes the line of a wet and overgrown trackway running parallel to and below the metalled road and reaching the river some forty yards west of the present bridge where the stone abutments of an old bridge of indeterminate age proclaim a crossing point. Some ten feet away, on the opposite side of the rapidly-flowing Clettwr, the early road continues until it once again picks up the metalled lane past Gwarcwm towards Pensarn Farm (SN669910), passing on the way the remains of a disturbed Early Bronze Age cairn. *Bedd Taliesin*, as the cairn is so-called, is traditionally reckoned to be the last resting place of the sixth century poet, Taliesin. The association of this strangely evocative site with Taliesin provides for an attractive legend, but the story has no basis in fact and the cairn, like several others of similar type in the area may well mark the grave of a Bronze Age chieftain or some other man of distinction. Within the precincts of Pensarn Farm, a hundred yards or so below the cairn, travellers will notice the abandoned nineteenth-century chapel languishing among modern farm buildings of the usual unprepossessing type. This originally served the thriving community of miners who struggled to win lead from the Pensarn Mine (SN668912). The remains of the mine workings are visible in the fields to the north-west of the farm, a late nineteenth-century wheelhouse being built into the stone wall of a nearby lane.

Between Pensarn and Talybont, the assumed route is by way of the present minor road past Penpompren Hall and on to the crossing of the River Leri at the site of the bridge carrying the A487 out of the village (SN655892). While there is no doubt that the roads from Pensarn and Erglodd crossed the Leri at this point, there is virtually no field, no place name, no photographic or other evidence to lend substance to the claim that the above road represents the precise Roman line. On the other hand it is difficult to imagine any alternative since, if they had tried to forge even a slightly more direct route, the Roman engineers would inevitably have had to confront the problem of crossing the very steep valley of Cwm Ceulan.

TALYBONT TO PENLLWYN AND TRAWSCOED

In the mid-nineteen seventies, an aerial photographic survey revealed the subterranean remains of one of the largest Roman forts in western Wales. For some time archaeologists had postulated the probable location of a fort guarding the crossing of the River Rheidol, and the discovery of Penllwyn (SN650806) overlooking the river from a west-facing slope behind the village of Capel Bangor, established both the river crossing and the line of *Sarn Helen*. Excavation of the seven acre site, whose remains are barely visible on the ground, suggested that the fort was occupied during the Flavian-Hadrianic period and deliberately demolished when abandoned.

The Roman road linking this fort with the Leri crossing unquestionably takes the line of the present minor road between Talybont and Capel Bangor by way of Penrhyncoch, a road given some prominence on Thomas Kitchin's map of 1752. Known locally as 'The Roman Road', it leaves the A487 some 300yds south of the Leri to run past the Iron Age camp at Llettyllwyd and then to the west of Elgar Farm (where a field called *Cae sarn* runs close to the road at SN651862) before running into Penrhyncoch. Apart from the complete lack of evidence of any alternative roadline, it has been carefully laid out to avoid excessive slopes and also offers the most direct and easy route between the two points. South of Penrhyncoch, a village notable for the extreme dullness of its more recent architecture, the road runs through gentle, undulating country of ancient hedgerows and well-maintained farms. As it does so it exhibits several markedly Roman features including a particularly well-engineered gradient near Penyberth (SN646837) and *Cae sarn* and *sarnau* name elements at SN647809 and SN647820. A straightish alignment south of Penyberth comes to a junction with another old road between Capel Dewi and Bancydarren (SN647830). From this point the Roman course runs along a hedgeline a few yards to the east until it picks up the enclosed lane to Felin-wen on the bank of the little Peithyll stream (SN64827). After zigzagging up the steep slope past the farm buildings the Roman line is apparently continued by way of a green lane (which may well justify excavation) to rejoin the minor road at SN648823.

This part of Cardiganshire is criss-crossed by scores, if not hundreds of miles of trackways of uncertain vintage and it is hardly surprising that other courses for *Sarn Helen* have been postulated. Before the identification of the Penllwyn fort, there was a strong local tradition of

Above: Aerial view of the Roman fort at Penllwyn, Capel Bangor

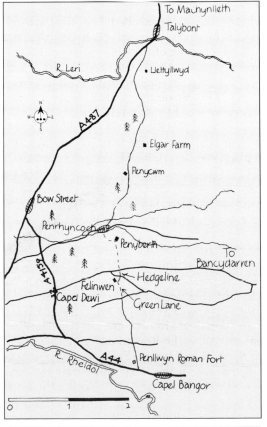

Below: Green lane on the line of an assumed Roman course above Felin-wen

Sarn Helen. Talybont to Penllwyn

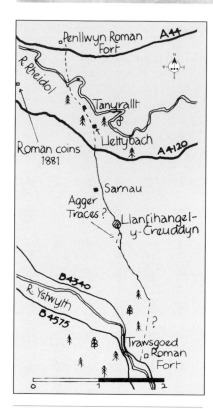

Sarn Helen. Penllwyn to Trawsgoed

a Roman crossing of the Rheidol opposite Pwllcenawon Farm on the south bank of the river (SN640805). This tradition derives from the unearthing, in 1885, of the remains of a 12ft-wide 'metalled road' some ten inches below the surface of a field near Cwmwythig Farm to the north-west of what is now known to be the Roman fort. This road fragment, apparently, aligned directly with Pwllcenawon and also with Tynycwm (SN644827) to the north and it was assumed, in the absence of any other evidence, that this alignment represented the original

Aerial view of the Roman fort at Trawsgoed. See page 30

Roman route. Several years before this stretch of roadway had been revealed, a hoard of several thousand third-century Roman coins came to light near an old lane to the south-west of Rhiwarthen-Isaf below Pwllcenawon (SN639795). This was quite sufficient to persuade local antiquaries of the existence of a Roman road whose subsequent course ran through land belonging to Nantybenglog and Penuwch Fawr Farms to arrive at the village of Llanfihangel-y-Creuddyn (SN665760). The latter certainly lies on the route for the major fort at Trawsgoed (SN671727), but it is highly improbable that Roman surveyors would have laid out such an indirect road line as that described above. The discovery of the coin hoard is no evidence in itself as this might represent a random burial made in the turbulent years following Roman withdrawal. Moreover, forty years before these were found, a copper pot containing a further 200 coins was ploughed up at Bwlch (SN608793) almost two miles to the west and well away from any likely road line. Given the location of the newly-discovered Penllwyn fort there can now be no question

The probable Roman road near Penpompren Hall

Sarn Helen near Penycwm, between Talybont and Penllwyn Roman Fort

of the Tynycwm-Pwllcenawon-Penuwch Fawr course representing the line of *Sarn Helen* and the 'metalled' road (of which all traces have long since vanished) remains a mystery.

Movements of the bed of the mature River Rheidol along with agricultural activities over the centuries will have removed any remnants of Roman road material immediately to the south of the fort. A straight continuation of the highway from the north would have extended to a ford across the river several hundred yards above the modern bridge accommodating the minor road to New Cross. Here the Roman surveyor was faced with the problem of negotiating the very steep bank of Rhiw Arthen, which he seems to have solved by taking his road along the base of the hill, roughly corresponding to the track of the Vale of Rheidol light railway. As the railway passes the smallholding of Tanyrallt (SN657789) a terrace ascends towards Llettybach (SN659785) through fine woodlands of oak and beech. Carefully engineered to ensure a steady ascent and to avoid the steepest slope, the narrow terrace rounds the shoulder of the ridge at Llettybach, where a backwards glance offers a splendid view of the incomparable Rheidol Valley. From here its course is difficult to trace through the woodlands, but it almost certainly linked with the old road running from the top of the hill through gentle pastoral country towards Llanfihangel-y-Creuddyn.

Half-a-mile or so down this metalled minor road is Sarnau Farm below which, according to the National Monuments Record, aerial photographs reveal slight traces of agger in the fields to the right. They are not, however, visible on the ground. The supposed alignment of these *aggere* remains would have carried the road over the deep gulch of a narrow stream and it is difficult to see why Roman road makers should have preferred this slightly more westerly route to the present line, which crosses the watercourse before it gouges out this awkward channel. At the top of the next hilltop ridge, Llanfihangel-y-Creuddyn comes into view, its fine church dominating the cluster of whitewashed houses. Beyond the village the Roman road can be seen to work its way round the next hillside on the line of an enclosed metalled road with a Roman-type zigzag towards the crest of the hill (SN665755). Another more pronounced zigzag effect occurs after another half-mile where a steep slope runs down to the lovely vale of the Ystwyth (SN670748). From the top of this slope, the fort of Trawsgoed, rather more than a mile distant, would first have come into view, smoke from the chimneys of its timber and wattle-and-daub type garrison buildings rising into the clear air of the wooded vale (SN671727).

Except for the broad bank in the field to the south of the gardens of Trawsgoed House which represents the remains of the rampart, there is little evidence on the ground of the 5.4 acre rectangular fort containing all the services necessary for a garrison of 1,000 men. Aerial photography, however, backed-up by excavation, has highlighted details of the internal structure, the street grid of the *vicus* immediately to the north and the orientation of roads from the four main gates. It seems also that the basic defences of the fort remained of an earth and timber nature from its origins in the late 70s until its apparent abandonment around AD130. Trawsgoed was ideally located to control the crossing of the nearby River Ystwyth, to provide excellent views of the surrounding hilly countryside, and to serve as a staging post for patrols operating out of Penllwyn. These patrols would have approached the fort on the *Sarn Helen*. Unfortunately all traces of this road, as it crossed the lowlying vale have been lost, although it presumably ran on a straight alignment from the bottom of the hills to the north.

A thousand years after the Romans left Wales, a local chieftain by the name of Adda Vychan married Dido, daughter of Ieuan Goch ap Gruffydd of Trawsgoed and thereby started the 600-year association between the family of Vaughan and Trawsgoed, only to be broken in 1947 when the running of the estate passed into the control of the Ministry of Agriculture. Like many Welsh gentry families, the Vaughans reached their apogee in the late eighteenth century when they were raised to the peerage as Earls of Lisburne. On the basis that social grandeur necessitated elegant trappings, the third earl pulled down his home in 1795 and built the Regency house forming the eastern wing of the present building. He also proceeded to lay out the fine grounds, planting azaleas, monkey puzzles, wellingtonias, cypresses and all manner of exotic species to complement his parterres, fountains and other delightful contemporary conceits. Sadly the effect was destroyed in 1891 when the sixth earl built an exquisitely vulgar west wing in pseudo-French chateau style. As if this were not enough, the Ministry of Agriculture, whose Agricultural Development and Advisory Service occupied the building until very recently, threw up further extensions in quite scandalously bad taste. Nevertheless, the grounds are worthy of a visit while the ceiling of the library in the Regency house, if somewhat crudely executed, is a charming riot of acanthus leaves and putti.

TRAWSGOED TO CARMARTHEN

From the western gate of the Roman fort lying in the field adjoining the Trawsgoed gardens, a road issued forth and zigzagged down the steep slope towards the River Ystwyth. Now only visible from aerial photographs, this was the southwards continuation of *Sarn Helen*, engineered to align as closely as possible with the fortlet underlying the farm of Taihirion-rhos some 6 miles to the south-west (SN645651). Running through what are now thickets of rhododendron and stands of Douglas Fir, the road seems to have forded the river at a point aligning with a field boundary joining the farm lane of Hendre Rhys close to the remnants of Trawsgoed railway station (SN665725). From this unkempt and dreary blight on a fine landscape the Roman roadline continues past Hendre Rhys before turning abruptly south and taking the form of a deep track pursuing a steady ascent along field boundaries until it reaches the modern road at the base of the afforested Banc Cwmllechwedd (SN662719). While the road

Above: Ascent of assumed Roman road from Trawsgoed

Sarn Helen. Trawsgoed to Taihirion-rhos

Left: The B4578 south of Lledrod lies on the course of Sarn Helen

clearly ran towards the piles of stones and enclosure banks which are all that remain of Sarn Ellen Farm (SN656704), its actual course over Banc Cwmllechwedd is obscured by a network of forestry roads. Beyond the ruins of Sarn Ellen though, the Roman line is marked by a continuous series of straight and massive hedgebanks carrying it to the east of Penlan Farm on the old road between Lledrod and Ystrad Meurig (SN655696). Careful inspection of these hedgebanks as they cross pastureland and unreclaimed bog, suggests that they were constructed on a terrace extending in parts between 5ft and 6ft either side of the bank. As this, in all likelihood, comprises the remnants of Roman agger it may merit excavation.

At almost 900ft above sea level, the point of intersection of the Roman and minor roads offers panoramic views of the low, rolling hills to the south where improved pasture alternates with brown, ill-drained wetlands and the poor quality of the older farm and cottage architecture reflects the combined poverty of the agriculture of the last century and the building materials available at that time. A stretch of the Roman road was apparently visible between this point and Llwynmerchgwilym (SN654685) in the 1930s but a grass mark on the aerial photograph at SN654694 represents the only clue to its course over the next half-mile. Below Llwynmerchgwilym, however, the Roman road briefly follows the modern B4578, until at SN653676 the latter turns south-east before rejoining the same alignment a quarter of a mile to the south. The Roman engineers maintained their road on its straight course along a twenty yard wide causeway running almost rush-free through boggy ground for more than a hundred yards. The causeway is discernible on the ground at its northern end and identifiable from aerial photographs at the point where it once again picks up the straight line of the more recent road which carries it over the little Camddwr river.

The aerial photographic record shows clearly the straight continuation, marked on the ground by fieldbanks, of the *Sarn Helen* for the mile or so between the Camddwr to below Taihirion-rhos, the junction with the modern A485. S.R. Meyrick in his *History and Antiquities of the County of Cardigan* of 1808 maintained that stretches of the road were still visible at the time of writing. A hundred and fifty years later local antiquaries excavated several sections to reveal a variety of metalling types ranging from boulders capped with layers of soil and clay to a mixture of clay and stones to a depth of 10 inches resting on a peat base. Today, however, apart from the slightest indication of agger in the field to the east of Taihirion-rhos there is little to highlight the passage of a major Roman road between the river and the fortlet.

Left: Bremia, the remains of the bath house

Taihirion-rhos is roughly equidistant between Trawsgoed and the important auxiliary fort overlooking the River Teifi near Llanio-isaf Farm several miles due south (SN644564). Tentatively identified with the *Bremia* mentioned in the early eighth century collection of place names known as the *Ravenna Cosmography*, this fort occupied an area of rather more than 3.8 acres and was located on a gravel terrace to the north of the Teifi. Its surface features have been virtually obliterated by centuries of cultivation, but excavation has shown that the essentially earthwork and timber complex was founded in the 70s, refurbished in the early second century and abandoned sometime between AD125 and 130. The abandonment of the fort was followed by the decay of its associated *vicus* and also, presumably, of the bathhouse, whose stone and tile remnants a hundred yards south of the fort share with Tomen-y-Mur in Merioneth the distinction of being the only visible remains of such a structure in this part of Wales.

Bremia apparently, was garrisoned by the Second Cohort of Asturians. Soldiers from the Asturias, an important goldmining district of Spain, would, it has been suggested, have played an important part in the exploitation of the gold workings near Caeo to the south-east. Unfortunately this rather attractive idea ignores the fact that the 'national' characteristics of Roman auxiliary regiments were ephemeral, to say the least, and the Asturians may with equal likelihood have comprised soldiers from other parts of the Empire besides Spain. Consequently we must regard their stationing at Bremia as quite incidental. *Bremia* has been known since the

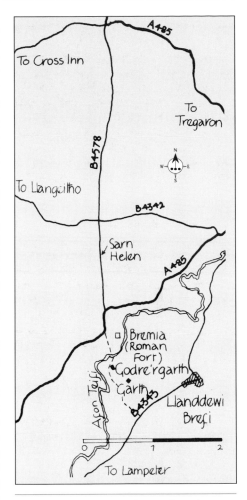

Sarn Helen; Taihirion-rhos to Bremia

seventeenth century and like other similar sites has long been a happy hunting ground for antiquaries, collectors and treasure hunters like Richard Fenton who, in the first decade of the nineteenth century purchased for 1s ' ….a very ancient Pickaxe' at Tomen Llanio not far from the fort. This he 'bore in Triumph to Tregaron' marvelling as he did so at the richness of the surface material around *Bremia*: 'All the fields, every hedge and pile of rubbish pregnant with bricks and tiles of every kind, as likewise cement and pieces of pottery.' The enthusiasm with which he and his fellow antiquaries plundered Roman sites may explain why so little remains today of even the more substantial Roman structures in this part of the Principality.

For the first mile-and-a-half from the point where it joins the A485 below Taihirion-rhos, the course of *Sarn Helen* to *Bremia* roughly follows the modern road to the crossroads at Ty'ncelyn to the northeast of which Dr J.L. Davies identified remains of Roman metalling in the early 1970s. South of the crossroads the B4578 takes up the approximate Roman line as it twists and winds through pastureland before adopting a fine, straight alignment directly for *Bremia*. South of the junction with the A485 at SN642572, the Roman road is shown by aerial photographs to run close to the house to the west of the track to Llanio-isaf Farm before heading for a crossing of the broad, shallow River Teifi at SN643559. Traces of the agger were

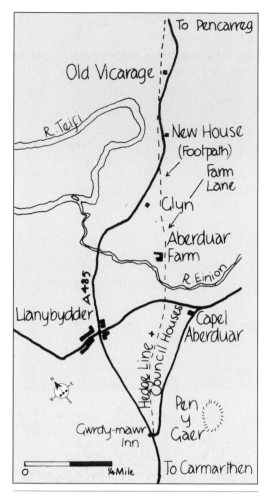

Course of Roman road around Llanybydder

readily visible from the railway bridge close to the farm back in the 1930s and can still just be made out today, in particular where the road crosses the meadow alongside the riverbank. On the opposite side of the Teifi an ancient looking track climbs the slope on the edge of a strip of woodland and then runs round the contour (its course marked by massive hedgebanks) past Godre'rgarth and Garth Farms (and two fields called *Cae pensarn* at SN64555) to join the modern B4343 which is generally believed to represent the southerly continuation of *Sarn Helen* towards Lampeter. This road takes a gently meandering course through low-lying riverside meadows, the land steadily rising to the east. Such terrain, with few difficult gradients, would have presented the Romans with an ideal opportunity to construct a classically straight road. This they would certainly have done and one can only assume that the fruits of their labours have been obliterated by progressive movements of the Teifi riverbed. Perhaps detailed local fieldwork will eventually reveal remaining stretches of the original on the western side of the B4343.

It is usually maintained that the Roman course for the journey through the quiet pastoral landscape between Lampeter and Carmarthen is taken by the present A485. Once again, while there is no question that this road pursues the *overall* Roman line, as evidenced by short straight traverses across the steeper hills, angular realignments and place names, the precise course will be elucidated only by intensive fieldwork. At present it is possible to identify a clear deviation of the Roman from the existing road where it runs from Pencarreg and through the gloomy little town of Llanybydder to the village of Llanllwni to the southwest. Back in the late nineteenth century a stretch of the original metalled road was uncovered near Neuadd, Pencarreg, a house previously occupied by the vicar of the nearby parish church (SN533451) and also in the gardens of the Old Vicarage a quarter of a mile or so to the south (SN532448). Both these sightings align with a footpath leaving the A485 at SN528444 which itself aligns with a section of the paved road surface revealed in 1820 by drainage operations in fields to the northwest of Capel Aberduar outside Llanybydder (SN525439). The footpath is continued by an old unused lane which, before it reaches Aberduar Farm, turns abruptly to the west (SN528442). The Roman line is maintained for a straight, steep descent past the farm buildings and across the meadows on a slight raised agger of almost 15ft wide, on line with the stretch near the chapel described above. This would have been reached after a short, sharp climb up the south bank of the Einion stream, presumably forded at the point where the agger joins the north bank. Beyond the chapel a continuous hedgeline (now broken by a council estate) originally marked the position of the Roman road as it passed by the base of the hill fort of Penygaer to rejoin the A485 at the Gwrdy – mawr public house (SN521435). The coincidence of the two roads does not last for long since traces of the Roman surface have been found in *Cae dan-yr-efail* on Abercwm Farm (SN503407), in *Cae Capel*, Maesnoni Farm (SN497397) and in three fields belonging to Pensarnhelen, Llanllwni (SN486392) where it seems once again to have joined the modern main road. Rather more than half-a-mile south of here the latter makes a sharp angular turn to negotiate a hillside in a typically Roman manner (SN479385), doing so once again below Gwyddgrug (SN461355) close to a field named *Sarn Elen*. Further fieldwork may cast light on the exact location of the original course of *Sarn Helen* over the final few miles to Carmarthen through Rhydargaeau (with fieldnames *Sarn* and *Sarnebach* at SN438254 and SN438256) and Sarnau village. For the time being, however, drivers through this lovely countryside can rest assured that they are motoring along a road in part at least, familiar to the footsoldiers and cavalrymen trudging towards *Moridunum* nineteen hundred years ago.

BREMIA TO LLANDOVERY

The eastern branch of *Sarn Helen* linked *Bremia* with a large fort on the outskirts of modern Llandovery a dozen or so miles to the south east (SN703527). This road parted company with the main *Sarn Helen* to Carmarthen at the village of Llanfair Clydogau where a Victorian bridge carries the present B4343 across Nant Clywedog (SN624511). Just beyond the bridge a narrow minor road climbs steeply out of the Teifi valley, eventually running along a series of very straight alignments through pinewoods and into high, silent and cairn-strewn country. Deep in the forest at SN640493 the remains of a Roman practice camp have been identified while an unfinished practice camp languishes in the open moorland on the left-

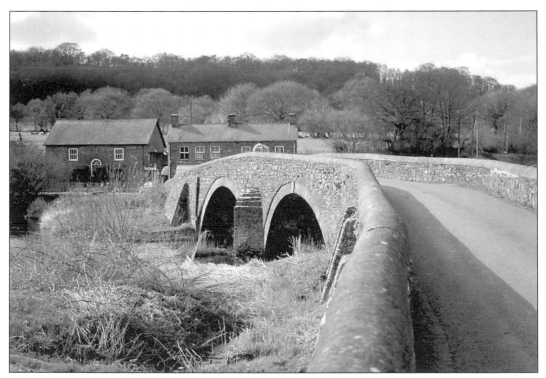

The Victorian bridge over Nant Clywedog at Llanfair Clydogau

hand side of the road half-a-mile on towards Llandovery (SN647485). Rectangular or square with rounded corners, practice camps are usually to be found in close proximity to a Roman road and rarely more than a few hours march from an auxiliary fort. The two on this particular road, which, by the way, are the only examples of this earthwork type in West Wales, may be the result of exercises carried out by detachments from *Bremia* or the fort at Pumsaint in the Cothi Valley (SN655405).

The long, straight stretch of road comes to an end beyond the second practice camp and then winds round the side of the hill to a point above the Twrch valley where aerial photographs have suggested a stretch of the original agger. Traces of this can be picked out on the ground as it cuts through the heather to the right of the minor road (SN643472-644476). Roman columns marching this way could now, if they bothered themselves with such things, contemplate the peaks of the Brecon Beacons rising magnificently on the southern horizon before they tackled the steep descent into the Twrch valley. Now a landscape of enclosed pasture, the valley would probably have been heavily wooded in Roman times, and this may well have concentrated the minds of the soldiers on the possibility of ambush as they approached the ford across the little River Twrch before heading for Ffarmers and Pumsaint. On the outskirts of the village of Ffarmers (whose Drovers Arms pub reminds us of the associations of the area with the cattle trade) there appear to be remnants of agger in the fields to the left of the present road before it once again crosses the Twrch to run due south towards the modern A482 (SN650442).

The new Ordnance Survey map shows the Roman road joining the A482 near the Royal Oak Inn. However, the original Roman line seems to have diverged from the minor road a hundred yards or so to the north of the pub and run along a deep old lane towards Brynmaiog Farm,

where it is marked by a hedgebank taking it to a junction with the A482 near a chapel below the pub. The subsequent course of the Roman road to Pumsaint, a mile-and-a-half distant, is unknown although it is probably marked by the A482.

Below and inset: Sarn Helen South east of Llanfair Clydogau

Above: Twrch Valley

Watching the heavy lorries thunder across the elegant modern stone bridge on their way to the industrial valleys of South Wales, it is difficult to think of Pumsaint as an important Roman centre. Yet here, at the confluence of the Cothi and Twrch rivers, a Roman fort enclosing 4.75 acres was identified in 1972-3. There is little to see today, but visitors walking to the Dolaucothi Hotel from its adjacent carpark will pass over the remains of the fort which excavation revealed to have been founded in the late 70s and subsequently abandoned in the mid-second century. The fort, tentatively identified with Ptolemy's *Luentinum*, later served to protect the gold mines at nearby Caeo from which bullion may even have found its way to the Imperial mint at Rome. A good deal of gold from the mines also came into local hands if finds in the area are anything to go by. In 1796 numerous gold ornaments of the second and third century were found near Dolaucothi House thirty years after a hoard of several thousand copper coins reputedly came to light in the same vicinity. More recently, 682 *radiates* coins ranging from the time of Decius (AD249-251) to Carusius (AD291), were uncovered during work on a Forestry Commission road near Erw-hen (SN676436).

The Roman emperors enjoyed a monopoly of bullion and no expense (or sweated labour of slaves) was spared in exploiting to the full the

Roman road; Llanfair Clydogau to Pumsaint

Above and left: The Lower and Upper levels of the Roman mines at the National Trust site at Dolaucothi near Pumsaint, between Lampeter and Llandovery. It is well worth a visit.

potential of the gold-bearing pyrites three-quarters of a mile south-east of Pumsaint. Here depressions in the ground and great gashes in the shaly rock indicate that both opencast and underground mining were carried out while a series of brilliantly-conceived aqueducts, one of them seven miles long, were cut into the hillside to carry water for washing the crushed ore and breaking down beds of pyrites. The remains of water tanks and reservoirs, an underground gallery drained originally by a large wooden waterwheel, and the 'Carreg Pumsaint', a great block of diorite apparently used for crushing the ore, may all be seen at this National Trust-owned site. Later mining has obscured much of the original Roman activity and some scholars have recently questioned the Roman provenance of sections of the aqueduct system. The great oak waterwheel, however, of which parts are now on view in the National Museum in Cardiff, are undoubtedly of Roman origin as

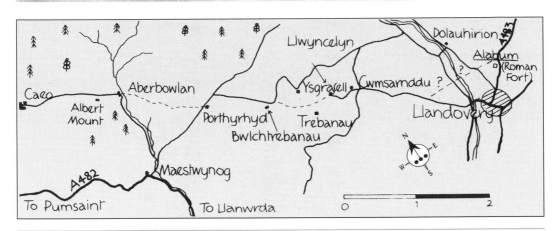

Roman road; Caeo to Llandovery

indicated by radiocarbon dating. Associated with the gold mines was the Roman bathhouse whose original location was to the south-west of the Pumsaint fort. Containing two hypocausted rooms, the bathhouse was built after the abandonment of the fort thereby suggesting that it was created for the use of mineworkers rather than the military garrison. Judging from coins and other finds, Roman or Romano-British miners were still performing their ablutions here in the late fourth century.

The country road to Caeo village (SN676399) runs through the gold mines and is generally reckoned to represent the original Roman line. Caeo itself is a charming place. Visitors will find little evidence of Roman activity, but they will enjoy the splendid church with its massive tower dominating the surrounding cottages. This part of Wales yields few interesting churchyards, yet here at Caeo we can see headstones whose materials and quality of execution emphasise the prosperity of the minor gentry families living in the area in the past. In a vault near the church lie several of the Johnes family of Dolaucothi who, like so many Welsh county families, contributed much to the affairs of nineteenth-century Wales and to the wider British Empire. Along side John Johnes, Lord Lieutenant of Carmarthenshire (died 1815), rests James Beck, a young officer who married a daughter of the family before being carried away by dysentery in Jamaica in 1864. Close by moulder the remains of another John Johnes whose career as Recorder of Carmarthen and a county court judge was brought dramatically to a close by a bullet from his deranged butler's gun. The most distinguished of this company was surely Sir James Hills-Johnes, VC, an old India hand who survived numerous Imperial battlefields to become Military Governor of Kabul during the Afghan War of 1879-80. He died, full of honours, in 1918, the closing years of his exciting career having been devoted to county matters and the governorship of the University College of Wales at Aberystwyth. In the latter post his experience at Kabul may have served him well!

From Caeo, a steep climb carries the minor road south-eastwards to the little farm of Aberbowlan on the River Dulais (SN696390). Here the Roman road fords the Dulais and heads across the hills on an alignment for Porthyrhyd (SN710378). Initially proceeding as a deep lane with a typical Roman zigzag on its steepest part, the road eventually becomes a sunken trackway across the open hill with occasional traces of embanking on either side. However, as it once again descends the hill to rejoin the minor road opposite the Drovers Farm in Porthyrhyd, it takes the form of an enclosed lane.

Between Porthyrhyd and Llandovery there are few clues in the literature or from aerial photographs as to the actual course of the Roman road. There is a very strong tradition that it ran along the present minor road as far as Bwlchtrebanau (SN722370) and then deviated to cross the tributary of the little Mynys stream at the bottom of a deep valley before running on towards Llwyncelyn (SN727636) and rejoining the minor road to Llandovery at SN742363. Unlike the modern road, curving widely as it does to avoid the steep-sided valley of the Mynys, this course would have offered the advantage of directness. At SN725370, a point beyond Bwlchtrebanau where this curve begins, a gate leads off the road to a narrow unused lane which seems to have been the original access to Trebanau Farm (SN725366). After a few yards this lane turns sharply southwards and deteriorates into a hollow way leading across the fields for the farm. According to local tradition the Roman road followed the early stretch of the farm track before continuing on a straight alignment to descend through the woods and across the valley on the line of the more recent Trebanau Farm lane.

Despite the lack of evidence on the ground, this seems probable since, at SN728366 where the farm lane heads north-west for the minor road, an overgrown track, aligned with the lane leaving the same minor road near Bwlchtrebanau, zigzags through woodland towards Llwyncelyn, westwards of which it becomes incorporated in the council-maintained country road to continue past Cwm-sarn-ddu (SN740364) and directly towards the River Tywi on the outskirts of Llandovery. This road has several characteristic features, including a long, straight section on the run into Llandovery, but only tradition and directness can be cited as evidence for its Roman origin. The problem with the final straight stretch is simply that it does not directly align with the fort to the north-east of Llandovery and an alternative crossing of the Tywi opposite Llwyn Howell has been suggested (SN761354). From here the Roman road would have struck out to connect with the Llwyncelyn-Bwlchtrebanau section at an unidentified point. Only intensive fieldwork and excavation in this area is likely to resolve the problem and establish the precise location of the last few miles of the eastern branch of *Sarn Helen* between Porthyrhyd and Llandovery.

The Llandovery fort was vitally important in the communications and military organisation of Roman Wales. Occupying around 5 acres and providing services for a garrison of 1,000 men, the fort controlled roads running eastwards and westwards for settlements at Brecon and Carmarthen and northwards for the forts of Bremia and Castell Collen. In common with several other forts in the area, Llandovery was originally built as an earthwork and timber edifice and after much alteration, rebuilding, and eventual reduction in size, was abandoned in the mid-second century. As usual, only the imagination can serve to remind us of the formidable nature of the original structure, with its wooden towers, barracks and storehouses dominated by the great *principia* whose site is currently occupied by St Mary's Church. Apart from various small finds, including a broken altar and scraps of Samian ware, the remnants of the *vallum* in the field near Llanfair House, and a Roman cemetery at Caefelin to the south-east (SN770347) there remains little by way of a monument to the troops occupying this remote corner of the Empire.

LLANDOVERY TO BRECON GAER

An important road linked Llandovery with the auxiliary fort at Y Gaer, near Brecon. Traces of the early stretches of this road as it heads for the River Brân on a south-easterly alignment for Mynydd Bach Trecastell are shown on aerial photographs as crop marks in the field immediately below the fort. Also, remains of the original causeway are visible in the eroded river bank and again as a long raised mound running across a sportsfield towards a gate opening on to the A40 opposite the White Swan pub (SN772344). After a second crossing of the Brân the Roman road takes up the line of the pre-1780s turnpike road between Llandovery and Brecon by way of the hills south of the Tywi Valley. Climbing out of Llandovery and past Picton Court, the turnpike makes a wide curve to avoid the steepest part of Allt Rhydings

Aerial view of the Roman marching camps of Y Pigwn

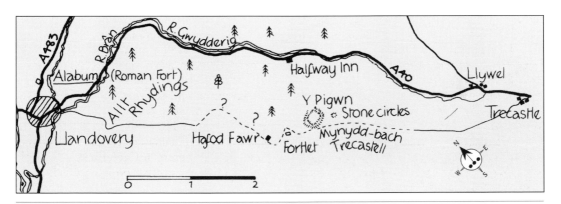

The Roman road from Llandovery to Trecastle

(SN780335). There is no field evidence to indicate any other course, so one must conclude that the turnpike surveyors were following the Roman road at this stage. They certainly did so for some way beyond Allt Rhydings where straight alignments towards Cefntelych eventually give way to a winding stretch of road heading for Hafod Fawr at the base of the mountain (SN814313). Henceforth the road climbs in an almost zigzag fashion to the top of the wastelands of Mynydd Bach Trecastell, passing close to a Roman fortlet at SN821310 and then, at the western end of the ridge, more or less alongside a series of old tile-working mounds to the south of the fine pair of superimposed Roman marching camps of Pigwn (SN827313).

At this remote and desolate point over 1,300ft above sea level, detachments of troops

Right: Gateway of the Roman fort; Brecon Gaer

Below: The Roman road (seen on the left) from Llandovery towards Trecastle, with Llandovery in the mid-distance

originally enclosed an area of more than 37 acres by means of earthworks and ditches, later superimposing a second camp of 23.5 acres. The earthworks of the camps are still traceable on the ground today, the *claviculae* or curved banks defending the openings in the ramparts of the inner camp being easily detected by the keen observer. Marching-camps like these were built during the early phases of the Roman conquest so as to provide an easily-defended temporary camping-site, the ramparts being supplemented by a fence of sharp wooden stakes. An undertaking of this sort must have involved a good deal of hard labour which, in common with that required for the building of practice-camps, would have been far from popular with the soldiers. Troops stationed in Wales no doubt detested the work and cursed it in a variety of languages as they rested in their heavy leather tents behind the earthen ramparts. Unlike the legions in lower Germany though, they stopped short of openly rebelling against the task. Of the latter, Appian wrote: '....They complained about the hardness of the work and specifically about building ramparts, digging ditches, foraging, collecting timber and firewood and all the other camp tasks that are either necessary or are invented to keep the men busy.' Grumble they might have done, yet here at Y Pigwn on the Brecknockshire-Carmarthenshire border, the Roman soldiers left behind an enduring monument to their vigour, discipline and profession-alism. Indeed, they left behind a monument which represents one of the few tangible pieces of archaeological evidence for the initial thrust of the campaign to bring the Welsh tribes to heel.

Aerial photographs of the site indicate the original Roman road as a thin line to the south of the old turnpike. It forms a well-engineered terrace running from just above the fortlet (which eventually came to replace the marching camps) to rejoin the turnpike some 500yards eastwards (SN821311-824310). In the mid-eighteenth century at 'a spot called the Heath Cock', approximately a hundred yards inside the Carmarthenshire border, was located a milestone bearing the name of the Gallic Emperor Postumus (AD258-68). This stone, now lost, was probably sited on the road when it was being repaired by the civil authorities undertaking responsibility for road maintenance after the bulk of the troops had been withdrawn. The turnpike, now a rough track through bleak mountain grasslands until it is taken up by a metalled road to the village, has for long been assumed to follow the overall course of the Roman road to Trecastle. However, excavation has identified a road, well-surfaced with chippings of Old Red Sandstone, to the north of the turnpike. This road clearly pre-dates the turnpike, though whether its origins lie in the Roman period or in early mining activities at Y Pigwn is not altogether clear. Equally, the course of the Roman road for most of the remaining 8 miles or so to Y Gaer is rather obscure. While logic suggests a route along the Usk valley, there are neither cartographic nor place-name clues, nor is there any evidence on the ground. Local antiquaries interested in establishing the details of this section of the Roman road should not ignore the traditional belief that it ran, in part at least, along the minor lanes to the north of the Usk, passing through the church near Llwyncyntefin (SN920280) and then to Parc-mawr (SN944300), Trallong (SN965296) and alongside the churchyard at Aberyscir (SN999297). Unquestionably the deserted lane immediately to the west of Aberyscir church, lying as it does in direct alignment with a ford over the Yscir and the west gate of the fort at Y Gaer, represents the initial stretch of the road.

Brecon Gaer, situated magnificently at the confluence of the Rivers Usk and Yscir in what is surely some of the finest countryside in Britain, was one of the largest and most important forts in the Principality. Occupying some 7.8 acres, the earthwork and timber fort was garrisoned sometime between AD75 and 100 by a 500-strong Spanish cavalry regiment. Eventually the earthworks and some of the wooden internal buildings were replaced by stone structures including a commandant's house and granaries, while a substantial *vicus* was later established outside the northern walls. When he excavated the site in the 1920s, Sir Mortimer Wheeler was able to identify much of the internal layout. Unhappily the entire area within the ramparts has been ploughed out so that apart from a stretch of the splendid north wall and the remnants of two angle towers, the stone gateways in the east, west and south walls are virtually all that remain immediately visible. The site is worthy of a visit for the gateways alone, their massively-constructed guardhouses reminding us once again of just how formidable these larger Roman forts must have been to the local inhabitants.

CARMARTHEN (MORIDUNUM) TO LLANDOVERY

As the Roman armies gradually withdrew from Wales once the fortification process had been completed, a limited degree of autonomy was established under local leaders. Many of these had been successfully cajoled into adopting the habits and way of life of the conquerors and *Moridunum* originally may have developed from a *vicus*, wherein native Demetae had observed and emulated Roman ways. Like *Venta Silurum*, the town was probably constituted as a cantonal capital following Hadrian's visit in AD122 and in any event soon became a highly sophisticated centre. First recognized from the street layout of the modern town, *Moridunum* has been extensively excavated since the 1960s, so that we now know that it occupied a well-defended 32-acre site with the planned layout typical of a Roman town. The wealthier citizens lived in underfloor-heated houses, their larders well stocked with amphorae of wine and olive oil from the Mediterranean and their tables set with fashionable high-quality Gaulish Samian ware. Their less opulent brethren owned flagons, kitchen bowls, dishes and jars made at pottery sites in the central and eastern parts of Britain. Both would have regularly strolled down to the 5,000-seat amphitheatre, cut out of the natural slope outside the east wall. Such a large structure, far in excess of the population of the town, may have served the dual function of being a civic entertainment centre and a meeting-place for natives from the local area. The latter, unlike their countrymen in the remoter hill-country, must inevitably have felt the cultural effect of the Romanized life style emanating from this brilliant centre which continued to flourish into the late fourth century.

Visitors to Carmarthen will find an excellent museum, Records Office and tourist information centre, all providing a great deal of useful material about Roman *Moridunum*. Today's town is dominated by nineteenth-century buildings, many of them dating from the time when it was a bustling agricultural centre and an important port for coasting vessels. By 1829 the place boasted no fewer than eighty-four registered ale houses, many of ancient lineage. Several of these, under the questionable pretext of making the flesh more tender before slaughter, maintained the old sport of bull-baiting with dogs, although this came to an abrupt halt early in the nineteenth century when a spirited bull killed the landlord of the Boar's Head. This house, The Talbot, The Nag's Head and the Ivy Bush were among the more notable coaching inns of Carmarthen, whose parlours several of the town's more famous sons knew well. Richard Steele (1672-1729) died in the house which later became the Ivy Bush Hotel, while the architect John Nash's earliest commissions included Carmarthen Gaol (demolished in 1938) and several local mansions. Another Nash, Richard 'Beau' Nash (1674-1762) was educated in the town before going up to Jesus College, Oxford and subsequently launching out on his remarkable career as master of ceremonies and arbiter of taste at Bath.

The Ivy Bush typified the fine old inns of the coaching age. Standing at the top of the town with the Vale of Tywi to the rear, it was the epitome of comfort for man and beast. Here, at the meeting place of the 'upper' and 'lower' turnpike routes to Milford Haven, travellers could briefly forget the rigours of travel as they watched porters clumping across the cobbled yard with heavy baggage and ostlers rubbing down sweating horses as they cursed the devil-may-care coach drivers. With a bumper of claret in hand and the aroma of succulent roasting beef lending an edge to the appetite, the prospect of the onward journey may have seemed just a little less formidable to the jaded visitor.

Carmarthen in the early nineteenth century

For many years it was assumed that the turnpike traveller between Carmarthen and Llandovery more-or-less followed the earlier Roman road currently marked by the A40 highway along the Tywi Valley. More recently, however, the work of Professor G.D.B. Jones, among others, has identified several significant divergences from this general line, the first of these occurring to the north-east of Abergwili railway bridge beyond the crossing of the River Gwili. Here the line of the Roman road drops away from the A40 to be carried on a causeway through pastureland in the direction of Nantgaredig. For a mile or so the course is now lost (presumably owing to the shifting of the bed of the Tywi) only to reappear as a series of continuous hedge boundaries between Tanyrallt Farm (SN478227) and 'The Berriwns', a group of houses below Nantgaredig School. These can be readily viewed from the A40 at Tanyrallt while a little further along the road below Llechwenny, parts of the original agger seem to have been incorporated in the field boundary. Aerial photographs from the 1960s reveal a cropmark at SN492216 which apparently locates the course of the road from the end of the hedgebank series towards 'The Berriwns', in direct alignment with the lane towards Glyneiddan Farm. This shows up on the ground as the slight depression of a hollow way

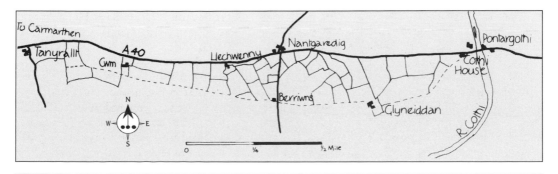

The Roman road from Carmarthen to Pontargothi

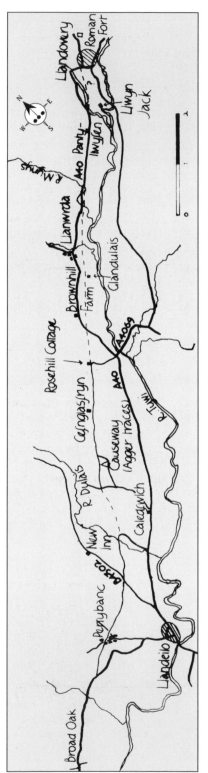

Left: The Roman road from Broad Oak to Llandovery (see page 47)

Right: The Roman road through Abermarlais Park, near Llanwrda (see top half of left hand map)

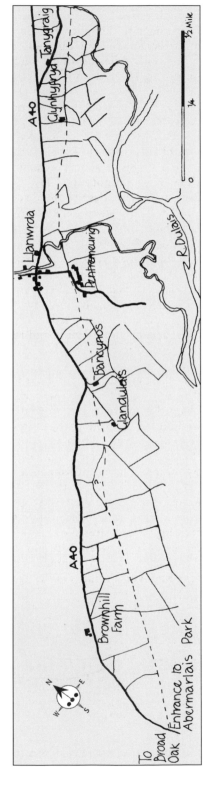

through re-seeded pastureland. A massive hedgebank now takes up the Roman line east of Glyneiddan to the spot where it joins an old lane near Cothi House, several yards to the west of the bridge carrying the A40 over the River Cothi at Pontargothi.

For some miles beyond Pontargothi the details of the Roman route are far from clear. According to most authorities the A40 follows the Roman original as far as Wern Garage (SN535214) whence it runs above the main road on a lane rejoining the latter at Nantarwenllis to the east. Thence straight alignments carry the A40 for 2 miles to Broad Oak, beyond which minor roads are thought to represent the Roman line to the hamlet of Penybanc north of Llandeilo (SN619240). This route, and its subsequent continuation towards Abermarlais Park several miles to the north-east, runs through the beautiful rolling country on the northern side of the Tywi valley and would have certainly provided a more direct approach than the later A40 along the valley bottom. The earlier stretches of the minor road system offer little evidence of Roman activity, despite the discovery many years ago of a milestone of the time of Tacitus (AD275-6). However at SN646255, beyond the crossing of the River Dulais south-east of New Inn, the country lane takes a sharp turn southwards to rejoin the A40, the earlier road being continued by way of a narrow deserted track through woodland to link up with the minor road heading straight for Abermarlais (SN655268). The directness of this section and the command-ing views which it offers of the Tywi Valley and the high land above the Dulais support a probable Roman origin, while the broad 20ft-wide causeway at SN663274 undoubtedly represents the remains of the agger. This causeway, to the north-east of the junction of the road for Caledfwlch, was particularly well-preserved in the 1960s, but is now less obvious in consequence of ploughing and re-seeding.

From this point travellers along the present road past Cefnglasfryn in the direction of Abermarlais Park are unquestionably on the course of the Roman road. At Rosehill Cottage (where an eighteenth-century tollhouse indicates that carriages took the same course during the early phases of the turnpike era) the road makes a virtually right-angled turn towards Llangadog. Here, at the original western entrance to Abermarlais, the Roman road continues straight through the park, running for several hundred yards on a raised causeway. It then descends towards a stream, with traces of metalling nearby, before being taken up by a footpath aligning with the eastern gateway of the park opening onto the A40. Sometime before 1851 a gold intaglio ring of Roman make was found close to the spot during drainage operations. Beyond the entrance to the park aerial photography has highlighted a cropmark carrying the Roman road south of the A40 to join a continuous hedgeline (along which is evidence of a causeway) to Bancynos Farm (SN69300-709310). From the south-eastern corner of the farm buildings a long stretch of the original agger heads straight across the fields on a pronounced causeway of between 30ft and 35ft in width eventually joining the lane past Pentremeurig (SN710311-715315). Immediately eastwards of Pentremeurig changes in the Dulais riverbed have removed all traces of the agger. However, it appears once again in a road running below

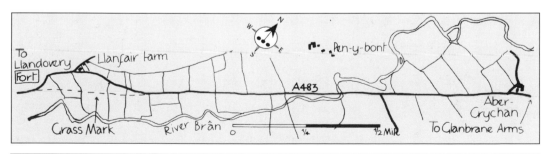

The Roman road from Llandovery to Aber-Crychan

the A40 close to Glynhyfryd (SN722318). A slight causeway on an alignment with the Pentremeurig lane leaves the field directly westwards of Glynhyfryd to join the metalled road, where traces of the causeway may still be identified on either side. Where this road turns north to join the A40, there is the slightest suggestion of a causeway maintaining the easterly progress of the Roman road (SN724319). Significantly this lies on a precise alignment with the field at SN735324 where, in the 1970s, ploughing turned up remains of agger and metalling and thus established the point where the Roman road coincided with the A40 for the final seven miles past Ystrad and into Llandovery. In all probability this was the stretch of road identified by the antiquary Fenton in 1800. 'Its surface [is] so altered', he wrote in a manuscript currently in Cardiff City Library, 'and so intersected with numerous enclosures in every direction that only by snatches can you follow it'. Keen observer as he was, Fenton failed to locate the remains of the Roman villa at Llys Brychan near Llangadog, some way to the south of the road. Unearthed in 1961, this late fourth-century structure, with its hypocaust system and walls bedecked with painted plaster, represents the sole example of a villa in this part of Wales and may have been built as the official residence of some Roman or Romano-British dignitary.

The long straight run of the A40 carrying the Roman road past Ystrad House ends at Pantyllwyfen (SN749333), where in the 1870s traces of the road metalling were recorded before being dug out by the tenant of the farm. This implies a straight continuation of the Roman line to cross the Tywi above Llwyn Jack and thence to proceed directly north-east to the auxiliary fort on the outskirts of modern Llandovery. The discovery, in 1825, of massive piles of oak in the bed of the Tywi between Blaenos House and Nantyrhogfaen Farm has led to speculation about a crossing further north. This would have involved the road engineers in what seems, superficially at least, to be a rather pointless realignment of their road. On the other hand this stretch of the Tywi may have occupied a rather different course in Roman times such that it was considered a more practical proposition to make a ford (or even a bridge) at the northern location. In all likelihood this will remain a matter for speculation since the meandering of the river over the centuries, coupled with the growth of modern Llandovery, will have removed any material evidence of the Roman road as it ran east of the Tywi for the fort.

LLANDOVERY TO CASTELL COLLEN

The fort at Llandovery played a pivotal role in the supervision of the Tywi Valley and of the several smaller valleys adjoining it, besides being an essential component in the chain of communications with the forts of the north, notably that of Castell Collen near Llandrindod Wells (SO056628). The Roman road running towards Castell Collen from Llandovery can be identified on aerial photographs by means of a crop mark in a north-easterly alignment through

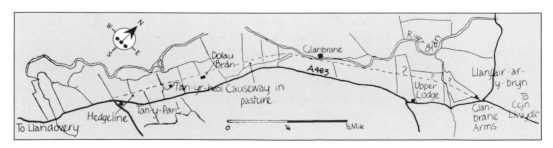

The route of the Roman road through the Glanbrane estate

Left: Roman road towards Caerau

the grassland immediately below the fort. At SN776356 the crop mark picks up the line of the A483 trunk road which carries the Roman road for the next mile-and-a-half past Aber-Crychan to Tan-y-Parc Restaurant (SN794375). Here the modern and the Roman roads diverge, the former continuing along the edge of the tree-lined hillside, the latter proceeding through the meadows of the Brân Valley. Initially incorporated into a series of hedge boundaries running towards Dolau Brân (SN797381) the Roman alignment was in the direction of the Glanbrane Arms, the old drovers' pub at the head of the valley (SN809396). A dominant feature of the Roman roadline is a massive causeway, some 30-35ft wide, clearly visible in the fields to the north of Dolau Brân and again alongside the river as it heads through the Glanbrane estate (SN803391). The causeway can be traced from Dolau Brân for the best part of a mile, although from time to time (for example, at SN801388) it has been eroded by movements in the course of the river. In the field to the northwest of Upper Lodge however, the causeway has been ploughed out and we have only the evidence of aerial photographs and parching in the dry season to show its onward progress (SN807392). The little stream of Nantcwmneuadd has obliterated any evidence on the ground, yet the alignment of the causeway coincides precisely with the minor road running in a north-easterly direction from the Glanbrane Arms on a steady ascent of the slopes of Cefn LIwydlo (SN811396). This road, degenerating into a rough and undriveable track through the Crychan Forest at SN841415, clearly represents the overall course of the Roman route, which, prior to local afforestation, would have offered excellent visibility to all points of the compass. Towards the top of the ridge, at SN849415, lie the remnants of an earthwork whose general appearance and location relative to the chain of Roman fortifications bespeak a possible fortlet, but this has yet to be substantiated by excavation.

Beyond Sarn Cwrtiau (SN872435) the road leaves the forest to join the minor lane past Gellicrugiau, Cefngorwydd and Aberdulais in the general direction of the River Irfon. While it possesses few immediately obvious Roman characteristics, this road certainly follows the general Roman line to the Irfon ford near Glancamddwr (SN920470) whence a northerly

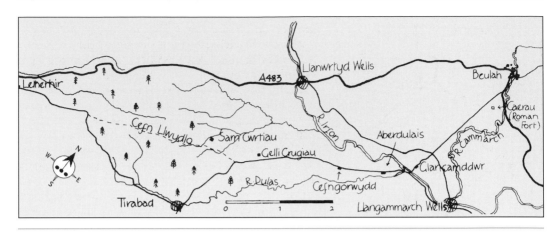

The Roman road across Cefn Llwydlo to Beulah

alignment heads for the auxiliary fort at Caerau near Beulah. To motor-bound travellers, incidentally, the Glancamddwr ford is impassable at all but the driest times of the year and those wishing to pick up the Roman road north of the river need to make a detour by way of Llangammarch Wells. Pedestrians cross the Irfon on a modern footbridge which, it has to be said, is a rather ill-proportioned piece of work for so charming and elegant a river.

A fine and remarkably straight piece of road (coinciding directly with the Roman line as evidenced by aerial photographs revealing traces of parallel ditching in the adjoining fields) runs through rolling countryside from the Irfon to the Caerau fort some two miles to the north. Standing on a low hill close to the road and overlooking the river plain, Caerau was an ideal 'half-way house' between Llandovery and Castell Collen. Excavation has uncovered a timber building (possibly the commandant's house) of the Flavian period underlying a later stone granary, its floor supported on small stone pillars. Also, pottery fragments found at the fort and at the adjacent civilian settlement in the fields to the north-east indicate an occupation period from AD80-140, after which the site seems to have been abandoned. At some time within this period the area of the fort was reduced from 4.2 to a mere 3 acres, suggesting, in common with several other contemporary forts, a possible demotion in status or simply a scaling down of garrison size. Today farm buildings and a medieval motte occupy the *principia*, and the ramparts of both the original and reduced fort are preserved under the springy turf of the surrounding fields. Outside the north-eastern rampart, where the ground drops away towards the River Cammarch, a ledge may mark the original site of the bathhouse, while the *clavicula* and northern and western earthworks of a large temporary marching camp can be seen to the west of the fort at SN919507.

It used to be thought that the continuation of the Roman road from Caerau followed the modern B4358 as it twisted and wound its way towards Newbridge-on-Wye several miles to the north-east, although it is difficult to see why this should be so since the local terrain would have allowed a more direct course. Indeed there is growing support (and growing evidence) for a totally different roadline independent, for the most part, of the B4358. Marked for part of its route on the new OS 1:10,000 map, this connects Caerau with the farm of Simddelwyd (SN941521) and thence to Glandulas (SN946531) and Sarn Helen Farm (SN970543), in line with the fort at Castell Collen. The straight modern by-road carrying the Roman line past Caerau proceeds northwards to join the A483 at SN922506 and immediately before this intersection traces of the older road may still be made out in the boggy ground to the left. The Roman road then began its north-easterly course, crossing the River Cammarch, ascending

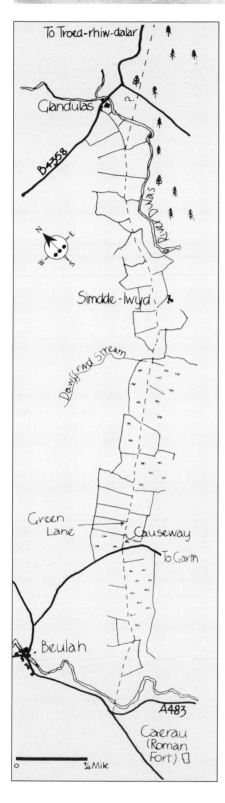

through rather wet land and following a series of continuous hedgebanks as far as spot height 253 on the Beulah-Garth road (SN928513). Aerial photographs provide clear evidence for the earlier course, while excavation in the late 1950s (at a point approximately half-a-mile north-east of Caerau) unearthed a road of 18-19ft wide made up of 9in of rammed stone on a bottoming of 7in of red clay. A glance over the roadside hedge at SN928513 reveals the continuation of the road by way of a very pronounced causeway leading directly into an old green lane on the same alignment.

This lane peters out after a few hundred yards, the roadline being preserved in the hedgebank series running towards the ford over the Dawffrwd stream beyond which it is carried past Simddelwyd by another deserted green lane of 10-20ft wide. At SN947529, below Glandulas in the delectable Dulas Valley, a causeway in a nearby field identifies a probable north-easterly deviation of the Roman road from the green lane in the direction of Troed-rhiw-dalar. For the next half-mile the original Roman course is less clear although local topography hints at a roadline broadly coincident with the B4358 past the early eighteenth-century Troed-rhiw-dalar Chapel and on as far as Penrhiwdalar (SN956536). Here, in all probability, (and according to local tradition), the road followed the footpath to Esgair-goch (SN967542) and thence to *Sarn Helen*. It must be emphasized, though, that however logical this course may appear, the unearthing of a few traces of metalling in the fields north of *Sarn Helen* constitute the only available evidence for Roman road building in the immediate vicinity. The same applies to the final 6 mile stretch running towards a crossing of the River Wye and on to Castell Collen. The orientation of the metalling fragments near Sarn Helen Farm implies an alignment in direct coincidence with the straight run of the B4358 as it heads for the fort. Alternatively, the Roman fortlet at Penmincae (SO006539) on the east bank of the Wye may mark a crossing point on the river in which case the subsequent course would have run north-north-east towards Newbridge-on-Wye before joining the B4358. Beyond the fact that this modern road probably follows the Roman line between SO024587 and SO035610, little more can be said save to suggest that local historians and field workers might care to focus their attention on the problem.

The Roman road from Beulah to Glandulas

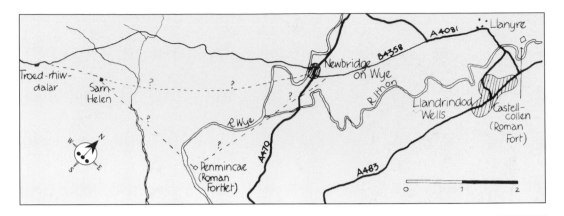

Possible routes of the Roman road to Castell Collen

The Castell Collen fort has been much excavated. Immediately before World War I some rather haphazard digging uncovered several fragments of inscribed stones and a set of Castor Ware cups besides establishing the location of the *principia* and the main walls. Later work in the 1950s directed towards unravelling the history of the fort, located a large extra-mural bathhouse (with provision for bathing in both moist and dry heat), the *praetorium* (commandant's house), *horreum* (granary) and details of timber barrack buildings. Scholars are generally agreed that the fort was originally constructed of turf and timber by Julius Frontinus's troops during the course of the struggle against the Silures in AD75-78. At some time in the mid-second century the defences were revetted with stone, stone gates with projecting semi-circular gate-towers were built, and some of the more important internal buildings were replaced with

Remnants of the Roman fort at Castell Collen

Troedrhiwdalar Chapel

robust masonry structures. This preceded a period of abandonment followed, in the early third century, by reconstruction and reduction in size so that later in the century, when the defences and gates were once again renovated and the ditches re-cut, the site was occupied by a squarish fort of 3.6 acres capable of accommodating about 500 men. In other words it was now only half the size of the earlier fort, reflecting the changing realities of the political and military situation in Roman Wales since Julius Frontinus's early campaigns.

From the rather dishevelled remnants of Castell Collen (which surely merits further excavation, or at least an attempt to render the remains more immediately comprehensible to the visitor), the spa town of Llandrindod Wells comes into view. Locally celebrated for the curative properties of its waters as early as Restoration times, Llandrindod achieved more widespread recognition when an ambitious entrepreneur by the name of Grosvenor attempted to capitalize on the growing demand for the waters by flatulent and overindulgent country gentlemen and built an elegant hotel in the village during the 1750s. Unhappily this building was officially closed by the local authorities in 1787 on the grounds that the 'entertainment' offered the clientèle amounted to more than a chaste cup of tea and a dry biscuit! Development of the town as a watering-place was limited by poor road access and it was only the arrival of the railway that prompted the building of the hotels, the boating lake, the golf course and all those other facilities which contributed to make Llandrindod so fashionable a retreat in the High Victorian era. The medicinal springs no longer attract much interest, yet the town is well worth a visit. It still retains that air of cloying elegance and respectability common to many of Wales' Victorian towns, behind whose bay windows and lace curtains Mr Grosvenor and his raffish friends would have been far from welcome. Indifferent to the ramshackle remnants of an earlier empire just down the road, the Victorian developers of those tall, serviceable houses seem to have built with a confidence that *their* empire and *their* way of life would last for ever.

2 SOME MEDIEVAL AND EARLY MODERN ROADS IN CARDIGANSHIRE

> Like one that on a lonesome road,
> Doth walk in fear and dread,
> And having once turned round walks on,
> And turns no more his head;
> Because he knows a frightful fiend
> Doth close behind him tread.

S.T. Coleridge
The Rime of the Ancient Mariner, 1799

For medieval man long-distance travel was a hazardous affair. The ever-present danger of highway robbery, the miserable condition of the road surfaces and the real possibility of passing unwittingly through a plague infested area were enough to persuade the prudent to settle their affairs at home before embarking on a lengthy journey. Once Roman Britain had fallen into disarray and the hordes from northern Europe and Scandinavia had imposed their way of life on lowland Britain, there followed a virtually complete collapse in trade which was not to recover until the ninth and tenth centuries. By the sixth century, those communities in Wales that had come to accept the customs and laws of Rome had, by and large, abandoned them, and throughout the long centuries between the departure of the Romans and the Norman Conquest the economy was essentially a Celtic one wherein pastoral farming predominated. Nevertheless arable agriculture based on settled farmsteads continued to play a role in the agrarian economy. Analysis of pollen samples indicates fluctuations in the relative significance of corn growing and shows, for example, that arable farming was particularly important in Roman times and again after 1150, though it certainly did not disappear in the intervening period.

As far as the living conditions of the people were concerned, scholars have tended until recently to draw heavily upon the works of medieval chroniclers, notably Giraldus Cambrensis, who recorded his impressions of life in Wales in the late twelfth century; 'They do not live in towns, villages or castles, but lead a solitary existence deep in the woods. It is not their habit to build great palaces or vast and towering structures of stone and cement. Instead they content themselves with wattled huts on the edges of the forest, put up with little labour or expense, but strong enough to last a year or so.' Reading this one cannot help feeling that the bulk of the population lived in isolated and rather spartan conditions largely without material comforts. This was certainly so in many cases, yet archaeologists are now beginning to discover that there were occasionally more sophisticated settlements. Indeed, excavation of two of the numerous drystone or rubble-built circular huts in North Wales has revealed paved floors and a simple drainage system. Furthermore, there is growing evidence of continuity of occupation both of Iron Age hill forts and Roman sites well into the early medieval period, so that at a location like *Venta Silurum*, burials in the extra-mural cemetery continued into the ninth century. Giraldus's mention of the 'solitary existence' of the native Welsh has also been called into question on the realisation that there was a tendency towards siting settlements around the old Celtic churches and on the western coastal fringes. In short, we cannot yet make overall generalisations about the pattern of settlement any more than we can be even remotely exact about the size of settlements in the pre-Norman period.

Of one thing, however, we can be sure; the Roman concept of a series of well-defined roads was lost. Wooden bridges gradually rotted and were swept away by winter flood waters; trees fell across metalled highways, drainage channels became blocked and with the abandonment of repair work much of the network decayed, save for short stretches used by local traffic. In other words, throughout the Dark Ages communications became distinctly difficult and movement over long distances must have been tedious in the extreme, above all during the winter months. Even so this is not to imply that roads ceased completely to exist. In upland areas where a considerable proportion of the land on the lower mountain slopes had long been enclosed into hedged or stone-walled fields, there were innumerable local lanes used as access roads by farmers. Again, on the open mountain, unfenced tracks forged by the seasonal movements of livestock provided well-trodden courses for local people to travel in search of bracken and peat and for packhorses to move between farmsteads and hamlets. It has been suggested elsewhere, with reference to Devonshire, that virtually all the farms and their associated trackways on the Ordnance Survey map for that county would have appeared had the map been drawn a thousand years ago. There is good reason to believe that the same would apply to much of the northern and western parts of Wales, particularly as the laws of Hywel Dda (Hywel the Good) specify in some detail the legal requirements regarding highways and by-ways.

At the time of his death around AD950 Hywel, a close friend of the English King Alfred, was ruler of a substantial part of Wales and he has traditionally been credited with codifying the customs of Wales into a single set of laws governing virtually every aspect of daily life. The earliest copies of the laws date from some two hundred and fifty years after Hywel had left the scene and some scholars have questioned the tradition that he and his chieftains were responsible for this massive undertaking. Whether it was Hywel Dda or some later luminary who took on the task, he clearly understood the role of roads and highways in economic development and effective government. Each *tref* or township, the laws state, should have a road running across and along it, while every habitation requires two footpaths, one leading to the church and a second to the watering place. Moreover, the same habitation should have a by-road of 7ft in width giving access to the common land of the *tref* and the *tref* itself should be separated from its neighbour by a meer of 5ft wide. In addition, the large administrative unit, the *cantref* consisting of 100 *trefs*, was to be delineated by a meer of 9ft wide. According to the laws, the ruler reserved for himself the punishment of persons committing felonies (such as robbery and the felling of trees) on the king's highway, which was to be maintained at a width of 12ft.

We find then, in the century before the Norman Conquest, a complex of local roads and trackways between villages and towns which had grown from habitual lines of travel by means of the movements of traders, pilgrims, tax-collectors and ecclesiastical and secular officials. It is important to realise that such roads were rarely 'built'. An occasional causeway over boggy ground might have been constructed, yet as a rule a medieval road represented a right of way along an existing trackway maintained by the passage of generations of men. As such, particularly where they ran through open hill country, these 'roads' would often be of great width since a horseman would always be on the lookout for an unbroken surface to ride on, as would the packhorse trains and strings of panniered horses which provided the principal means for the transport of goods. To this traffic the boggy, unmade surfaces would have offered relatively little obstacle. Even if the great magnate or court official travelling in a heavy covered waggon had cause to complain about the surface of the road, the fact that the extraordinarily mobile Norman and early Angevin kings did not bother to re-forge a definite road system implies that the existing roads were adequate for their purposes.

It also suggests that however decayed they may have become, some of the old Roman roads still played a part in local and long-distance communications. This is borne out by the evidence of the celebrated 'Gough' map of 1360, the first to give the general directions of roads, wherein of almost 3,000 miles of road shown, some forty per cent ran along the lines of recognized Roman roads. In Wales there are plenty of examples of Roman roads persisting in use through the medieval period and for centuries later. We find references in eleventh-century charters relating to properties in south-east Wales indicating that these lay both on local trackways and alongside what we now know to have been the course of Roman roads. Again, the Roman road from Llandovery to Brecon remained in use as a principal highway until the late eighteenth century, while a medieval Bishop of St Davids arranged for produce to be sent from his Brecknockshire farm to his Pembrokeshire palace by way of the Roman road through Carmarthenshire.

In the absence of a fully serviceable road network the movement of large numbers of troops in the more remote parts of Britain could present a field commander with prodigious logistical difficulties. To facilitate military activities in North Wales, Edward I cut a 30-mile highway from Chester to the River Conwy by way of Flint and Rhuddlan in 1277. Apart from the roads forged by the great Cistercian houses, this proved to be one of the few 'constructed' roads of medieval Wales and necessitated the employment of scores of sawyers, masons and charcoal burners. Significantly Edward ordered that the woodland on either side of the road was to be cleared to the width of one bowshot, a principle enshrined in the Statute of Winton of 1285 wherein a clearance of 200ft on each side of the king's highway was specified.

By the sixteenth century woodland occupied little more than 10 per cent of the total area of Wales, yet in the remote valleys the proportion was considerably higher and in these and the mountainous regions, travel, even on horseback, was very difficult indeed. As he rode through the Principality with Baldwin, Archbishop of Canterbury in 1188, Giraldus Cambrensis experienced at first hand the narrow tracksways, treacherous fords and steep mountains which, coupled with the inhospitability of the natives, meant that every mile of the journey carried with it the prospect of some incident or another. Even in the 1780s things were not that much better for, as Walter Davies observed, men and beasts tackled the hills and mountains, ' . . . more by a spirit of daringness than by craft or circumvention'.

Among the fundamental obligations of the medieval landholder to the Crown was that of maintaining the main highways of the land to facilitate the free passage of the king and his subjects. In theory then, the lord of the manor and his tenants were obliged to keep local roads and ways in serviceable condition. In practice, because relatively few people benefited directly from road maintenance, this task was tackled with less than tepid enthusiasm. Also, such were the effects of the Black Death and the devastation wrought by the Wars of the Roses in the following century, that manpower availability throughout much of Britain was so reduced that road maintenance became virtually non-existent. As trade began to grow in the sixteenth century an effort to rationalize matters was effected in the concept of 'Statute Labour' whereby every parishioner occupying land was obliged to provide a cart with horses or oxen and two able-bodied men to help with road repairs, non-landholders being expected to work on the roads for four, and later six, days each year. Normally carried out under the supervision of a parish-appointed surveyor who probably knew little about roads and cared less, Statute Labour was extremely unpopular and hopelessly ineffective. By-roads were almost entirely neglected, inter-parish disputes led to the abandonment of whole stretches of highway, and in most cases where maintenance was carried out at all it was done in so desultory a manner that little in the way of improvement resulted.

Despite the exhortations of the Council of Wales and the Marches, the secular authorities in the remoter reaches of west Wales paid little attention to enforcing the 'Statute of the Mending of the Highways'. Occasionally, where a large acreage of a parish lay in the hands of a magnate who believed his interests would be served by ensuring adequate road surfaces, some

Strata Florida Abbey; The great gateway

effort was made to improve matters. In general, though, the nature of the lanes and trackways comprising the road network changed little between Roman times and the end of the sixteenth century.

The situation on the estates of the Cistercian abbeys was very different. With a domestic economy based on sheep farming over many thousands of acres and the constant need to provide for the requirements of pilgrims, the Cistercian monks concerned themselves closely with creating adequate communications on their territory and within its vicinity. This chapter will consider some of the roads associated with the abbey of Strata Florida on the edge of the bleak mountains of eastern Cardiganshire (SN746658).

By the end of the sixth century much of Wales had been converted to Christianity by those remarkable Celtic saints whose names are enshrined in church dedications and parish names throughout the Principality. Their early settlements on the coastal fringes of Dyfed, constantly under threat from Viking sea-raiders operating from Ireland or the Isle of Man, became havens of culture and civilization in a turbulent countryside in which the people struggled to exist and the princes engaged in their favourite activity of fighting among themselves. By the twelfth century the energies of the Welsh princes were concentrated on the ultimately unsuccessful attempt to repel Norman encroachment from the east. But even this fearsome threat was not enough completely to stop inter-tribal strife. For the next two hundred years west Wales bore witness to sporadic military activity and neither people nor Church could avoid becoming involved as the fortunes of one prince waxed and another waned and the formidable Anglo-Norman cavalry strove to bring the country to heel.

In 1164 a small group of Cistercian monks from the Abbey of Whitland in Carmarthenshire set out for the remote wastes of central Cardiganshire with the object of building a monastery on land provided for the purpose by Robert FitzStephen, Lord of Pennardd. In accordance with

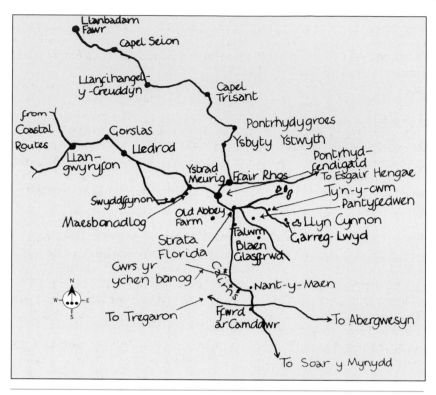

Roads associated with the abbey of Strata Florida, Cardiganshire

the Cistercian principle of teaching the virtues of a hard life governed by strict rules, the monks had chosen to settle in a barren place, 'far removed from the concourse of men'. Bounded on the west by the peaty morass of Cors Caron and on the east by a great block of inhospitable mountains, they could hardly have selected a less promising locality. Yet, like other Cistercian groups in Wales, the monks of Strata Florida created an agricultural settlement which made a major contribution to the economic development of the area. Initially they occupied a site to the south-east of the present ruins, not far from the old Abbey Farm. However, twenty years after their arrival in Cardiganshire, the great prince Rhys ap Gruffudd granted to the monks large tracts of land stretching virtually from Pumlumon in the east to Aber-arth on the coast of Cardigan Bay. This prompted a shift in the monastery site and heralded the beginning of fifty years of building, the cruciform abbey being completed in the mid-thirteenth century. Constructed of stone brought by sea from Somerset to the little port of Aber-arth, the new abbey of Strata Florida proved to he the largest, if not the grandest, monastic building in medieval west Wales.

As they struggled to build the abbey, the monks concurrently developed their demesne farm, laid out gardens and orchards and directed attention to the more distant outposts of the foundation's lands. At the centre of a large mountain estate with granges throughout Cardiganshire and in the neighbouring counties of Brecknock and Radnor, sheep farming, aided by King John's grant of a licence to export wool, became the mainstay of the monastic economy. The monks' success with sheep did not go unnoticed by the native peasantry and there are indications that by the early thirteenth century sheep began to increase in importance in an agricultural economy wherein animal husbandry had previously been dominated by cattle. Meanwhile, the monks found fish to be readily available in the lakes on the upland granges while weirs constructed in the streams passing through the abbey lands and on the coast at Aber-arth provided further opportunities for fishing. Also, the possession of granges on lower-lying land at Morfa Mawr, Anhuniog and Blaenaeron meant that oats and barley could be grown for consumption by both humans and livestock.

As a market for their surplus produce and that of their tenants and as a source of income from tolls, the monks founded the great fair at nearby Ffair-rhos (SN742680). This proved eminently attractive to visitors, as a visit to the fair could be combined with a pilgrimage to the abbey. To Ffair-rhos on St James Day, the Feast of the Assumption and Holy Rood Day, flocked local farmers, pedlars, pilgrims and the usual gang of ne'er-do-wells along with traders in cattle, sheep and wool. A similar clientèle attended the fair at nearby Ystradmeurig, established under the patronage of the Knights Hospitallers and an important trading centre until the early nineteenth century when the principal fair in this part of Cardiganshire became centred on Pontrhydfendigaid (SN705676).

For almost two hundred years Strata Florida Abbey was a major economic and cultural centre, surviving military activity, lightning, fire and the changing fortunes of the medieval economic climate. It was dealt a severe blow during the Glyndŵr rebellion when (and for years later) its precincts housed a royal garrison. Subsequently, bickering between the monks and other Church officials and the break up of the traditional medieval economy resulted in the abbey's falling into decline and the demesne lands being let out to lay tenants. Its fortunes had reached such a low ebb that on the eve of the Dissolution, Strata Florida supported a mere six monks and an abbot, and had a rental income of no more than £50.

In its heyday, though, the abbey was the venue of hundreds of pilgrims, ranging from 'professional' palmers travelling from shrine to shrine, motivated by a combination of religious devotion and wanderlust, to the ordinary citizen for whom a pilgrimage provided both a holiday and a means of observing the requirements of the Church. By the late Middle Ages, domestic pilgrimages had become increasingly popular and the papal dispensation that 'twice to St Davids' was equivalent to 'once to Rome', meant that Welsh shrines enjoyed a considerable vogue. Strata Florida was conveniently sited near the meeting place of several ancient tracks with the coastal highway linking the shrine of St David with the holy island of Bardsey, both important centres for pilgrimages. A particular attraction of Strata Florida was a small, much-worn wooden cup, reputed to be a fragment of the True Cross or, according to another tradition, to be that most holy of relics, the cup used at the Eucharist. The cup, eventually came into the possession of the Powell family of Nanteos near Aberystwyth, and is considered by some authorities, (though doubted by others) to have been with the monks even before they moved from the earlier abbey site. The cup apparently possessed miraculous properties and those drinking from it could be cured of all manner of ills. Small wonder, then, that it attracted a multitude of pilgrims to the abbey, particularly in years when plague and pestilence stalked the land.

Towards the end of the pilgrim era, Henry VIII's antiquary John Leland visited Strata Florida and travelled extensively in the surrounding countryside, his horse carrying him through a landscape by now substantially deforested. Since 1280 when the King's Justiciary of West Wales had been ordered to destroy the woodlands, 'where robberies, homicides and other enormities against the King's peace have been wont to be committed', the English kings had striven to reduce forest cover and thus to deny the Welsh a base for guerilla operations. This policy, along with the growing demand for charcoal for lead smelting operations, meant that by the mid-fifteenth century the bulk of the remaining forests on the lowlands of mid-Cardiganshire had yielded to plough and pasture. Readers of Dr Rachel Bromwich's splendid edition, in both English and Welsh, of the works of the great fourteenth-century Cardiganshire poet Dafydd ap Gwilym, might gain a rather different impression. Dafydd's description of his amorous adventures with the local ladies makes frequent reference to forest and woodland

Left: The memorial to Dafydd ap Gwilyn under the allegedly 1400 year old yewtree in the churchyard adjacent to Strata Florida abbey. His leg is buried near-by.

where he wandered in pursuit of passion. It is important, however, to differentiate between the term 'forest' in its modern and medieval senses. Within a medieval 'forest' large areas of cleared land used for agricultural purposes were interspersed with groves and blocks of woodland of varying sizes and mix of species.

The mountain sides though, were almost exclusively under rank, open grasslands which, according to Leland, '.....be so great that the hunderith part of hitt rottith on the ground and maketh sogges and quikke more by long continuance for lak of eting of hit'. Here the peasants dug peat for their fires, poached the occasional trout and eel and tended their herds during the summer months, living as they did in 'vari poore cottagis for somer dayres for catel'.

The early eighteenth-century maps delineate a roadline from Machynlleth to Ponterwyd across bleak open mountain via Glaspwll, Gwaunbwll, Dolrhuddlan, Bwlch y Styllen and Dinas (SN745007-748808). The young Michael Faraday, with some trepidation, trekked between Ponterwyd and Machynlleth in 1819, describing this trail in his diary as having, '....(1) no roads (2) no houses (3) no people (4) rivers but no bridges (5) plenty of mountains'. Five hundred years previously it would have been little different when groups of pilgrims, preferring this to the longer (if less arduous) coastal route, trudged their way to Ponterwyd to meet like-minded travellers entering Cardiganshire from the east.

The tracing in detail of the routes taken by these medieval pilgrims to Strata Florida and those followed by the monks to their outlying granges is bedevilled by difficulties. Besides the absence of contemporary maps and the scantiness of the printed literature, it has to be appreciated that many of the roads and trackways of mid-Cardiganshire had been in use for centuries and it is difficult to differentiate between 'prehistoric', 'dark-age' and 'medieval' roadlines. Nevertheless, the countryside is replete with evocative field and place-names providing valuable clues as to areas with pilgrim or monastic associations. Combined with evidence on the ground, such names, gleaned from the nineteenth-century Tithe Apportionments, enable roadlines to be established with some accuracy and the remainder of this chapter seeks to describe just a few of the many routes leading to and from the abbey of Strata Florida.

PONTERWYD TO STRATA FLORIDA

Pilgrims heading south from Ponterwyd pursued a route which was direct and kept to the higher ground to avoid the rushy morasses of the vales. The available evidence suggests that the medieval road as far as Devils Bridge followed the course of the present A4120 separating

The countryside between Ponterwyd and Devils Bridge

Ponterwyd village. From here pilgrims turned south to reach Strata Florida

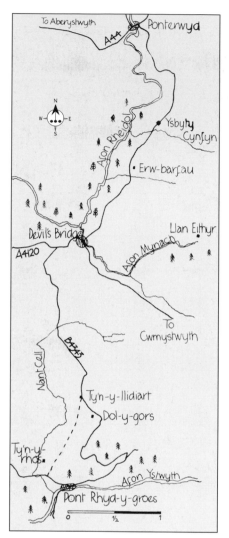

Medieval route from Ponterwyd to Pontrhydygroes

the lovely Vale of Rheidol from the grim mountains to the east, and past Ysbyty Cynfyn for the entire length of the journey (SN753791). The word *Yspyty* and its corruptions *Ysbyty*, *Spital* and *Spite* occur frequently in this part of Cardiganshire. Besides the villages of Ysbyty Cynfyn, Ysbyty Ystwyth and Ysbyty Ystrad-meurig, there is a *Spite* and a *Tavernspite* on the line of the Roman *Sarn Helen*. There are also numerous house and field names of this type on the Cardiganshire coastal road, the course of the major pilgrim route between Bardsey and St Davids. One of these, Spytty Hâl, on the site of three demolished cottages at Llanrhystud (SN39698), was located on land granted by Rhys ap Gruffudd to the Knights Hospitallers of St John, who also administered property at Betws Ifan, Betws Leucu and Pontarfynach (Devils Bridge) from their headquarters at Slebech in Pembrokeshire. The derivation of the Welsh *Ysbyty* from the Latin *hospi-tium* has been questioned by some scholars, but it is not without significance that these name elements oc-cur at strategic points on several established pilgrim routes. In any event, hospitality was a basic duty of all monastic bodies and in the absence of the *hospitia*, where news was exchanged, legends created and friend-ships forged, medieval travel would have been a far from pleasant business.

Of recent years scholars have begun to doubt the traditional assumption that Ysbyty Cynfyn itself is of monastic origin. They have, moreover, tended to dis-miss the view that the location of the church within a circular enclosure incorporating several large standing stones is indicative of continuity of site from pagan times, pointing out that the present shape has its origin in church and churchyard expansion at various times during the nineteenth century. There is no direct evidence to link the Cistercians or Knights Hospitallers with the site, nor, for that matter, with Ysbyty Ystwyth and Ysbyty Ystrad-meurig. Yet the strength of local tradition in this respect cannot be entirely neglected. For example, approxi-mately half-a-mile to the east of the present church lay a chapel of ease, locally believed to have been associated with Strata Florida. It may even have been this site of which Lewis Morris wrote in 1755: '.... once a year... they remain all night in the chapel and try their activities in wrestling, all the benches being removed and the spectators generally young women and old champions who are to see fair play.' Furthermore, at Llaneithyr on the banks of the River Mynach to the south east is *Cae Ffynon Saint* (Field of the saints' spring) traditionally supposed to represent the location of an ancient church. Unfortunately no field evidence remains (SN762772).

Circular cemetery enclosures embracing the older churches are quite common in west Wales and it has been suggested that at least some of these pre-date the church with which they are associated. The place-name element *llan*, commonly found in conjunction with early churches,

Standing stones built into the wall of Ysbyty Cynfyn churchyard

appears originally to have referred to the enclosure as opposed to the church itself. Evidence for this is provided by those farmsteads and other secular structures which have *llan* in their names and circular enclosures associated with them.

From Ysbyty Cynfyn the pilgrims passed the farm of Erw-barfau (mentioned in a deed of 1590) to arrive at Devils Bridge where the confluence of the Rheidol and Mynach created those remarkable scenic effects that were to move to rapture artists and writers of a later period (SN742770). Of the three bridges over the Mynach gorge only the lowest need concern us as it is usually claimed that this was built for the benefit of pilgrims by the Strata Florida monks in 1087 and provided a convenient crossing place for Giraldus Cambrensis on his odyssey a century later. While Giraldus was travelling through Wales, the monks of Strata Florida would have been busy with their new abbey and it seems rather unlikely that they would have gone to the trouble to build a relatively sophisticated stone bridge at this time in what was, after all, a rather remote spot. It is much more probable that they bridged the Mynach initially with a temporary wooden structure and replaced this with the present one at a later stage in the abbey's history.

Beyond Devils Bridge the pilgrim route pursued the present B4343 towards Pontrhydygroes (*rhyd* = ford; *groes* = cross; *pont* = bridge) as far as the farm of Ty'n-y-llidiart (SN742746). Here it deviated from the present road winding past Doly-gors and Pant-y-craf to take an ancient lane running directly south. Leaving Ty'nyllidiart as a rather marshy enclosed way some six yards wide, the lane runs along a causeway across the hilltop beyond Dol-y-gors whence it descends for a hundred yards or so as a deep green lane enclosed by high banks surmounted by wych elm trees. Subsequently it follows the line of a deep ditch (created by recent farm drainage work) towards the valley of Nant Gell where it joins a narrow lane opening into the Aberystwyth road approximately one hundred yards to the west of the bridge over the Ystwyth at Pontrhydygroes (SN739728). There may be some significance in the fact that as this lane descends towards Pontrhydygroes it aligns directly with Ysbyty Ystwyth church on the southern side of the Ystwyth valley where, in the fourteenth century, Moelgwyn Fychan is supposed to have granted land to the monks for the building of an *hospitium*.

After crossing the Ystwyth, presumably by way of a wooden bridge, pilgrims and other travellers followed the B4343 through Ysbyty Ystwyth and over rather gloomy countryside towards Ffair-rhos, passing the farm of *Llwyngwyddel* (Irishman's Grove) on the way (SN741686). This is one of several sites with *Gwyddel* (Irish) or kindred name elements in this part of Wales, many of which may have been associated with Dark Age Irish settlements. We know little of the density of Irish settlement in the fourth, fifth and sixth centuries, yet the presence of ogham inscribed stones throughout south-west Wales and the inclusion of Irish names and traditions in later Welsh genealogies implies that at least some of the Irish raiders

The pilgrims' way
from Ty'n-y-llidiart

who crossed the sea in search of slaves found things sufficiently to their liking to remain permanently. It is even possible that local chieftains offered them land in the hope that this would curtail the blood-letting and rapine accompanying their regular visits to Welsh shores. What is fairly certain from the evidence of inscriptions and place-names is that in the sixth century at least, much of southern Dyfed was Goidelic in character and language. While a great deal can be gained in this connexion from the study of place-names, *Gwyddel* calls for an element of caution since some locations may derive their names from those of itinerant Irish harvest labourers of the eighteenth and nineteenth centuries. No such interpretative problems occur with *Llwyngwyddel* which appears by name in a Chancery suit of 1532. Anyhow, it is noteworthy that by medieval times the word *Gwyddel* had come to be recognized as a term of derision, rather like 'Paddy' today, and may have occasioned a wry smile on the part of passing pilgrims.

After Ffair-rhos, whose local importance as a trading centre was emphasised by its

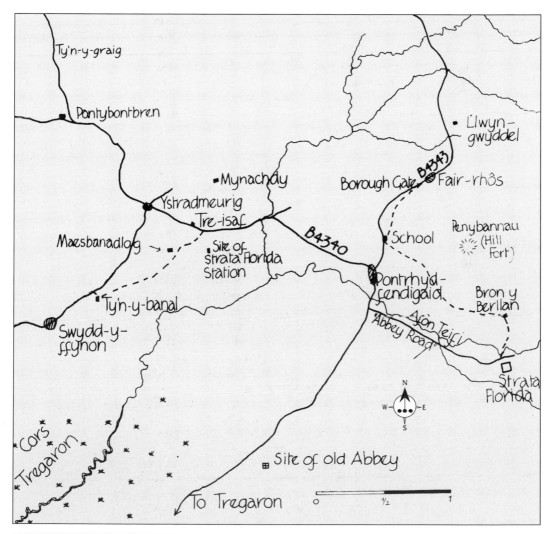

Pilgrims' routes to Strata Florida

The old Monk's Lane, now Lôn Nantaches, commencing by the school on the B4343, half a mile north of Pontrhydfendigaid

delineation on Speed's and Seller's maps of 1610 and 1695, the road continues for several hundred yards in the direction of Pontrhydfendigaid (Bridge over the Blessed Ford) to Borough Gate. From here to the village, the B4343 follows what is clearly a relatively recent course on a line suggestive of an enclosure road. Medieval travellers approached Pontrhydfendigaid more directly by leaving the existing road and heading south-west for the village school along what, by tradition, represents the course of an old road. Though recent field rationalisation and agricultural activity have removed any evidence on the ground, this road joined what was almost certainly the original approach to the abbey.

In medieval times, the present 'Abbey Road', if in use at all, would have passed through boggy meadowland, difficult to negotiate even during the summer months. It is reasonable to suppose, therefore, that visitors to the abbey and the monks themselves would have sought a drier, and if possible, more direct approach from the north. In all probability this was by way of the old lane running from the village school to the ford over the Teifi immediately to the north of the abbey. *Lôn Nantaches*, the present name of this lane, is apparently a corruption of *Lôn y Fynaches* (Monk's lane) by which it was known earlier this century. *Lôn Nantaches* leads off the B4343 from a gate adjoining the school and after a few yards of tarmac continues past the remains of an old well as a deep, green lane with banks planted with wych elm, hawthorn and hazel (SN735663). Varying from two to five yards in width it passes through the woods of Coed Penybannau below the Iron Age univallate hill-fort and its adjoining hut circles, and then traverses open fields on a causeway running above some abandoned lead workings towards the nineteenth-century ruins of Bronyberllan (SN746662). Here the abbey first came fully into view and visitors no doubt marvelled at its splendours, the massive limestone walls and finely executed tracery contrasting starkly with the crude vernacular architecture of the surrounding countryside. After a brief pause to stand and stare and perhaps even to offer a prayer of thanks upon the safe completion of their journey, the pilgrims descended along the ancient hedgeline south of Bronyberllan to ford the Teifi at a spot close to the present footbridge leading to the ruins of the abbey.

LLANFIHANGEL-Y-CREUDDYN TO PONTRHYDYGROES

The great church of St Padarn at Llanbadarn Fawr near Aberystwyth, an ancient foundation at the time of the establishment of Strata Florida, was an ecclesiastical centre of importance in medieval times and a port of call for pilgrims and church officials as they travelled through this part of Cardiganshire. From Llanbadarn the route to Strata Florida would have been by way of the Devils Bridge road beyond Capel Seion and thence to Llanfihangel-y-Creuddyn, the meeting place of a complex of deep lanes running through leafy countryside (SN665760).

Leaving this village, medieval travellers ascended the present road past Penybanc, occupying the course of an old upland trail to Capel Trisant, and thus avoided the steep slopes of Banc Cwm Magwr and Banc Nantrhiwgenau (SN717757). To the east of Blaen Cwm Magwr this road meets a number of old lanes, one of which, from Pen Bwlch Crwys to the north, was used by pilgrims working their way to Strata Florida from the Rheidol Valley (SN707765). Beyond the junction a deep narrow lane leads to the farm of Rhyd-y-pererinion (*pererin*, *pererinion* = pilgrim/s). Thence, instead of continuing down the lane to Mynydd Bach, the pilgrim trail followed a hedge line due south to rejoin the road above Capel Trisant, to pass Fron-goch Pool and on through broken hill country now rendered rather desolate by the remnants of nineteenth-century lead workings. Today's traveller might consider the rather scruffy remains of the many lead mines in the area to be a blight on the scenic beauty of Cardiganshire. It should be remembered, however, that the lead industry contributed significantly to the economy of the county over many centuries and the last vestiges of the mines are as worthy of preservation as any other class of monument. Each year the mines sink further into decay as shafts and leets are filled in and surface material is removed. This is a matter of growing concern to officers of the Royal Commission on Ancient Monuments and National Monuments Record (Wales) whose Aberystwyth headquarters would welcome public interest in the conservation of mines and other remnants of our industial past.

The old miners cottages at New Row, near Pontrhydygroes

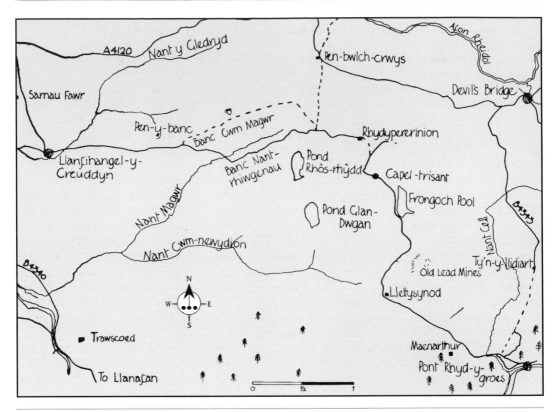

Medieval routes near Devil's Bridge

Beyond the lead workings, past Lletty Synod (which occurs in an indenture of 1571) and the miners' cottages at New Row, the pilgrims' road forded Nant Cell where it left the existing road for the old lane to Pontrhydygroes shared by the route from Devils Bridge. Apart from accommodating pilgrims, the way from Capel Trisant to Pontrhydygroes was of considerable importance to local farmers in the late Middle Ages, as indicated by the frequent mention of the corn mill at *Maenarthur* in fifteenth-and sixteenth-century documents (SN729728).

LLANGWYRYFON TO PONTRHYDFENDIGAID

Travellers leaving the coastal route for St Davids with the intention of visiting Strata Florida had the option of following one of the many ancient trackways winding inland from Llanrhystud and Llanddeiniol towards Llangwyryfon. In respect of Llanddeiniol it is worth noting the location of *Spite* on the A487 to the west of the village and the farm of *Palmon* (= palmer?, pilgrim?) on the banks of Afon Carreg to the east (SN569722).

There is no field or place-name evidence to substantiate it, but a very probable course would have taken pilgrims along the lane from Llanrhystud, skirting the earthworks of Caer Penrhos and across the dry land above Cwm Wyre to Llangwyryfon (SN599708). East of the village the present road meanders past Gors-las before moving away to the north-east and then turning south towards Lledrod. Approximately a hundred yards to the east of Gors-las a gate on the right-hand side of the road lies at the end of a raised causeway cutting across the open fields (SN622712). This descends the steep slope of the Wyre Valley to *Felin Saint* (Saints' Mill) and

Rhyd Saint (Saints' Ford), both of which occur on the Tithe Maps, while *Melin Rhyd-y-saint* appears in a legal covenant of 1599 (SN624709). Of the mill, used as a dwelling-house until the early years of the present century, only a pile of debris in the woodlands in the valley bottom now remains. From the ford by the mill a green lane climbs steeply up the side of the valley towards Pantybarwn where it turns abruptly left along a hedge line to meet a gate on the metalled lane leading to Lledrod past Ystafell-wen and Rhiwafallen (SN645703). Since the local mill was of major importance to the community and the lane adjacent to it provided the most direct route between Llangwyryfon and Lledrod, this, like those connecting with other mills in the area, was probably an important trackway in medieval times, while the name 'Saints' Mill' itself is indicative of pilgrim connexions.

An indenture of mid-seventeenth-century date refers to *Tythin yr Artal Mawr*; a farmstead located at the time near Bwlch-y-geufron to the south of Lledrod. *Artal* and its derivatives *Rattal*, *Ratshole* and *Ratsol* may represent a corruption of *Rhastl* (a rack or crib) or *atal* (to stop or prevent, in the sense of being an impediment). If *atal* is the correct interpretation, it is interesting that this word tends to occur as a place-name element on roadlines where the traveller faced a stretch of boggy ground, a rocky defile or some other obstacle to movement. *Atal* is merely one of many much-corrupted place-names whose deciphering awaits the advent of a Welsh scholar with an interest in historical geography and the stamina to tramp the highways and by-ways of this part of the world.

To the north-east of *Tythin yr Artal Mawr* lies *Spite Cottage* beyond which the pilgrims headed eastwards for Ystrad-meurig along one of two possible routes, the first following the present road past Penlan and across the Roman *Sarn Helen* to enter the village from the north. At Penderlwynwen below Pant-y-bont-bren are two fields, *Cae dan rhydgaled* (*rhydgaled* = paved ford) and *Cae pwllcleifion* (*cleifion* = invalids), the latter term being of particular significance in view of the association of Ystrad-meurig with the Knights Hospitallers and the tradition that a hospital was maintained at Hafod-y-cleifion near the site of the old Strata Florida railway station (SN712672). While this is some distance from the abbey itself the prevalence of plague and leprosy in the Middle Ages meant that the locating of a quarantine 'hospital' near the junction of several routes to the abbey would have seemed eminently sensible. Here, or perhaps at *Tir-llety y cleifion*, (by the seventeenth century an alternative name for nearby Tre Isaf Farm), sick or invalid pilgrims and other travellers could be 'screened' before being allowed into the abbey.

An alternative route for Ystrad-meurig and Pontrhydfendigaid involved turning south off the previous road beyond Gilfach-las and crossing open common land to pass by the earthwork

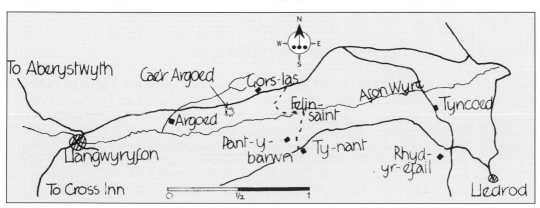

Trackways towards Strata Florida from the west

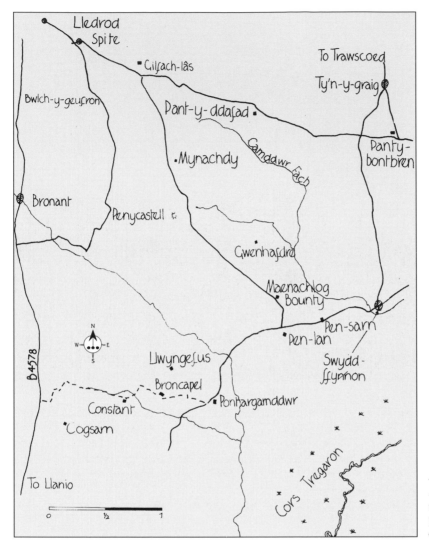

Alternative routes
towards Strata
Florida from the west

of Penycastell with its large round motte and counterscarp bank (SN663675). Now served by a metalled road, this course passes through rather melancholy countryside punctuated by clumps of trees representing the sites of abandoned farmsteads, notably Mynachdy Ffynnon Oer with its associated wayside spring. Further on, at Gwernhafdre Uchaf, are two fields called *Maenachlog Bounty* (*Maenachlog/Mynachlog* = monastery) below which the road turns left for Swyddffynnon along the lane from Castell Flemish (SN692662). It is widely believed that this lane, in part, lies on the easterly route taken by pilgrims leaving the Roman road of *Sarn Helen* at a point close to Cog-sarn, whence it passed through Constant and Broncapel to join the Castell Flemish–Swyddffynnon road at Pontargamddwr (SN669648). Although the Tithe Map of the area shows a causeway at Constant (SN657649) and a *Ratshole* to the north-east, it is difficult, given the nature of the terrain, to see this as a regularly-used pilgrims' way. However, at *Cae Demer*, Broncapel, were originally the remains of a chapelry served by the Strata Florida monks who must have approached the place by way of Swyddffynnon, the great bog of Cors Caron preventing the forging of a more direct route.

From the tiny village of Swyddffynnon, today's travellers approach Ystrad-meurig along the

The road to Ystrad-meurig from Lledrod

metalled road past the remains of the important (and much-fought over) Norman stronghold eventually dismantled by Maelgwyn ap Rhys in 1202 (SN702675). However, at Ty'nybanal, approximately half-a-mile towards Ystrad-meurig an ancient lane leaves the road and skirts the wet land on the northern flank of Cors Caron to run past Maesbanadlog, before joining the B4340 west of Ystrad-meurig Post Office (SN710673). In view of the preponderance of evocative field names in the vicinity it is likely that this lane, varying from 10ft to 30ft in width and enclosed by high banks, originally provided a more direct route to Pontrhydfendigaid and thus to the abbey.

MOUNTAIN WAYS TO THE EAST

Eastwards of the River Teifi much of Cardiganshire is high country of peat-capped plateaux cut by deep, rocky valleys. For much of the year when rain-sodden winds sweep off Cardigan Bay, these lonely uplands comprise an inhospitable environment for both man and beast. Yet, since time out of mind, men have driven their sheep and cattle to the mountain grazings during the brief summer months, the ruins of enclosures and simple *hafod* dwellings bearing silent witness to this practice. Until well into the eighteenth century the transhumance system whereby livestock was transferred for the summer from the lowland *hendre* to the mountain *hafod*, accompanied by the women and older menfolk, remained an important feature of the farming economy. So effective was the *hafod/hendre* system in terms of optimum utilisation of pasture that it was readily adopted by the Cistercian monks on their granges in the heart-lands of Wales. The need for the monks and their lay assistants to move readily from the abbey to the upland granges, and for that matter, to the various chapelries on the remoter

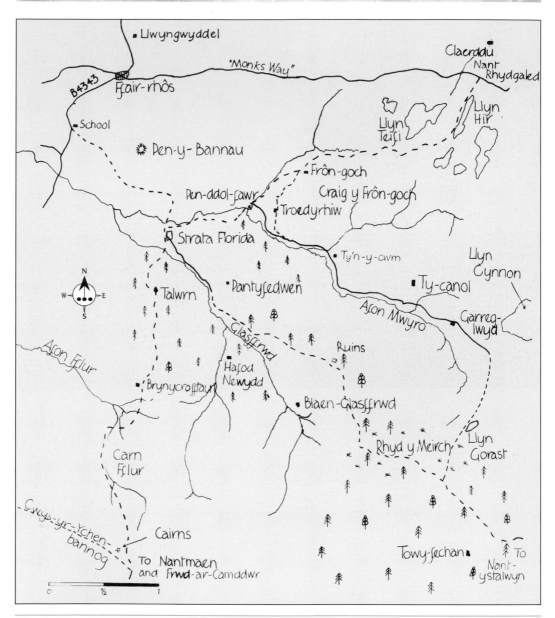

The 'Monks Way' and other tracks to Strata Florida from the East

parts of their property, meant that over the years recognized trackways became established. Many of these trails, followed by countless pack-horse trains throughout the several hundred years of Strata Florida's history, probably followed the lines of trackways forged centuries previously. As with so many roads, however, it is virtually impossible to be sure of their origins. In later centuries some of these long-distance cross-country routes came to be used by cattle drovers heading for the English border; later still they became incorporated into the network of Forestry Commission roads.

Singer's map of 1803 shows a road from Ffair-rhôs running to the north of the Teifi Pools

The 'Monks Way' fording the Claerwen

and south of the isolated mountain farm of Claerddu (SN793687). This road, known locally as the 'Monks Way', forms part of the ancient route linking Strata Florida with its granges of Nannerth and Cwmdeuddwr on the River Wye and eventually with the sister foundation of Cwmhir near St Harmon in Radnorshire. It is possible nowadays to drive along the road to a point just beyond Llyn Hir at 1,400ft above sea level, crossing *Nant Rhydgaled* (Stream of the paved ford) on the way. As they laid their stepping stones in the little stream, the monks probably reflected upon the desolate nature of the terrain which could hardly have been further 'removed from the concourse of men', the rock-strewn countryside silent save for the moaning of the wind.

As the modern tarmac comes to an abrupt halt, the 'Monks Way' deteriorates into a rough track. Recent traffic has changed the nature of the surface, yet careful inspection reveals the remains of clearance cairns and, at points where the road passes over a peaty depression, evidence of the carefully placed flat paving-stones some distance below the present surface. Half-a-mile beyond the ford over the River Claerddu the 'Monks Way' leaves the track across the great blanket of peat to the south of Claerwen and heads in a northeasterly direction by way of a path across the boggy slopes of Esgair-Hengae (SN805677). Here and there the course of the path seems to be defined by marker stones, although these may be merely incidental. Certainly for most of its course the route is rather difficult to follow, except where it occurs as a sunken way or a terrace around a contour. To the north-east of the ruins of the ancient upland farmstead of Hengae, the 'Monks Way' fords the River Claerwen before ascending the slope of Esgair Cwynion as a green way into Radnorshire (SN824682). Here again there are occasional suggestions of crude paving where the way crosses a patch of peat on the open hillside. From the brow of Esgair Cwynion the road can be seen as it passes to the south of Llyn Cerrigllwydion Uchaf. It then runs on for several miles to the River Elan ford (SN899719) where it crosses the old Rhayader-Aberystwyth turnpike and negotiates further hills before finally reaching the banks of the River Wye.

The Tithe Map for the parish of Gwnnws marks a road passing through Troedyrhiw and Fron-goch to the north-east of Strata Florida and joining the 'Monks Way' above Llyn Hir (SN791682). This was the path taken by Leland when he set out from the abbey in the 1530s to view the Teifi Pools and Claerddu River, only to find, 'in no place within sight no woodd but al hilly pastures'. It has changed little; a landscape treeless as far as the eye can see with frost shattered rock, moorland peat and rough pasture being its dominant features. Leaving the abbey, this old road passed Dolau-fflur and then followed the line of the present road to Penddôl Fawr. Here it forded a tributary of the Teifi and ran up the valley to Troedyrhiw, not far from where a medieval long-hut and associated enclosures have been identified (SN764663). Looking westwards from Troedyrhiw the observer cannot fail to be impressed by the numerous ruins of farmsteads dotted about the hillsides. These are likely to have originated as *hafodydd* serving farms in the Teifi Valley east of Pontrhydfendigaid, and provide evidence of the

Medieval hollow way beyond Pantyfedwen

relatively dense occupation of this countryside prior to farm amalgamation and the creation of self-contained upland holdings.

Between Troedyrhiw and Fron-goch, a distance of rather more than half-a-mile, recent agricultural improvements have obscured the course of the road. However, from behind the house at Fron-goch it can be followed round the northern side of Craigyfrongoch along a rough track cleared through the stone-strewn upland pastures. This eventually descends to ford the infant River Teifi before climbing towards Llyn Hir along a hollow way, now only discernible in parts. Leland remarked upon the excellence of the trout and eels of Llyn Hir, Llyn Teifi and the other lakes of the Teifi Pools group, and it seems that the route described, certainly representing the most direct and easily negotiable way between the abbey and the lakes, was that taken by the monks of Strata Florida to their mountain fisheries. There is a local tradition that the monks also took fish from Llyn Cynnon to the south of the Teifi Pools where a medieval complex, including a long-hut linked to the lake by a slabbed trackway under the peat layer, has been reported by the Royal Commission on Ancient Monuments. The Commission suggest that what appears to be a slab-lined store cut into the hillside was used for holding fish before carrying the catch back to the abbey. If this was so, the monks would have reached the remote lake by way of the lane from Ty'n-y-cwm, south-east of Troedyrhiw on the trail to the Teifi Pools (SN771655).

This ancient track, running along the vale of the Myro to Garreg-lwyd, passes through a stretch of countryside offering yet another reminder of the relative density of the population of these uplands in former times. The valley bottom and the bracken covered hillsides are dotted with the remnants of houses, farm buildings and livestock enclosures, some abandoned over the last hundred and fifty years during times of agricultural depression and others long before that. Many, connected by a network of trackways, may themselves be of considerable antiquity, while others yet may represent early settlement sites. On the hillside below the ruins of the early nineteenth-century farmstead of Ty-canol, for example, are the remains of a single-storey house and several small enclosures. Was this an earlier Ty-canol; and if so, when did it originally come into being? What area of land did its occupiers cultivate and what caused them to abandon the site? The problem with questions of this sort is that few of these ruins contain datable artefacts. Also, because there are no *known* surviving farm buildings of Dark Age or medieval construction in Cardiganshire (and a mere handful in the Principality as a whole), it is difficult to decide on the provenance of a ruin unless its architecture proclaims it to be of a recent period. The possibility remains, though, that a ruined farmstead, even of Victorian origin, may mark the location of a settlement with Dark Age and perhaps prehistoric origins. Only a combination of careful and exhaustive local studies by historians and excavation of selected sites by archaeologists will help to give the true picture.

A particularly important route used by the Strata Florida monks was that connecting the abbey with the chapelry of Ystrad-ffin and the grange of Nant-y-bai in Carmarthenshire. From the abbey site the rocky lane behind the adjacent farm fords the Glasffrwd near the present footbridge and climbs through old woodlands of oak and silver birch. At this stage the precise line of the trackway is difficult to follow owing to the cattle tracks running around and across it. However, the approach to the ruins of Talwrn at the edge of the woodland is by way of an enclosed lane lying on the line of the monks' road (SN745649). As it continues southwards beyond the farm, the antiquity of its banks and the diversity of tree species growing upon them, suggest a possible early origin for this road. Passing through a further stretch of woodland into unenclosed countryside beyond the fields south of Talwrn, the banks disappear and the road becomes a hollow way of 4-5ft deep.

Here, if one takes the trouble to scrape away the oak, birch and, more lately, coniferous debris of the centuries it appears, in places, to have been paved with small, regular stones set in the underlying clay. Beyond this deciduous woodland the road enters wet open hills and runs through a recent Forestry Commission plantation. Today its course through the young plantation is difficult to identify and the walker's progress is severely hampered by luxuriant growth of rushes and bracken. In the Middle Ages, however, when the track would have been regularly used, the going was no doubt easier and groups of monks would have regularly tramped their way into the gloomy hills of the south, perhaps turning round from time to time to contemplate the fine views over the upper reaches of the Teifi. Rather more than a mile beyond Talwrn the track skirts the ruins of Brynycrofftau (SN744633). Incorporating massive stones, some of them carefully faced, this complex of buildings seems to have been erected without the use of mortar and certainly gives the impression of being of some antiquity. To the southeast of the house are the ruins of what has been identified as a small corn-drying kiln of eighteenth- or nineteenth-century origin with a stone-lined drying chamber and stone-capped flue. This should remind us again that we tend to think of upland Wales as being dominated by an almost exclusively pastoral economy, yet cereals were grown in these hills and valleys in times past. During the Napoleonic Wars, the high price of wheat meant that it was profitable to grow that crop in these ecologically marginal areas while eight hundred years earlier, the need for subsistence led to the cultivation of wheat, barley and oats for human and animal consumption and of flax for making linen. We do not know, and are unlikely ever to know, the relative significance of arable and pastoral farming in the Welsh uplands in medieval times, although it is worth recalling that at the end of the twelfth century climatic conditions in this part of the world were rather more favourable to cereal growing than they are today.

As one looks directly west from Brynycrofftau towards the site of the Old Abbey three miles away, further ruined farmsteads come into view. These scattered holdings, with their tiny enclosed fields carved from the hillside, appear on architectural grounds to be of eighteenth- or nineteenth-century date, but some of them at least, might represent medieval settlement sites. Alternatively they may mark the position of *hafodydd* of indeterminate date or, yet again,

Continuation of the hollow way skirting the hillside

the location of eighteenth-century squatters' dwellings. If they are in fact of medieval origin, this particular stretch of countryside would have seemed rather less empty and melancholy to the traveller than it does to us today.

After descending the slopes of Carn Fflur to ford the River Fflûr, the road once again begins to climb and after two miles across open mountain it passes to the east of a complex of Bronze Age cairns at 1,776ft above sea level (SN741610). It is likely that these and others of the many cairns in this part of Cardiganshire owe their survival to their having served as markers on routes and trackways. Hundreds, if not thousands, of those cairns in less accessible places have been taken for building material, a practice which, if it continues, will yet further impoverish our already threatened corpus of field monuments. Beyond the cairn complex the road runs southwards to join the line of the ancient earthwork of Cwys-yr-Ychen Bannog. The earthwork, visible to the east of the cairns, forms the dividing line between the parishes of Upper and Lower Caron and is believed to have been built by the monks of Strata Florida to define the extent of the land granted them by Rhys ap Gruffudd. The Cwys is certainly a boundary marker of some description, but there remains some doubt as to its origins, the most widely held view at present being that it dates from the Dark Ages.

Below the cairns the road is clearly visible on aerial photographs, although rather difficult to follow on the ground as it runs in a south-easterly direction towards Nantymaen (SN762585). The general course, though, was across the slopes of Bryn Cosyn and Esgair Ambor, thereby avoiding the dangerous bogs of Blaen Camddwr. Now and again, especially between the two cairns at the foot of Bryn Cosyn and Esgair Ambor, the road follows a modern fence line and on the descent to Nantymaen it runs alongside the remnants of an earthwork, presumably the southern extension of Cwys-yr-Ychen Bannog. At Nantymaen the road is incorporated with the farm lane heading for Ffrwd-ar-Camddwr on the intersection with the older drovers' road between Tregaron and Abergwesyn. From the ruins of Ffrwd-ar-Camddwr, a farm cited in the marriage settlement of James Pryse and Ellynor Gwynne in 1589, the monks' road continued along the banks of the Camddwr on the long journey south past Soar-y-mynydd to Ystrad-ffin.

Yet another road from the abbey of Strata Florida crosses the mountains in a south-easterly direction to join the Tregaron-Abergwesyn trail at Nantystalwyn, involving a journey of some ten miles. Once again this road is marked on Singer's 1803 map and features prominently on the Tithe Maps of the parish of Caron, while aerial photographs taken in the 1940s, before the Forestry Commission began planting in the area, showed its course very clearly indeed. Needless to say, the roadline is now obscured by the criss-cross of access and service roads following in the wake of afforestation. Nevertheless, for at least half of the exhausting journey to Nantystalwyn the original road can still be followed by the energetic walker. Between the Abbey Farm and Pantyfedwen (both incorporating material from the abbey in their buildings) the road is metalled. A gate at the edge of the forestry opens on to a plethora of tracks, the original road being the one which steadily ascends the planted hillside by way of a rocky lane lined with gorse, heather and whinberry. To the right the lane runs side-by-side with a forestry road with branches leading off to the farms of Hafod Newydd and Blaenglasffrwd, the latter lying close to a cairn cemetery and an early complex of huts and enclosures (SN767633).

Passing through ranks of conifers for almost a mile the road runs by the remains of a deserted farmstead to a gate and the open mountain. From this gate it continues to climb alongside the forestry as a shallow green lane which, in common with earlier stages along its length, shows clear signs of having been embanked on its western side in order to ensure a relatively level ascent. After approximately half-a-mile yet another gate carries the road into the forestry and the descent into the marshes around Nant Rhyd-y-meirch (SN779627). Tradition has it that this lonely spot witnessed the passage in 1094 of the troops of Rhys ab Owain and Rhydderch ap Caradog, princes of South Wales, as they journeyed to do battle with the sons of Cadwgan ap Bleddyn, who had been responsible for the murder of their grandfather. A group of platform houses of probable medieval origin and a short length of revetted road leading from this complex into boggy land near the ford have been identified recently on the rocks near Nant Rhyd-y-meirch. From Rhyd-y-meirch the road's course is rather obscure, but it is likely to have followed the line of the track flanking the Tywi forest along the banks of Nant Gwineu to its confluence with the Tywi river at the farm of Moel Prisgau (SN806612). It then seems to have extended due south along the rocky Tywi Valley past Nantystalwyn to join the drovers' road between Tregaron and Abergwesyn (SN804569).

Left: Stones from Strata Florida incorporated into nearby farm buildings

Like some of the others described in this chapter, the road to Nantystalwyn was used by cattle and sheep drovers until the development of the railway system in the mid-nineteenth century heralded the beginning of the end of the age-old droving trade. Victorian cattlemen may not have appreciated it, but they and their animals were often travelling along trackways well-established centuries before the Norman knights landed in England. Continuity of use also applied to many of the farm and settlement sites alongside and in the vicinity of the tracks. Given the choice, the wise farmer will always select well-drained, south-facing land for settlement and cultivation. Such land is normally relatively easy to work and warms up quickly in the spring months thereby triggering off crop growth. The early farmer would soon have learned the vital importance, in terms of getting as high a yield of food as possible from his holding, of selecting an 'early' site and his successors down the years would have had little reason to abandon that site unless forced to do so. True, there would be movement *within* the site as buildings became redundant and the farmer responded to agrarian change, and the area cultivated may also have increased with time. The fact remains, nevertheless, that the original place of settlement may in many cases have remained occupied for centuries. It is significant in this context that Rhys ap Gruffudd's grant to Strata Florida, dated 1184, mentions the farms of Moel Prisgau, Dolfawr, Tref-y-Gwyddel, Mynachty Ffynnon Oer and several others which were still occupied in the early years of the present century. Other sites in the uplands and mountains of Cardiganshire may represent the remains of *hafodydd*, while others still may be squatters' holdings of eighteenth- and nineteenth-century origin. Only when the archaeologists have investigated the ruins will the present-day traveller along the roads of Cardiganshire and of other parts of the north and west of Wales be able to obtain a true idea of the settlement history of the surrounding landscape.

Looking towards the Altar, Strata Florida

3 PRE-TURNPIKE ROADS IN RADNORSHIRE

These high wild hills and rough uneven ways
Draw out our miles and make them wearisome -

William Shakespeare
Richard II

Welsh roads remained largely free of wheeled vehicles before the latter part of the seventeenth century. Occasionally a great magnate trundled through the countryside in an unsprung horse-drawn carriage on a grand, if uncomfortable progress to his mansion, overtaking, perhaps, a local carter, his ox-wagon loaded with goods destined for a country fair. Overall, though, the roads remained the province of the packhorse and mule or the well-shod mare of the parson, squire or man of business. Once they had left the immediate proximity of the village or town most roads were unfenced and tended 'to grow better of themselves' through the combined action of the weather and of travellers turning aside to the surrounding farmland to avoid potholes. It was to the confined roads close to centres of population that most of the legal papers relating to road conditions refer, one such road being in the mind of Sir John Wynn of Gwydir when he penned an *aide-memoire* in 1616; 'Call Petty Sessions and take a mise on the Highways'.

Statute Labour and local enterprise had done little to improve the pitiful surfaces of the roads which had remained with few exceptions in *status quo* since medieval times. This was a serious matter to the authorities because poor communications had the dual effect of limiting the expansion of trade and of impeding the progress of both official and private posts. A primitive postal system for the transmission of the king's mails and those of his more favoured courtiers had existed in Tudor times, but the private individual or merchant had relied on messengers, trusted travellers or drovers to carry gifts, letters and money the length and breadth of the country. Drovers, in particular, played an important part in this traffic. In the spring of 1585 Sir George Chaworth explained to the Countess of Rutland that, '.... I have done my best to procure you some money to be paid in London, but I could not do so as most of the drovers who were likely to serve you had already gone to London.' A rather anguished letter received by the Anglesey squire, Richard Bulkeley, emphasises the problems for correspondents resulting from drovers' activities being limited to the spring and summer seasons. 'We pray you', wrote Bulkeley's cousin in 1637, 'that our money be paid by November 1st as we cannot return our money (to London) ....otherwise than by drovers.'

While the importance of the drovers as messengers persisted until well into the eighteenth century, the appointment, by Henry VIII, of Sir Brian Tuke as Master of the Posts was followed, in 1561, by the first line of posts through Wales for which official records are available. Initially this was a temporary affair connecting London with Holyhead which by now had replaced Chester as the main port of embarkation for Ireland. By 1598, however, the Holyhead mail was rendered permanent by an Order in Council confirming the positions of John Ffranccys, Piers Conway, William Prichardes, Rowland ap Roberte and Robert Pepper as postmasters respectively of Chester, Rhuddlan, Conwy, Beaumaris and Holyhead, towns whose commercial and social status was considerably enhanced by being located on a mail route. Much the same applied to Chepstow, Newport, Cardiff, Bridgend, Swansea, Carmarthen and Haverfordwest when the first post to Milford Haven was forged three years later. Innkeepers now enjoyed a rich harvest of trade, especially when their particular houses were designated as the official posts, when they were paid 1s 8d daily for maintaining a change of horses and ensuring that official letters were safely forwarded to the next post. John Aprice of Holyhead, Richard White of Beaumaris and Nicholas Hookes (famous as the forty-first son of his father and himself the sire of twenty-seven children) were just some of the stalwarts occupying much-sought after positions as postmasters in the late seventeenth century. In addition to keeping at least three horses for the use of King's Messengers, the innkeeper/postmaster enjoyed the monopoly of letting horses to travellers requiring them for an onward journey. This was a useful concession and compensated the postmaster for the fact that the Privy Purse was often less than prompt in paying his salary and expenses. As he was dealing with official, and often secret mail, the postmaster needed to be a man of honesty, tact and discretion and though we find the Brecon postmaster being hauled over the coals in 1672 for tampering with the mail, most of these men carried out their duties diligently and effectively.

Being a charge on the Privy Purse, the posts, officially at least, were used only for Royal mail. But as the seventeenth century progressed, private letters came to be sent along with official mails and as trade grew the need for a public postal service was emphasised. Recognition came in 1635 when a royal proclamation established for 'his Majesties subjects', a postal service from the principal mail routes to the market and shire towns, to be paid for by a fixed level of charges. From now on a letter sent by a man in London to a relative in Wales would be carried by a 'post-boy' (a rather unsatisfactory term for what was usually a mature, if not elderly man) to the most appropriate town on the Holyhead or Milford Haven route. The letter could now either be collected by the addressee, or, if he was particularly affluent, be delivered to his private address on arrangement with the postmaster. Before 1700 letters despatched from North Wales to addressees in the south of the Principality travelled firstly to London on the Chester road and thence to South Wales by way of Bristol and Chepstow. This was a time-consuming and costly process. By 1700, though, a route had been forged between Bristol and Chester passing through Ludlow and Hereford, while a cross-post for mid-Wales through Radnorshire serving the far-flung centres of Tregaron, Aberystwyth and Machynlleth was established at Montgomery under Mrs Elizabeth Davies whose services were rewarded with the not inconsiderable annual sum of £45.

As the 'post-boy' pursued his lonely journey through Radnorshire he would, if not unnerved by the prospect of highway robbery, have enjoyed the delights of one of Britain's loveliest counties. As Radnorshire continues to offer the modern traveller a multitude of pleasures in terms of scenery, architecture and historical associations, I have chosen to write in this chapter of some of its roads during the immediate pre-turnpike era. Bounded by the rivers Wye and Teme and to the west by the great mass of the Cambrian Mountains, the centre of the county is dominated by Radnor Forest. In medieval times this was an area of unenclosed country reserved for hunting, but its nature has been entirely altered in recent years by teutonic coniferisation. The towns, villages and inter-connecting roads of this thinly-populated pastoral county tended, from the sixteenth to eighteenth centuries, to lie around the Forest which could be approached only on foot or on horseback at that time. Since the mid-fifteenth century when the shattered remnants of Jasper Tudor's Lancastrian army had dispersed through the hills beyond Presteigne after the Battle of Mortimer's Cross, the Radnorshire countryside had become renowned as the haunt of thieves and outlaws and though in the next century Bishop Rowland Lee had mounted a vicious campaign to extirpate them, travel in the county remained a dangerous venture. Even as late as 1720 a lady proposing to travel from Presteigne to London explained in a letter to her daughter that, 'there being such robbery of travellers and carriers that I shall not venture to bring or send a penny of money any other way but what will barely defray the expenses of my journey'.

Around the Forest and in the broken hilly country to the south of the county were numerous tracks and paths connecting the villages and farms. Skirting manorial boundaries, occasionally following prehistoric tracks used since time immemorial, circumventing steep inclines and fording streams and rivulets, these were usually quite adequate to meet the needs of the pastoral economy. A post-boy would occasionally travel from Presteigne, Hay-on-Wye and Knighton into the heartland of the county, or a pedlar carry his backpack to one of the country fairs, yet traffic consisted for the most part of ox-drawn sledges bringing wool, hay or peat from the isolated hill farms. This agricultural traffic might perhaps be accompanied by panniered horses carrying grain from the market of Presteigne to a village mill, or salmon from the Wye to some gentleman's household. Gentlemen, in seventeenth-century Radnorshire, were few and far between if the lament of a Parliamentary Commissioner sent to the county to collect fines from Royalists is anything to go by:

Radnorsheer, poor Radnorsheer,
Never a park and never a deer,
Never a squire of five hundred a year
But Richard Fowler of Abbey Cwmhir.

Shortage of gentlemen and of human beings in general made travelling a very lonely business. Richard Symonds, writing of Charles I's wanderings after his defeat at Naseby, recorded rather

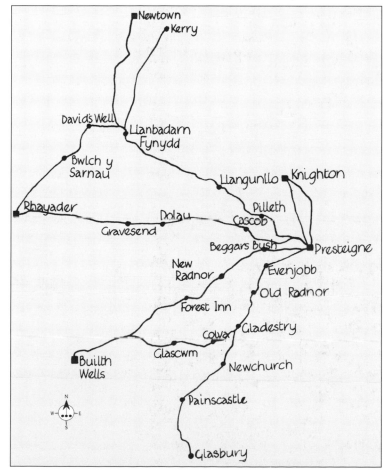

Some Pre-turnpike roads in Radnorshire

disconsolately that when the king and his party set out from Presteigne on September 19th, 1645 and travelled towards Newtown in Montgomeryshire, '.... except in the first three myle wee saw never a house or church over the mountaynes'.

Though not dealing specifically with Radnorshire, the account of John Taylor (The Water Poet) who rode through Wales on horseback at the age of 74, gives a vivid impression of the frustrations and dangers of travel in Stuart times. Riding from Lampeter to Carmarthen in 1653 he found, 'the way continually hilly, or mountainous and stony, insomuch that I was forced to alight and walke 30 times'. With about four miles to go, darkness descending and little idea of the way, his nerve began to fail and he decided to spend the night in a nearby field of oats, only to sink into a quagmire with his horse! Managing to grope his way back to the road he was fortunate enough to meet a horseman who led him on to Carmarthen and 'good and free entertainment at the home of one Mistris Oakley'. Unable to obtain a tobacco pipe at any price, Taylor was nevertheless impressed by Carmarthen and in particular by the low price of provisions. A happy place it must have been with its numerous taverns, oysters available at one hundred for ld, a $2^{1}/_{2}$ft salmon for $12^{1}/_{2}$d and beef at $1^{1}/_{2}$d per pound!

The solitary traveller in rural Wales had to deal both with the language problem and, quite often, with rough treatment at the hands of servants and landlords in the taverns along the way. Poor old Taylor was no exception and he was beside himself with rage as he left a Swansea inn where it seems that he was treated in a less than civil manner: 'If my stay in that house that night would save either Mr. Shallow-pate or Mrs. Jullock from hanging... I would rather lie and venture all hazards that are incident to hors (sic), man and traveller than to be beholding to such unmannerly mungrils'. As if dangerous roads and poor accommodation were not enough, the traveller also faced the problem of securing provender for his horse, often a difficult matter in a dry summer. When the weary Taylor arrived at Harlech he was mortified to discover that the town was unable to offer grass, hay or oats so that he was obliged to move on to Barmouth where he dined on 'a hen boyld with bacon, as yellow as the cowslip' and his horse on grass cut by two boys who travelled two miles to find it!

So much for the rigours of travel, of which a man making a journey would be aware in advance. However, before Charles II appointed John Ogilby and William Morgan to survey and map the roads of England and Wales, our traveller had to rely upon guides – to a greater or lesser degree extortionate in their demands – his own judgement and an element of luck, in order to find his way through the Welsh countryside. Saxton, Speed and others had produced maps of great beauty and cost, but these usually delineated only townships, villages and the occasional bridge, giving little indication of the direction of roads and trackways. Eventually, after many years work and at a cost of some £7,000, Ogilby published his *Britannia* in 1676, a fine road book in 'strip map' form, replete with information on routes, the local economy and dates of country fairs. Ogilby's work was to revolutionize travel and it was not long before other cartographers began to produce maps, 'delineations' and 'descriptions' of England and Wales. Notable among these were Morden and Taylor who published maps of Wales in 1704 and 1718 respectively, while Emmanuel Bowen and Thomas Kitchin's admirable atlas of the kingdom was progressively refined through several editions in the early eighteenth century. This was to remain the best available work before Cary's road books arrived on the scene towards the end of the century. These, and other contemporary sources, together with the Ordnance Survey sheets, have been used to define some of the more important pre-turnpike roadlines through Radnorshire.

Following the Acts of Union of 1536 – 42, New Radnor became the shire town of the newly-created county of Radnorshire. However, it enjoyed this privilege only until after the Civil Wars when the assizes were transferred to Presteigne whose importance in the county was thereby enhanced. As early as 1575 Saxton had been able to write that, 'Prestayn for beauteous buildings is the best in the shire', while a century later Ogilby found a well-built town of four

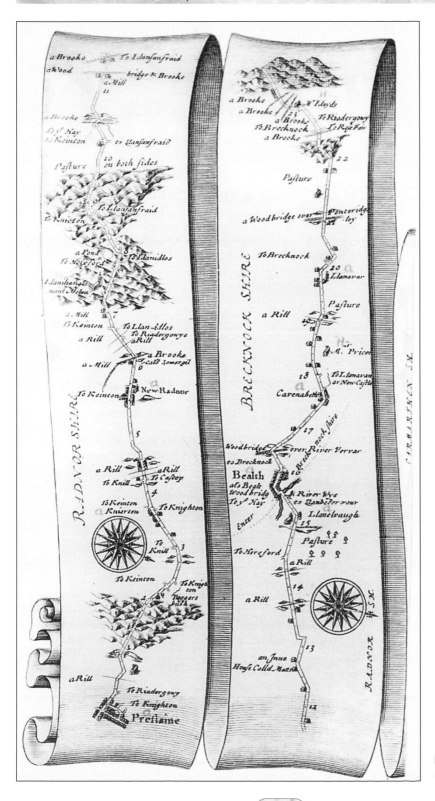

From John Ogilby's
Britannia of 1676

Hereford Street, Presteigne – the road to England

furlongs in extent with the usual markets and fairs, a reputation for excellent malted barley and several good inns including The Antelope, The Swan, The Duke's Arms and The Castle. The Radnorshire Arms, dating from 1616, was traditionally (and wrongly) reputed to have been the home of the regicide John Bradshaw. Presteigne, though, was strongly Royalist in its sympathies and was visited on two occasions by Charles I after the Battle of Naseby. Another distinguished seventeenth century visitor to the town was Henry, Duke of Beaufort who, as Lord President of the Council of the Marches, progressed through Wales in 1684. As he entered the narrow streets at the head of his entourage, 'The Magistrates in their formalities stood ready to receive his Grace, the streets, windows, trees and tops of the houses abounding with spectators giving shouts, acclamations and expressions of Joy.' Remote Presteigne may have been, yet his Grace's entertainment at the hands of 'the loyall Gentlemen of the County' was far from provincial, and he and his followers had their bumpers charged with 'foreign wine' to supplement the strong local cider.

PRESTEIGNE TO RHAYADER

Presteigne lay at the junction of a number of roads, one of the more important being the highway to Rhayader and across the mountains to the port of Aberystwyth. Designated 'The Great Road' by the early turnpike surveyors, it followed a route into west Wales with origins in the medieval period, if not before. Much of the course of the 'Great Road' was abandoned in 1767 when the Presteigne Turnpike Trustees decided to make a road to Rhayader by way of Beggar's Bush, Kinnerton, New Radnor and Penybont. Previously the line of road lay along the vale of the Lugg, skirting St Mary's Hill and following the present B4356 as far as Rock Bridge where it headed along the lane to Discoed, across Offa's Dyke and past Dyffryn to Cascob at the edge of Radnor Forest (SO239664). Cascob, where wolves roamed until

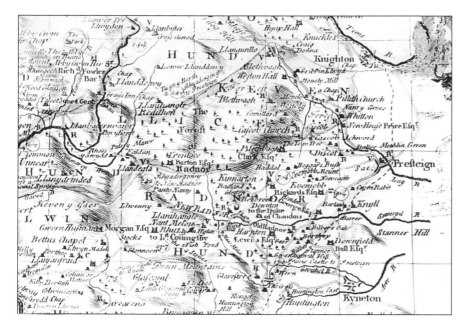

From Bowen and Kitchin's atlas (early 18th century)

Tudor times, was described by Ogilby as 'an inconsiderable village'. It had, though, enjoyed its moment of glory, for its fine little church was the benefice of Thomas Huett, translator of the Book of Revelations for William Salesbury's Welsh New Testament of 1567. Huett and his fellow Radnorshire clerics may have turned a blind eye to the persistence of pre-Christian beliefs and superstitions among their parishioners, many of whom believed firmly in the efficacy of incantations and invocations, exemplified by the charm currently displayed in the church. Frowned upon by the hierarchy of the Church, such charms were in common use in seventeenth-century pastoral society by people wishing to protect their livestock (and themselves) against 'the evil eye'. The tower of the present church at Cascob is constructed on an artificial mound, originally supposed to have been a Bronze Age barrow. However, like a similar earthwork at Bleddfa Church nearby, the mound is now thought to be the base of an earlier tower probably destroyed at the time of the Glyndŵr revolt in the early fifteenth century.

According to Ogilby, Cascob Church lay to the left of the 'Great Road', and its course can be followed along the sunken lane heading westwards in the direction of Cwmilward some 50yd below the churchyard gate. Beyond the steep ascent to Cwmilward the road reaches the brink of Radnor Forest and its subsequent route over the Forest (not negotiable by motor car) runs along the line of the track passing above Cwmilward towards the farm of Cwmygerwyn (SO191669). Here dwelt the Reverend Samuel Phillips, an eighteenth-century poet of some distinction, who lies at rest in Bleddfa churchyard with others of his family. A man of mordant wit, Phillips delighted in epitaphs and if the following extract of his commemoration of the life of a maiden lady is anything to go by, these were hardly notable as manifestations of Christian charity:

Scorning and scorn'd, she passed her life away,
An useless lump of animated clay;
Now spite and envy rule her frame no more,
But here it lies – more useless than before.

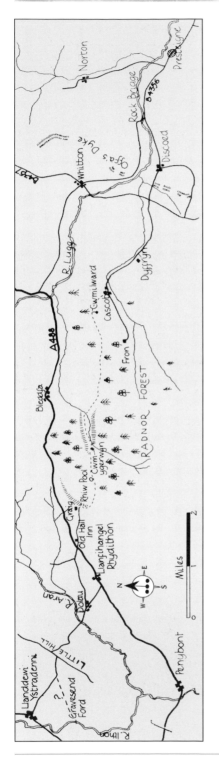

Above: The 'Great road' above Graig Farm

Above: The 'Great road' joining the Penybont Knighton turnpike at the 'Old Hall' Inn

'The Great Road'; Presteigne to Gravesend

Ogilby and later cartographers record the passage of the 'Great Road' beyond Cwmygerwyn and Rhiw Pool and its descent from Radnor Forest to Graig. However, such is the spider's web of forestry tracks that tracing the road to Rhiw Pool is very difficult, although further on it can be clearly seen as a raised causeway running alongside the forestry on Graig Hill, eventually being incorporated into a hedged lane as it descends towards Graig Farm (SO173673). From this substantial farm the road heads for the Knighton-Penybont turnpike (the present A488) crossing it at the site of the Old Hall Inn directly opposite the mid-nineteenth century Calvinistic Methodist Tanhouse Chapel (SO160674). Leaving the chapel on the right hand side the 'Great Road' follows the deep winding lane through the charming hamlet of Dolau, across the Aran River and over open country above Little Hill, whence it descends towards Llanddewy Ystradenni for almost half-a-mile before turning south-west along an undefined course to Gravesend Ford on the River Ithon (SO106673). While this one-mile stretch of the route is not easy to follow, both Taylor and Kitchin indicate it as crossing the Ithon at 'Grays Inn' or 'Gravesend' along a line past Penlan Farm.

Westwards of Gravesend, the older maps are not particularly helpful with Ogilby mentioning a 'direct road' to Rhayader, and Kitchin and others marking a route passing above Coedglasson to Rhiwgoch and thence to New Inn and Rhayader. Later maps, such as Cary's (1806) merely show a straight line connecting Gravesend and New Inn. However, by supplementing these sources with a study of the Ordnance Survey 6in maps and with local enquiry, it has been possible to piece together fairly precisely the course of this important pre-turnpike road. Initially, after fording the Ithon, it traversed the boggy land by Rhos Llawdden by way of the lane from the ford to its junction with the present A483. Here the 'Great Road' struck south-west along the A483 for approximately three-quarters of a mile before turning into the Abbey Cwmhir road and on towards Brynllycoed (SO083672). It now left the existing road, forded the River Clywedog and continued along a rough track enclosed by hedges to the south of Coedglasson, a farm located on several of the early maps. This track, known locally as 'Muddy Lane' can be traced across Coedglasson towards Bwlchbryndinam, becoming incorporated into the metalled road half-a-mile before the farm (SO062676). Apart from a stretch directly above Coedglasson, the 'Great Road' takes the form of a hedged lane, occasionally rather overgrown, for the whole of its length to Bwlchbryndinam Farm. Passing through the farmyard it crosses Baxter's Bank, skirts the forestry past the ruins of Rhiwgoch and thence across enclosed hill land to Lower Rhymney where it climbs steeply along a metalled lane to the junction of several tracks on the hills above Nantmel (SO041678). Instead of turning south for Cefn Nantmel on the modern road, the 'Great Road' originally proceeded

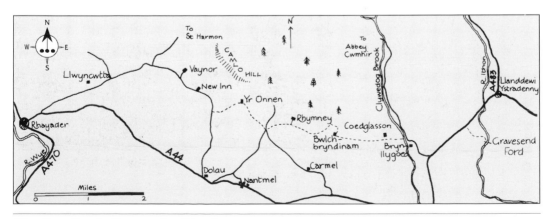

'The Great Road'; Gravesend to Rhyader

across open hill for Yr Onnen, its course, parts of which may still be traced, being marked by a sunken green lane running alongside the hill. This green lane passed Yr Onnen, along a line apparently represented by the present farm road, while the remainder of the route to Rhayader was along the country lane past Vaynor and Llwyncwtta passing, en route, the New Inn Farm, previously a hostelry important enough to be mentioned on many of the older maps (SO009697).

PRESTEIGNE TO LLANBADARN FYNYDD

At one point on its course the 'Great Road' crossed the ancient route through mid-Wales represented by the A483, upon which lay the village of Llanbadarn Fynydd, itself linked by a direct route to Presteigne. From the outskirts of Presteigne a traveller followed the 'Great Road' as far as Rock Bridge where he forded the Lugg and rode along the river valley, flanked on either side by exquisite meadows with land rising to the north in ancient fields, their lines broken up with gnarled oaks and plantations of larch. This road, currently the B4356, passes through Pilleth whose fourteenth-century church, standing on the slopes of Bryn Glas, witnessed the Battle of Pilleth fought on 22 June 1402 (SO258680). It was here that Owain Glyndŵr, guerilla fighter extraordinary, took prisoner Sir Edmund Mortimer after a battle claiming the lives of one thousand English soldiers. Glyndŵr's blood was certainly up. Previously he had sacked Abbey Cwmhir, burned several castles (including New Radnor where he hanged and then beheaded the bulk of the garrison) and he was now ready for an all-out fight. Once Mortimer's Welsh archers had deserted to his adversary's banner there was little doubt as to the outcome of the fight and the English were totally routed on Bryn Glas Hill, their corpses being subject to 'beastly shameless transformation' at the hands of Welsh women as they lay in the field after the battle. Shakespeare, in *Henry IV Part 1*, has Pilleth in mind when he has Westmoreland tell the battle-weary king of Mortimer's capture:

Mynachdy

A post from Wales loaden with heavy news;
Whose worst was that the noble Mortimer,
Leading the men of Herefordshire to fight
Against the irregular and wild Glendower,
Was by the rude hands of that Welshman taken,
A thousand of his people butchered.

Sir Richard Price, a local landowner, planted a square patch of fir trees on the side of Bryn Glas to commemorate the English dead, but their final resting place is reputed to be marked by the mounds in the river meadows below the road. This, however, would have been marshy ground in the fifteenth century and it is more likely that the unfortunate conscripts were buried where they fell: on the flanks of Bryn Glas Hill.

A mile or so beyond the melancholy field of Pilleth the road passes Mynachdy 'Monaughty' or 'Monely' on many of the older maps, whose compilers experienced the usual problems with Welsh orthography (SO238686). This fine late sixteenth-century house was built from materials taken from the Abbey Cwmhir grange of Mynachdy which originally lay in the meadows below Griffin Lloyd a mile to the north-west. Seventeenth-century travellers of curious disposition would have learned of the tradition that Mynachdy played host to Glyndŵr and his lieutenant Rhys Gethin (the Terrible) on the night before the Battle of Pilleth. They may, or may not have been aware that similar claims have been lodged for Monaughty Poeth in Llanfair Waterdine across the English border.

Beyond Griffin Lloyd the road meanders above the Lugg to Llangynllo, a village, according to one observer, '.... enhanced by the high average of comeliness among its children and young women'. Crossing the river in the village and again at the junction with the Knucklas road, the route to Llanbadarn Fynydd passes through oakwooded country, and into open sheep pasture. For much of its course, the old road tends to follow the B4356 although from time to time re-alignment of the modern road has revealed the original road boundary as a bank in an adjacent field. Passing over Little Hill the old road reaches The Pound and fords the Camddwr before deviating from the B4356 to follow a lonely course through open, bracken-infested hill country to the curiously-named Moelfre City, now a single house and an isolated telephone kiosk (SO119754). From this remote spot the same road winds down to Llanbadarn Fynydd, entering the village by Brook Cottage on the course of the modern A483 highway (SO098768).

Pre-turnpike route from Presteigne to Llanbadarn Fynydd

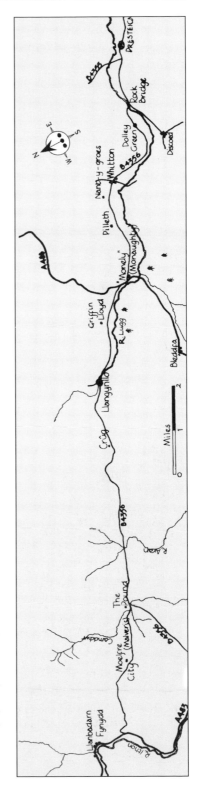

PRESTEIGNE TO GLASBURY

A much-used roadline connected Presteigne with Newchurch and subsequently with Glasbury on the River Wye to the south-west. Leaving Presteigne on the ancient trackway past Slough and Cold Oak, this road, in the form of a deep lane, ran over the hill to Evenjobb (SO263624). About half-a-mile from the village the traveller crossed Offa's Dyke where he would have enjoyed a fine view of Old Radnor across the cultivated vale of the Summergill. After its descent to Evenjobb the road headed south along the course of the B4357 to pass Hindwell, a pre-Flavian Roman site and home, in the early nineteenth century, of Thomas Hutchinson, friend of William Wordsworth. Here, Dorothy Wordsworth first learned to ride, while the poet himself, deeply moved by the glories of the Radnorshire countryside, visited the house in 1810 and 1812. William enjoyed the civilized company of the Hutchinsons and their circle and Dorothy, even if she reckoned the house to be one of the coldest in the land, wrote of Hindwell with great affection. She was particularly fond of the splendid pool in front of the house:

> 'You could hardly believe it possible for anything but a lake to be so beautiful as the pool before this house. It is perfectly clear and inhabited by multitudes of geese and ducks and two fair swans keep their silent and solitary state apart from all the flutter and gabble of the inferior birds'.

The Wordsworths must have travelled this road many times, their chaise bumping along the lane towards the crossing of the Summergill Brook and the present A44 highway before the steep climb across the side of Old Radnor Hill. The poet would have enjoyed Old Radnor and its pleasantly melancholy churchyard and like other travellers would have pondered on the

Old Radnor Church

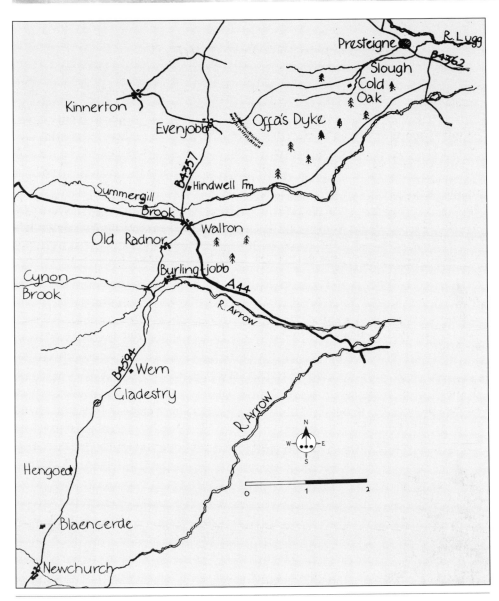

Presteigne to Newchurch

antiquity of a site where Celtic and Saxon churches had stood centuries before the present Perpendicular building. After viewing the unique Tudor organ case and fine linen-fold chancel screen, he might have wandered down to the remains of King Harold Godwinson's castle mound about 300yd to the south-east of the church. As with Charles I when he travelled this road in the nervous weeks after Naseby, these insubstantial remnants of the Saxon king's dominance of the Marches may have caused the poet to fall prey to thoughts of the transience of kingly existence.

Past Old Radnor the road crossed the Cynon Brook and proceeded through hilly country towards Gladestry, the original following the course of the present B4594 as a green lane enclosed on the field side by a high bank. The earlier road-banks are particularly apparent on the stretch of road

Gladestry: the meeting place of several old roads

a hundred yards or so past Wern Farm (SO239558). Gladestry, bounded on the west and east by Colfa Hill and Hergest Ridge, was the meeting place of several old roads, our particular one continuing along the B4594 towards Newchurch, passing Hengoed and Blaencerde along the way. Here again, road widening has obscured the earlier line although the original road banks can still be seen in the adjacent fields where they run parallel to the modern highway.

It was at Blaencerde that Charles I is reputed to have halted and drunk a jug of milk from the hand of a particularly beautiful local woman by the name of Mary Bayliss (SO218519). In 1870 Francis Kilvert met one William Pritchard who claimed to own the very jug from which the king had taken his milk. Moreover, he cited a well-attested tradition that Charles' entourage, riding two by two down the narrow road, extended from Blaencerde to Pontvane, a farm to the south of Newchurch prominently marked on Kitchin's map (SO210502). Past Blaencerde the B4594 descends steeply into Newchurch passing around the ancient churchyard flanked on the south by farm buildings of the fifteenth century. Crossing

The road from Presteigne to Slough in a deep holloway

the River Arrow and turning sharply right at the church, the old road is carried by the present country lane over undulating landscape towards Rhosgoch. On the higher ground above Rhosgoch Common, noted in the eighteenth century for its high quality peat, the B4594 incorporates the Portway, traditionally believed to be of Roman origin. There is little evidence to substantiate this, though the stretch of road is of unquestionable antiquity and in all likelihood first assumed importance in connexion with the medieval stronghold of Painscastle to the south-west. Rhosgoch Mill, south of the village, is currently a farmhouse (SO186475). Until the 1950s though, it had been run as a corn mill by members of the Powell family for over 400 years, and the Miller Powell who was contemporary with Kilvert claimed regularly to have seen fairies dancing on the mill floor. We shall never know how far this supernatural vision resulted from over-indulgence in the cider bottle. The mill, however, remains a magical place and Kilvert's description of '....the cosy old picturesque ivy' grown mill house with its tall chimney completely covered with ivy applies as well in 1983 as it would have done two hundred years before Kilvert wrote his admirable diaries.

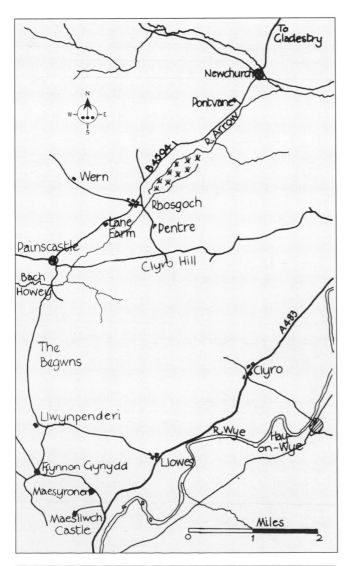

Newchurch to Glasbury

The old road, still represented by the B4594, enters Painscastle by the Maesllwch Arms, the sole and much modernised survivor of the six drovers' inns boasted by the village in its heyday. After the long and exhausting crossing of the Mynydd Epynt and the hazardous fording of the Wye at Erwood, these inns, with their associated enclosures, offered succour to man and beast before they continued their journey into Herefordshire and the English Midlands. An observer standing on the great mound overlooking the village would have seen the drovers approaching from the west as they urged on their cattle towards Painscastle. By the time Charles I passed through the village the same mound was virtually all that remained of Payne Fitzjohn's motte and bailey and of the castles subsequently built on the site by the rapacious William de Braose and by Henry III, the latter raising a stone building as part of his policy of strengthening the Marcher fortresses (SO160462).

If it was no longer an important centre for the cattle trade, mid-nineteenth-century Painscastle at

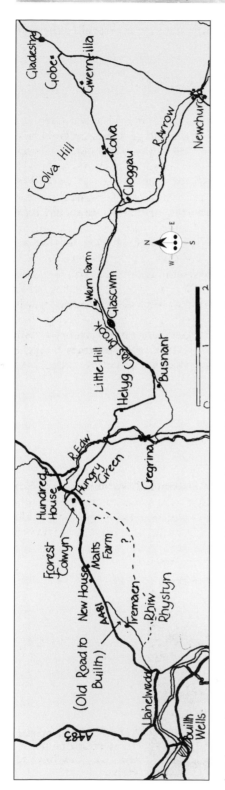

least achieved some celebrity as the home of one of Wales' most noted eccentrics, the Reverend John Price who lived out much of his life in three bathing-machines serving as study, bedroom and kitchen. Price, a man with an inordinate fondness for the literal interpretation of biblical stories, spent a great deal of his time seeking out vagrants and others, whom he paid 6d per head on condition that they attended his church services. Inside the church the good vicar provided oilstoves for his bemused flock to cook their food on during the sermon. A poor man himself, Price also offered 5s to each pair of vagrants 'living in sin' as a means of persuading them to go through the marriage service. Inevitably this gave rise to skullduggery because the short-sighted unfortunate was unable to distinguish between couples, and many were successfully married several times over! In 1895 Price began to decline in health, and went to stay at Talgarth in neighbouring Brecknockshire where well-meaning friends prevailed upon him to take a bath. The shock of it killed him! He was eighty-five years old and a much-mourned man.

Beyond Painscastle the older road no longer follows the course of the B4594. Instead, it ran south of the village to ford Bach Howey before a steep ascent into the silent open hill country of the Begwns. The traveller could now look back towards the gentle pastoral land-scape of Painscastle and westwards to the valley of the Wye, before ascending via a deep lane past Llwynpenderi to the hamlet of Ffynnon Gynydd (SO164413). Here the road turned abruptly left for the River Wye and Glasbury passing the plain little building of Maesyronnen Chapel (SO177411). Built on land bequeathed by one Lewis Lloyd in 1686, Maesyronnen was one of the earliest Nonconformist chapels in Wales and still retains the arrangement and many of the furnishings of the Com-monwealth period. Below the chapel, the brief final stretch of the journey to Glasbury pursued the course of the great highway from Hereford to Brecon, the modern A438. The seventeenth-century traveller along this part of the route would have been spared the sight of the Gothic folly of Maesllwch Castle with its riot of towers, battlements and arrowslits and would have journeyed to Ffynnon Gynydd through heavily wooded countryside. One such traveller was King Charles who rode out from Glasbury through this leafy landscape in August 1645. After dining with Sir Henry Williams at his fine Tudor house of Gwernyfed to the south-west, the king and his

Gladestry to Builth Wells

followers were conducted by their host over the Glasbury ford, whence they travelled the road over the Begwns for Painscastle, Old Radnor and Presteigne.

GLADESTRY TO BUILTH WELLS

From the quiet village of Gladestry a route struck out westwards for Builth Wells. Taking leave of the B4594 approximately half-a-mile to the south of the village, it passed Gobe and Gwern-illa and went on to Colfa, now little more than a farm and a thirteenth-century church overlooked by Colfa Hill and the great expanse of the Radnor Forest to the north (SO200531). Now an isolated spot, hemmed in by hills and wind-swept sheep pastures, Colfa's well-filled churchyard and the many ruins of farms and houses between here and Glascwm bespeak more populous days. Certainly the seventeenth century traveller on this route would have found more company along the way than he would today. Colfa parish is mentioned in one of the works of the medieval poet Lewis Glyn Cothi, when he cites the ancient legend that the church was founded by St David himself. There may be little basis to this legend, but it is nonetheless true that a church has stood on the same site since the eighth century.

A mile or so beyond Colfa the now metalled road runs by Cloggau, a farm at the base of Yr Allt whose bracken-covered upper reaches give way to neatly enclosed fields as the hill gently descends to the infant River Arrow (SO187526) . The countryside here has a timeless quality. It is a landscape of early enclosure and though fields may be larger, farm buildings more garish, and pastures of less floristic diversity, it has changed relatively little since Stuart times. Cloggau itself was reckoned by Kilvert to be one of the oldest inhabited buildings in the area and the spot moved him to verse:

> *The Cloggau on her greensward mount*
> *Sat like a queen for ever*
> *With tresses crowned with waving woods*
> *Green throned beside the river.*

Crossing the Arrow, the road ascends the treeless side of Glascwm Hill, forming a boundary between the heathery slopes of the hill and the deep valley to the north. The seventeenth-century road line – and, almost certainly, the road line for centuries previously – lays to the right of the present metalled road and can be followed along the flanks of the hill until it enters

Left: The eighteenth century bridge over the river Edw beyond Helyg

The seventeenth century road to the right of the current road on Glascwm Hill

Newchurch to Glascwm road descending to Glascwm village

The bridge over the River Wye at Builth Wells, 1815

the village of Glascwm past Wern Farm (SO161535). To the west of Glascwm it takes up the metalled road along the steep-sided Clas Valley towards Busnant, and beyond here, instead of continuing to Cregrina, it turns north and makes its way past Helyg, fording a tributary of the River Edw en route. Half-a-mile distant the old road crossed the same river by a wooden bridge, replaced in the eighteenth century by the present single-span structure. Approximately a hundred yards beyond the bridge it swung to the right to cross Hungry Green for Fforest Colwyn, its original course again pursuing the hedge line several yards to the right of the modern road.

The early maps leave some doubt as to the precise direction of the road for the remainder of the journey to Builth Wells. It certainly crossed Aberedw Hill via the track called *Rhiw Rhystyn,* though whether it climbed the hill from Hungry Green to Fforest Colwyn on the A481 (the Presteigne-Builth Wells turnpike road) is not absolutely clear. However, the well-trodden greensward track through the bracken on top of Aberedw Hill, marking the course of a nineteenth-century drovers' route, probably represents the earlier road line, while the descent of this track from the top of the hill by way of the *Rhiw Rhystyn* towards Llanelwedd definitely does so. The beginning of the descent by a rocky track much-eroded by the rainwater for which it is a natural catchment, presented marvellous views to the seventeenth-century traveller. To the west lay Builth Wells and the mature River Wye meandering magnificently through the enclosed pastures along its banks, while the grey mass of Radnor Forest was visible to the north. Leaving the open hill, the *Rhiw Rhystyn* runs towards Llanelwedd as a sunken lane with a well-marked hedge bank on its western side, until it merges with a lane bounded by hedges of considerable antiquity. An offshoot of this lane heads towards Tremaen Farm and marks the course of the pre-turnpike Presteigne-Builth Wells road (SO069522). The Rhiw Rhystyn crosses the present A481 at Crossway Cottage, approximately a hundred yards before the junction of this road with the modern B4567. It then pursues the course of a council-maintained lane to Coed Spoel and is taken up by a hedge line for several hundred yards before rejoining the line of the turnpike for the short journey to Llanelwedd and Builth Wells.

Travellers to Builth Wells in the late seventeenth century found little to divert them as the town was virtually destroyed by fire in 1681 and appeals for funds for rebuilding had met with little success. The remnants of the old town and the new houses that had mushroomed over the next hundred years were described by the antiquary Malkin in 1803 as being in a state of 'dilapidated antiquity', its main streets being 'as fashionless as miserable and as dirty' as anything he had seen. Eventually, though, the town came to enjoy some celebrity as a watering place despite the complaint of one traveller who reckoned that the waters tasted and smelt respectively of sulphur and gunpowder. To sample this malodorous liquid came the gouty, rheumatic and dyspeptic, their journey to Builth being much facilitated by the new turnpike roads of the nineteenth century and James Parry's magnificent six-arched bridge over the Wye, completed in 1779.

RHAYADER TO KERRY

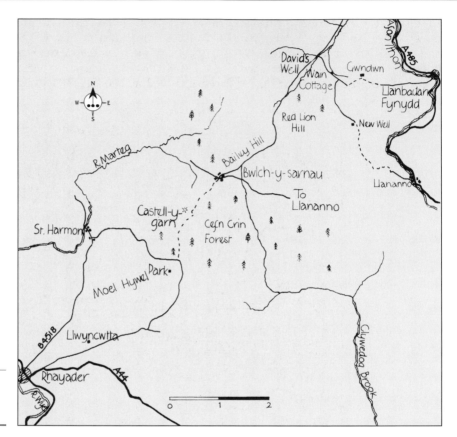

Rhayader to
Llanbadarn
Fynydd

By the seventeenth century the market town of Rhayader, with its cattle fairs and associations with the woollen industry was the junction of several roads, one of these heading north for Montgomeryshire through Kerry. After quitting Rhayader on the 'Great Road' the Kerry route joined the present lane to St Harmon at New Inn a mile beyond Llwyncwtta and proceeded north via a series of pitches and dingles to a point above Park Farm where it left the metalled road on what is now a forestry track (SO018719). This can be followed on foot between Pantybrwyn and Cefn-crin forests, passing to the east of Castell y Garn to enter Bwlch-y-Sarnau on the 'Glyndŵr Way' (SO029745). From this meeting place of ancient routes, that into Montgomeryshire is shown on the early maps as proceeding north-west across Bailey Hill through enclosed hill country towards David's Well, taking the course of the metalled road skirting Red Lion Hill. Little now remains of David's Well although its reputation as a healing well still persists and many people can remember the days, not so long ago, when the footsore and rheumatic flocked to the spot (SO059786). At David's Well the old road to Llanbadarn Fynydd turns directly south-east towards a junction of several lanes on the flanks of Red Lion Hill approximately a hundred yards past Wain Cottage (SO067779). A metalled and gated track past the ruins of Gwndwm marks the course of the road for a few hundred yards until, for no apparent reason, the tarmac peters out in the middle of the hillside. Here, an observer looking due east can see the original road line running across the open hill until it once again joins a metalled lane leading directly to Llanbadarn Fynydd a mile-and-a-half distant (SO075779).

The maps of Cary (1806) and Coltman (1813) delineate another route going southwards for Llananno from the junction above Wain Cottage. Running through the forestry on Red Lion Hill the road (now a forestry track) passes the charmingly restored Red Lion Inn, standing alone amidst the ranks of conifers, and then heads south-easterly for New Well. Owing to the complex of forestry tracks between the Inn and New Well it is not difficult to get lost and it is important for drivers and walkers wishing to remain on the old road to keep bearing left from the Red Lion on the track skirting the forest and fording the Crychell Brook, as this is the

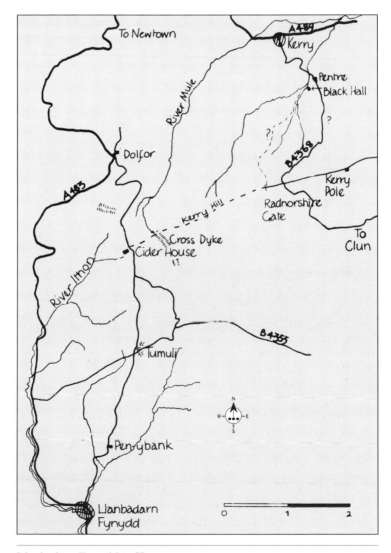

Llanbadarn Fynydd to Kerry

original road line. In the vicinity of the ford over the Crychell lay the village of New Well, complete with its school and cobbler's shop. In the nineteenth century, and presumably in earlier years, the chalybeate spring at New Well enjoyed a local reputation for healing scrofula and was visited regularly by invalids during the summer months when the curative powers of the water were at their most efficacious. Now, alas, little remains save the New Well house beyond which the old road originally crossed Yr Allt and entered Llananno down a narrow lane (SO072766).

Returning to Llanbadarn Fynydd we find that the old road into Montgomeryshire follows the modern 'B' road northwards along a tributary of the River Ithon and, after a mile or so, runs into wild, open hill of cotton grass, rushes and bracken. This is elemental country, of cairns and tumuli, curlew and sheep. On a warm day in late spring the views from the road are quite glorious, although a seventeenth-century horseman, travelling in mid-January may have thought otherwise! Driving along this stretch of road one is reminded of Hardy's highway across Egdon Heath: '....the long, laborious road, dry, empty and white. It was quite open to the heath on each side, and bisected that vast dark surface like the parting-line on a head of black hair, diminishing and bending away on the furthest horizon'.

Past the group of tumuli on Garn bryn-llwyd the earlier road continues to follow the B4355 as far as Cider House Farm. Here it turns abruptly east to leave the metalled road and take up the Kerry Hill Ridgeway which runs along a fence line immediately opposite the farm (SO109846). Of great antiquity, the Ridgeway had been used for several centuries by cattle drovers from west Wales as they plodded steadily on towards Herefordshire and the lush grazings of the Midland counties. It is even possible that the Ridgeway was in use as a drove route when the pre-Offan boundary dykes, clearly visible at its western end, were constructed (SO115850). By the seventeenth century, the ridgeway road was an important route to Kerry and thence to Newtown and the roads for North Wales. From the early maps it seems that the way to Kerry left the Ridgeway at Radnorshire Gate, past a tumulus on the left and thence by Black Hall and Pentre into the village (SO143862). Most Stuart travellers would not have known it, but sleepy little Kerry witnessed an episode of great drama in 1176 when a row broke out between the Bishop of St Asaph and Giraldus Cambrensis, Archdeacon of Brecon, over the consecration of the church, claimed by each to lie in his particular diocese. The dispute seems to have reached epic proportions, leading to each man excommunicating the other. The wily Giraldus finally won the day since, having been first to get possession of the church, he had been able to ring a triplet of bells thereby establishing an act of excommunication in advance of the Bishop!

PRESTEIGNE TO BUILTH WELLS

Turning off Presteigne High Street opposite the Royal Oak pub the pre-turnpike road to Builth Wells climbed steeply through Warden and past Rowley Farm to cross Offa's Dyke before arriving at Beggar's Bush on the junction with Rhos Lane (SO262642). The fugitive Charles I spent an uncomfortable night at Beggar's Bush Farm, a tavern lying within the bounds of the parish of Old Radnor in the 1640s. Sir Henry Slingsby, faithful chronicler of the King's travels and of the tribulations of his entourage, immortalised the now much-modernised house in his diary: 'In our quarter we had little accommodation; but of all ye places we came to ye best was at old Radnor where ye King lay in a poor low chamber and my Ld of Linsey & others by ye kitching fire on hay . . .' According to local legend the king himself conceived the name 'Beggar's Bush' after his servants and followers had begged the innkeeper for the remains of the single pullet and solitary cheese comprising the royal dinner! Since we know that the young Prince Charles visited Radnorshire and afterwards, as

Charles II, was known to his intimates as 'Mr Rowley', the name of Rowley Farm may not be without significance while that king's renowned association with oak trees might be reflected in the naming of the old Royal Oak inn at Presteigne.

For much of the way from Beggar's Bush the old road follows the B4372 to Kinnerton and thence along the flanks of Knowle Hill to New Radnor. However, for several hundred yards on the Kinnerton side of Knowle Farm the original road line appears to the right as a deep green lane overhung by venerable oaks. Soon, after journeying through glorious rolling pastureland, the modern traveller descends to the medieval town of New Radnor where Archbishop Baldwin and Giraldus Cambrensis enjoyed the hospitality of Rhys ap Gruffydd before their peregrinations through Wales. The town was granted borough status by Elizabeth I although, according to John Leland who visited the place in the 1530s, it was in a state of semi-decay by this time: 'New Radnor towne hathe been metely well wallyd and in the walle appere the ruines of iii gates. The buildynge of the towne in some part metely good in most part but rude, many howsys being thakyd. The castle is in ruine. . . .' So ruined was it that very little masonry remained at the time of Prince Charles's visit in 1642. The fate of New Radnor typified that of many of the border castles built by both Welshmen and Normans and of which only the mounds now remain. Half-hearted rebuilding after destruction in times of insurrection and the ravages of heavy artillery during the Civil War meant that the castles were relatively easy to dismantle following the abolition of the Marcher Lordships, whereupon their stonework became available for local domestic buildings. Today the streets of New Radnor are overshadowed by the great castle mound, a place of springy turf and harebells, no longer the malignant symbol of oppression which it must have seemed to the medieval inhabitants.

Beggars Bush Farm, where Charles I spent the night

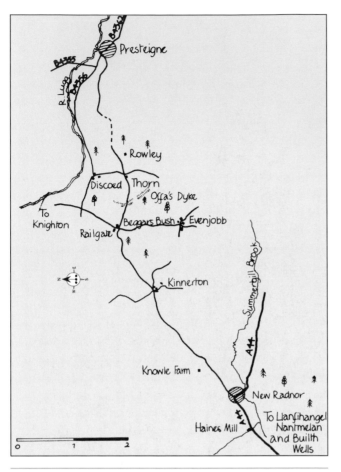

Presteigne to New Radnor

Our road follows Church Street past the toll house – a reminder that it was eventually turnpiked on the abandonment of the 'Great Road' – to join the A44 which now mercifully by-passes the little town. Ogilby's map shows the seventeenth-century road pursuing the course of the A44 across 'a Brooke cal'd Somergil' and past Haines Mill, whose ruins await the arrival of a wealthy restorer (SO203605). Overlooked by a hill to the south with the splendid name of 'The Smatcher', Haines Mill is cited in Letters Patent renewing the charter of New Radnor in 1642. Morris Draper, it appears, had been tenant in 1481. He was succeeded in 1508 by Thomas Davis who held the mill until 1534, when it was let to Anne Griffiths and her son for a term of twenty-one years at an annual rental of thirty shillings.

Skirting the hills to the north of Llanfihangel Nantmelan the road follows the Summergill Brook past Llanfihangel Nantmelan Church, within its ring of ancient yew trees, before leaving the A44 at the Forest Inn tollgate to join the A481 past Llyn Heulyn, referred to rather dismissively by Ogilby as 'a pond' (SO171585). It now curves its way down to Hundred House, named after the court where trespassers, small debtors and other minor offenders were tried by the Sheriff in medieval times. After it crossed the River Edw, Ogilby shows the road passing 'a House call'd Matts' (Matt's Farm) and then heading for Builth Wells by way of the Wye crossing at Llanelwedd (SO090537). However, Bowen's map of 1726 indicates a road line leaving the A481 a short mile after Matt's Farm and approaching Llanelwedd past Tremaen Farm on the lane joining the *Rhiw Rhystyn*. Apparently the original pre-turnpike road, this can still be followed on foot by turning off the A481 near Hope Chapel beyond New House (SO079530).

Like New Radnor, seventeenth-century Builth must have been dominated by grass-covered banks and mounds, the remains of Edward I's great stone castle. From the time of the first 'motte and bailey' to the final destruction of the Edwardian castle in the sixteenth century, this was the site of much violence, bloodletting and intrigue. William, grandson of Llewelyn ap Iorwerth was publicly hanged, drawn and quartered at the castle following a spell of marital infidelity, while other less distinguished persons met an equally grisly end within its walls. It was to Builth Castle that the great Llewelyn ap Gruffydd came to seek refuge from the English in 1282. Finding the gates closed against him he retreated into the countryside only to meet his death at the hands of a band of English soldiers. The unfortunate prince's body was buried

The monument to Llewelyn ap Gruffydd, near Builth Wells

in the grounds of the Cistercian foundation at Abbey Cwmhir, but not before the head had been struck off and sent to London for public exhibition. According to the chronicler Adam of Usk, the English soldiers washed the head in the nearby River Wye which, throughout the day, 'did flow in an unmixed stream of blood'.

PRESTEIGNE TO KNIGHTON

Knighton first came into prominence when the Normans built the nearby fortress of Bryn-y-

Castell soon after 1066 (SO290722). Granted to the powerful Mortimer family by Henry III, the town grew rapidly and after receiving its market charter in 1230 it soon became one of the major trading centres of the border country. Once Presteigne had become the administrative 'capital' of Radnorshire upon the transfer of the Great Sessions from New Radnor after the Civil Wars, pre-existing trackways linking the two towns developed into substantial highways.

They were in the late stages of this transition when King Charles passed through Radnorshire on his way to North Wales in September 1645. The king, arriving at Presteigne from Leominster and Weobley, slept for two nights at Lower Heath, the home of one Nicholas Taylor. Legend has it that after leaving the farmhouse and making appropriate farewells to his host, Charles headed westwards along the lane from the Heath until he reached the junction with the New Radnor road, where he turned north for Stonewall Hill at what has subsequently been named 'Kings Turning'. Afterwards, apparently, he progressed across the meadows

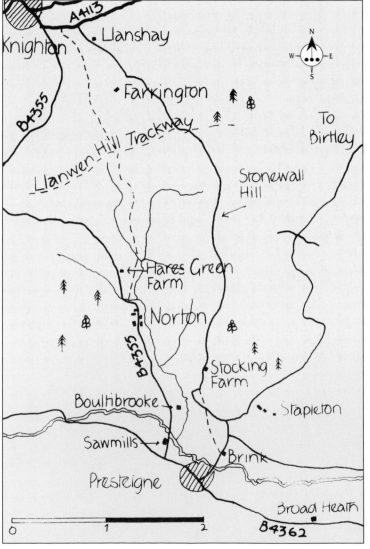

Alternative pre-turnpike routes from Presteigne to Knighton

Towards Stonewall Hill

alongside the Lugg before fording the river near Brink and riding on past Stapleton Castle for Stonewall Hill and Knighton. This would seem a logical route since the end of Brink Lane, running alongside the river from the medieval bridge in Broad Street, aligns directly with the castle (SO321646). A further tradition avers that the king rode down Broad Street, across the bridge and thence along the lane past Stocking Farm for Stonewall Hill, Llanshay and Knighton (SO315664). Whichever tradition one believes, the Stonewall Hill route was clearly of some importance in the seventeenth century, because by the mid-eighteenth, the Presteigne Turn-pike Trust was ordering that the Knighton road be laid out from Lugg Bridge past Stapleton Farm, Stocking, Oxenbrook and Stonewall Hill. Running south from a gate opening to the turnpike road approximately a quarter-of-a-mile before Stocking Farm there appears to be a trackway cutting across the open field to rejoin the road between the cemetery and the sharp turn north for the farm (SO315659). This seems to have crossed the meadows towards Brink and accordingly may mark the line of the original road to Stonewall Hill.

Interestingly, neither Ogilby, Morden nor Bowen indicate the Stonewall Hill road. Their route to Knighton left Presteigne beyond Warden and followed the B4355 to Norton, leaving Boultibrooke ('Fulbrook' in Ogilby) on the right. The present B4355 towards Boultibrooke crosses the Lugg by a bridge constructed in 1932. The earlier road, however, is a lane to the rear of the nearby sawmills, passing over a charming stone bridge of early eighteenth-century design which presumably replaced the wooden structure mentioned by Ogilby (SO309653).

North of the sawmills Ogilby's road continued along the B4355 to Norton and then, before reaching Hare's Green Farm, it deviated on to a lane running towards Farrington on the hills to the south of Knighton (SO302674). Today, for the first mile or so, the old lane is metalled, but it eventually deteriorates into a rough track bounded by foxgloves and gorse, the rigours of the ascent being amply compensated for by the splendour of the views to the north and west. Towards the top of the hill Farrington Lane crosses the 'prehistoric' Llanwen Hill trackway before the steady descent to Knighton in the Teme Valley (SO301699).

Like other towns throughout Wales, Knighton was ultimately served by a system of turnpike roads, some of them incorporating pre-existing road lines. The older roads escaping the attention of the turnpike surveyors continued to serve a useful purpose. Maintained, albeit rather poorly, by the local parish, they provided a system of communications of great value to farmer and tradesman alike. It is not generally recognized, moreover, that by the time Queen Victoria came to the throne, only 10 per cent of Britain's highways lay within the turnpike system and once travellers had left the turnpike, their journey took them along roads which had not changed materially for centuries. Like today's drivers along our country lanes they might have been so relieved at getting away from that nineteenth century juggernaut, the careering mail coach, that for a while at least, the rough and boggy surfaces would have seemed almost tolerable.

4 THE DROVERS

Begging politely to be excused on the plea that I was just about to take tea, I asked him in what capacity he had travelled all over England. 'As a drover to be sure', said Mr. Bos, 'and I may say that there are not many in Anglesey better known in England than myself – at any rate I may say that there is not a public house between here and Worcester at which I am not known.'

George Borrow
Wild Wales, 1862

Since he first attempted to exercise control over their feeding and breeding habits, man has needed to master the handling and driving of his livestock. An understanding of the peculiarities of group behaviour among the different types of domestic animals must have been as essential to the pastoralist of the Near East in the sixth millennium BC as was a knowledge of the location of suitable pastures and watering places. The present-day East African herdsman, often forced by climatic conditions to drive his cattle over thousands of miles, is heir to skills shared by the American cowboy, the Alpine shepherd, the long-distance drover in Britain and so on down through the millennia to the earliest livestock farmers in the foothills of Anatolia. In short, the 'art and mystery of droving' is an ancient trade, perhaps as old as the earliest of agricultural tasks, those of shepherding and herding.

In Britain, cattle, sheep and to a lesser degree pigs, have been moved from the highland to the lowland regions for many centuries. Until quite recently environmental and technical factors meant that sheep and cattle were rarely fattened on the hills and there developed a system whereby they were reared on the upland pastures and subsequently finished on the rich grazings and arable fields of the lowlands. Thus, from medieval times, if not before, beasts from the Scottish hills were finished on arable by-products in eastern England, and lean cattle and sheep plodded their way from the northern and western parts of Wales to the fattening pastures of the Midlands and Home Counties. Their common fate was the butcher's pole-axe, administered in the shambles of London, and by the early modern period those of other growing towns in lowland England.

This 'export' trade in livestock between Wales and England was of great antiquity. We know that Welsh cattle fed the Roman legions fighting in Gaul, and Dark Age documents provide evidence of an apparently legitimate trade in cattle across Offa's Dyke in the late eighth century. Cattle became the mainstay of the rural economy of much of medieval Wales and the abundant manuscript material of English lay and ecclesiastical estates shows that great magnates regularly sent their agents into the Principality to buy stock. We find also at this time the rapid growth of a mercantile class of Welsh cattle and sheep dealers who drove their animals to the fairs and markets of the English heartland. In 1253 a document relating to the granting of an annual fair at Newent in Gloucestershire mentions, '.....the Welshmen who come from the parts of Wales to sell their cattle', while, during the Hundred Years' War (1337-1443), cattle were purchased by the constables of the Welsh castles and taken by drovers to London and the ports of southern England. Many similar examples underline the importance of the livestock trade to the economy of both countries, epitomized by the special protection afforded to drovers by both sides in the Civil War.

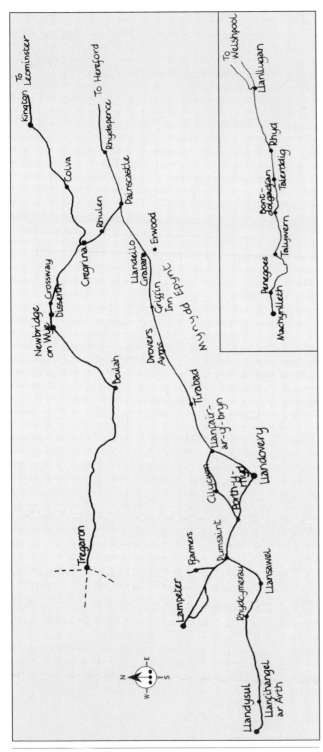

Drovers' roads from central Wales to the English border

Described by the early nineteenth-century commentator Edmund Hyde Hall as '......distinguished persons in the history of this country's economy', the Welsh drovers were a common sight in southern England as they followed their herds along the highways and by-ways, resting at recognized taverns and occasionally holding up at a village smithy while a bullock or pony was re-shod. In an attempt to exclude vagrants and other undesirables from the trade, Tudor and Stuart parliaments had enacted rigorously enforced legislation to regulate the activities of livestock dealers, particularly those involved with cattle. A cattle dealer, for example, had to be a married householder of over thirty and in possession of an annually renewable licence granted by Quarter Sessions. Further statutes imposed severe penalties on cattle stealing and driving livestock on Sundays and others laid down strict rules regarding trading conduct, pre-fair selling and the re-sale of stock within five weeks of the initial purchase.

Despite the frequent references in the contemporary literature to their roguery and dishonesty, based on a few much-publicised eighteenth-century cases of dealers defaulting on credit notes, the droving fraternity was essentially honest and scrupulous and was held in high regard throughout the community. As they were among the few ordinary people in Wales enjoying the opportunity of travelling far beyond their immediate locality, the dealers and their drovers formed an important link with England. Through them the Welsh countryman learned (and often disapproved) of the strange and wonderful happenings east of the border while the English yeoman, quaffing his beer at the roadside tavern, listened spellbound as the old

Left: Llanybydder Cattle Fair; late nineteenth century

Below: Two drovers; late nineteenth century

Painting on the side of the stand at Llandovery RFC ("The Drovers")

drovers spun the yarns and sagas of their travels. Generally literate and numerate, they carried back to the remote villages and hamlets of the north and west of the Principality news of social, political, cultural and religious developments in England, and in the days before the widespread availability of local news sheets their return must have been eagerly awaited.

From the seventeenth century onwards numerous dealers and drovers were involving themselves in the wider aspects of Welsh life. Some lent financial support to the publication of Welsh language books, others put their knowledge of English to good use and became established as schoolteachers, and others participated in local and county government. The pig-drover John Samuel is a typical example. He became a burgess of Carmarthen in 1818 and three of his descendants achieved the distinction of becoming sheriffs of the county. Similarly the father of the artist Thomas Jones of Pencerrig had been sheriff of Radnorshire in 1746 while *his* father had enjoyed a successful career as a drover before meeting his end at the hands of highwaymen. The fine seventeenth-century poet, Edward Morus of Perthi Llwydion regularly drove cattle between North Wales and Essex. Other drovers like William Jones of Trawsfynydd (1770-1837) and the celebrated Dafydd Jones of Caeo (1711-77) became Nonconformists, the latter translating the hymns of Isaac Watts and writing many moving hymns of his own.

When the French wars forced the Bank of England to suspend the redemption of its notes in cash in 1797, numerous local banking houses were established, many of them by individuals or groups of drovers. Among those surviving the financial collapse of the 1820s were the Black Sheep Bank at Aberystwyth and the famous Black Ox Bank at Llandovery, established in 1799 by David Jones (1756-1840). Jones was a cattle dealer with the good luck (or good sense) to marry the heiress to a considerable fortune. As he prospered he was created a Justice of the Peace and High Sheriff of Carmarthenshire, at the same time accumulating several substantial properties in the county. Typically, his descendants became firmly established in county society and a member of the family was returned to Parliament in 1868. It says much for the reputation of Jones and his bank that the directors of Lloyd's Bank (which absorbed Jones and Company in 1909) ensured that for some years its Llandovery branch maintained the old Black Ox symbol on its cheques.

These few examples may have given the impression that the drovers were a mild-tempered, bookish, slightly saintly group of men. Nevertheless, physical toughness, courage and stamina were the hallmarks of the typical drover who plied his trade in difficult and often dangerous conditions. Many people learned to their cost that the Welsh drover was not a man to be double-crossed, as the Somerset Quarter Sessions Records for 1657 dramatically reveal. 'William Jenkins with many other Welshmen treated at Thomas Hoddinot's home with Mr. William Knoyle of Sandford to buy a close of grass to put their cattle in and not agreeing they drew their swords and assaulted Mr. Knoyle, Hoddinot, the Tithing man's deputy, his wife and many of them who came to part them using violent language, cudgells and stones.' In 1850 when a Welshman was swindled by a group of Cockneys at Barnet Fair in Hertfordshire he took his revenge in a direct and quite memorable manner. Capturing one of his adversaries with the help of a fellow drover, he tied the unfortunate man over the neck of an unbroken colt and ran the animal four or five miles after which the Englishman was only too glad to purchase his freedom by paying the drover his due!

Tough, clever, articulate and financially astute, the larger drovers and dealers were able to make a good living from their trade. A number of droving families had entered the ranks of the county gentry by the nineteenth century and others had accumulated sufficient capital to be able to lend out money at interest to businessmen and even to local landowners. However, a sizeable proportion of the total volume of trade in livestock was in the hands of smaller men, some of them farmers or tradesmen attempting to supplement their incomes by dealing in livestock as a sideline. These people, most of them without access to capital, tended to operate on credit and were thereby a more risky proposition for farmers with livestock to sell. Sometimes a small operator would promise to pay for his purchased stock after their sale in England. But where the animals failed to sell for a satisfactory price he would be unable to meet his obligations at home with the sad consequence that, '.....many an honest farmer is duped out of his property in whole or in part'. It was at people of this sort that eighteenth- and nineteenth-century writers levelled their rather astringent criticisms.

In the early fifteenth century the Warwickshire famer John Broome of Baddesley Clinton recorded purchasing oxen of Gruff Hope Wallace from a drove of Welsh cattle on their way to Birmingham. Again, in 1687, the constable's accounts of the Midlands parish of Helmdon contain an entry relating to money being given to, '.....a poor Welshman who fell sick on his journey driving beasts to London'. These and many other examples testify to the presence of the drovers in villages throughout the Midlands and the Home Counties before the coming of the railways. A 'Welsh Road' passed through Staffordshire, Warwickshire and Buckinghamshire; a 'Welsh Way' by-passed Cirencester in Gloucestershire, while 'Welshman's Ponds', 'Welshman's Fields' and various corruptions of Welsh words occur regularly in field and place names. The names of Welsh drovers crop up in farm accounts of the eighteenth century as far apart as Stamford and Brighton, Canterbury and Chipping Sodbury and their own extant account books show that there were few parts of southern and central England east of the Severn estuary which did not echo to the drovers' cry at some time or other.

The cattle and sheep that found their way to England were purchased in large numbers by drovers at the spring and autumn fairs. By the mid-eighteenth century upwards of 30,000 cattle and 'innumerable' sheep annually travelled through Herefordshire to south-east England and in the following century Pembrokeshire alone supplied 25,000 cattle each year to the feeding pastures of Northamptonshire and the neighbouring counties. Cattle droves, often of several hundred head, were assembled at a central point and shod by smiths who moved from fair to fair for the purpose. They then set off on the long journey eastwards, usually taking several days to settle down to a steady two miles per hour. This leisurely pace allowed ample opportunity for wayside grazing and made sure that the drove covered between fifteen and twenty miles each day.

Originally drove routes would have developed by means of a compromise being effected between the quickest and least arduous way between two points and the availability of overnight accommodation and forage at farms or inns with adjoining paddocks. Given the antiquity of the trade, there is reason to suppose that before the development of turnpiking the same long distance routes, forged over open mountain and enclosed lowland, were used by successive generations of drovers down the centuries. The account books of drovers/dealers of the eighteenth and nineteenth centuries show clearly that while they strenuously attempted to avoid toll payments, many were quick to take advantage of the more direct access to the Midland counties provided by the turnpikes. By so doing they could reach the point of sale earlier than their competitors travelling along the old drove ways and thus obtain better prices for their stock. The accounts presented opposite, taken from the papers of David Jonathan, a nineteenth-century dealer from Cardiganshire, illustrate tollgate payments and other aspects of the costs of droving during this period.

	s	d		s	d
Lampeter gate		4	Ledbury gate	4	2
Cwmann gate		10	Beer	1	0
Beer at Porthyrhyd	2	0	Allowance at Folly		9
Llanfair-ar-y-bryn gate	5	5	Cash to D.Williams	2	6
Shoes and nails	2	0	Cash to D.Davies		9
Grass at Talgarth	11	6	Hollybush gate	2	10
Beer and lodgings	1	6	Bridge gate	2	10
Allowance	1	0	Tewkesbury gate	2	10
Beer	2	0	Doddington gate	2	10
Grass at Pugh's	16	0	Shoes and nails	1	0
Beer and lodgings	1	6	Lent at Croydon	2	9
Allowance		9	Expense paid	4	0
Keep for mare	4	6	Grass at Staplehurst	4	3
Rhydspence gate	2	9	Staplehurst gate	2	0
Willersley gate	2	9	Cranbrook gate	2	10
Hadmore gate	2	11	Cranbrook grass	8	9
Grass	6	0	Beer and lodgings	2	6
Beer and lodgings	2	9	Hire man	2	9
Shoe the mare	1	0	Beer for man		6
Brockhall gate	2	11	Fair and field	1	4
Shoe and nails	2	0	Fair gate		7
Grass at Hereford	16	0	Grass at Sandway	3	0
Beer and lodgings	2	9	Beer and lodgings		10
Hereford gate	2	11	Gate		7½
Tarrington gate	4	2			
			£8	6	½

Extract from the accounts of David Jonathan, cattle dealer, 1843

Drovers' account books, the early maps and the Tithe material, supplemented by place-name clues and local tradition, provide valuable sources for the tracing of drove routes. Many of them have now been incorporated into the present road network, or swallowed up by ever-expanding stands of mountain conifers, yet surviving drovers' roads may be recognized on the ground by various diagnostic features. Hill top tracks, like the Kerry Ridgeway, typify the sunken grass lane created where driven animals were confined to a relatively restricted area. Where there was less confinement, as with the route across Aberedw Hill near Builth Wells, the drovers' ways remain as wide turf tracks rendered bracken-free by the constant treading of driven livestock. Where old roads have been incorporated into modern cultivation systems, crop marks may record their original course. In enclosed country where many drovers' roads have evolved into modern highways, extra-wide grass verges are a characteristic feature, while those following farm or estate boundaries, or providing links between fairs, typically become narrow lanes flanked by hedged embankments.

TREGARON TO RHYDSPENCE

Most of the many hundreds of miles of tracks and by-ways in the western counties were used at some time or other by drovers. However, there evolved over the years a relatively limited number of recognized long-distance routes over the rugged terrain of central Wales to the English border. Among these one of the most important was that linking the market town of Tregaron in Cardiganshire with the ford across the River Wye at Erwood in Brecknockshire.

Birthplace of several eminent Nonconformist divines and of that great Radical and man of peace, Henry Richard, Tregaron's development in the eighteenth and nineteenth centuries was closely associated with the cattle and sheep trade and the cottage manufacture of stockings and other woollen commodities. By all accounts the town had little to commend it in the early nineteenth century, being a collection of ill-built houses and thatched cottages dominated by the church on its prominent mound and a wooden bridge spanning the River Berwyn

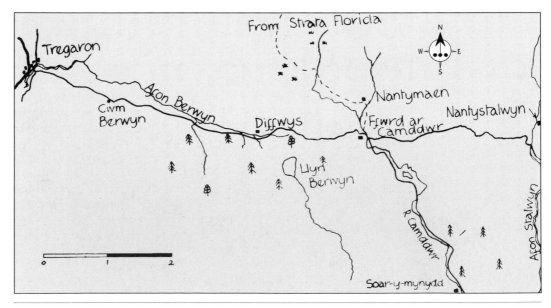

The Drovers' road from Tregaron to Nantystalwyn

Above: The Drovers road from Tregaron to Abergwesyn

Left: The Talbot inn, Tregaron

Below: The chapel at Soar-y-Mynydd

(SN680597). Here it was that many thousands of cattle and sheep converged each year, their drovers bringing welcome trade to the town's three shops and eleven pubs.

The Vestry Book for the parish of Lower Caron, covering the years between 1787 and 1846 makes frequent reference to the maintenance of 'the road across Tygwyn fields' and it seems that once the drovers' animals had been assembled in Pen Pica, the enclosure behind the present Talbot Hotel, they were driven through Tygwyn towards Cwmberwyn, a fine old farm originally the property of the Herbert family. The road to Cwmberwyn and subsequently to Abergwesyn was used both by drovers and by the Tregaron hosiers travelling to South Wales to sell their wares. Both would have appreciated that this road was free of tollgates, which may be another reason for the predominance of Tregaron as a droving centre in the turnpike era.

The drovers' road, now negotiable by car for the whole of its length to Abergwesyn, passes Cwmberwyn (frequently used as an overnight halt by drovers) and Diffwys and runs on towards the isolated ruin of Ffwrd-ar-Camddwr (SN762576). Here it was joined from the north by the ancient monks' road past Moel Prisgau, used by drovers bringing cattle from the fairs of North Cardiganshire. To the south the monks' road continued to the isolated chapel of Soar-y-mynydd, now on the edge of a great block of forestry, but in the last century (and centuries previously) the centre of a mountain sheep walk. Until recently this was one of the most isolated Calvinistic Methodist chapels in Wales and the point of convergence of many tracks used by farmers and others who came on foot or horseback for their weekly devotions (SN785533).

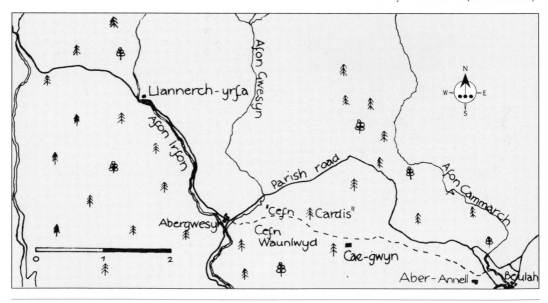

Drovers' road from Nantystalwyn to Beulah

From Nantystalwyn, further along the route from Ffwrd-ar-Camddwr, we notice several deeply sunken tracks leading to the mountain top in the direction of the Drygarn (SN805575). These may represent drift ways used when cattle from Nantystalwyn were driven to the open mountain. Alternatively they may be ways to the *Rhiw-y-Porthmyn* ('drovers' slope') which, according to the Nanteos estate map of 1819, left the road from Moel Prisgau and crossed the hill for Llannerch-yrfa (SN836556). The main drove road from Tregaron ran past the farm of Llannerch-yrfa, fording the River Irfon no fewer than three times, and on through wild, open country towards the hamlet of Abergwesyn (SN855528). After the long trudge across windswept mountain grasslands, the final approach to Abergwesyn through a lovely vale of oak woodland must have come as a welcome relief, especially on a morning in early autumn when shafts of sunlight through a break in the cloud heightened the golden colour of the bracken and the warm russet of dying leaves. Welcome too would be the refreshment provided at the Grouse Inn (now a farmhouse), the enclosure behind the inn being available for re-shoeing cattle that had lost their original shoes on the rocky track from Tregaron. Onwards from Abergwesyn the present country lane to Beulah does not lie on the

Above: Cattle shoeing enclosure, Abergwesyn

drovers' road, they preferring a more direct route across the hills. This crossed the fields in front of the Grouse Inn and forded the River Gwesyn before gently ascending the old hill track known locally as the *Cefn Cardis* (Cardiganshire ridge). In the early 1970s the hedged lane

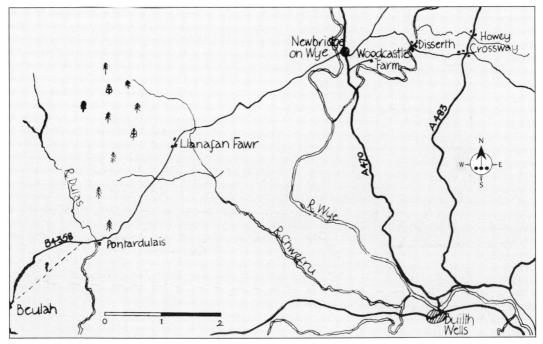

Drovers' road from Beulah to Newbridge-on-Wye

representing the beginning of the *Cefn Cardis* was still visible, but this has now disappeared in the wake of a modern farm road and a nearby bungalow, its course along the flank of the hill being now marked by a graded farm track. For much of its length the *Cefn Cardis* originally ran across open country which may explain why David Jonathan's accounts for 1839 contain a payment of 2s for the hire of an extra 'boy' at Abergwesyn. This local lad presumably helped

Below: Site of the ford across the River Wye at Newbridge-on-Wye

Disserth Church, dating from the fourteenth century, taken from the drovers road

to drive the herd across the hills until it joined the lane running past Aber-Annell for Beulah (SN915514). This is a lovely lane, varying from five to ten yards in width and enclosed by hedge banks planted with oak, ash and silver birch. In 1974 the narrow part of the lane towards Aber-Annell itself was fully hedged but, as is so often the case, supposed 'improvements' have subsequently led to the removal of the hedge.

As they left Beulah the drovers had the option of several routes to the English border. The first, entering England through Kington, seems to have run across Beulah bridge towards Pencrug before joining what is now the B4358 at Pontardulais to pass through leafy undulating countryside in the direction of Newbridge-on-Wye (SO015585). The ford across the Wye at Newbridge lay to the south of the present bridge, the drove road on the eastern side leaving the river banks to pass under the disused railway bridge and into a lane beside the church. By

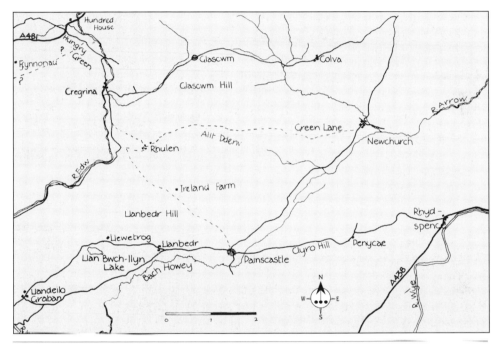

Drovers' roads from Newbridge-onWye to Rhydspence

this time a halt in the journey would be welcome and the bar of the Mid-Wales Inn (now a private art gallery) offered food and beer to the men, the banks of the River Wye providing ample grazing for the livestock. The onward journey carried the drove for several hundred yards in a southerly direction along the course of the A479 trunk road. However by the village school the drovers took the lane for Woodcastle Farm and thence across the fields to ford the River Irfon near the fourteenth-century church at Dyserth (Disserth), with its box pews and three-decker pulpit of the late seventeenth century (SO035584). Since the farmhouse by the churchyard was originally a pub (being licensed as such until 1897) it would have been regularly visited by drovers passing that way. The drove now joined the delightful country lane for Crossway which traverses the old Llandrindod-Builth Wells turnpike (the A483) before striking out across the gorse-covered southern slopes of Gilwern Hill. Subsequently it crossed the Hungry Green for Cregrina on the River Edw, passing the great mound used by John Wesley to preach one of his first outdoor sermons in Wales (SO123527).

At Cregrina, an important centre for cattle shoeing, the drove trail across Aberedw Hill joined the main route eastwards. Taking the course of an early road described elsewhere in this book, drovers heading for Cregrina ascended Aberedw Hill past Ffynnonau above which, so tradition has it, was a drovers' inn, known variously as *Tafarn Mynydd* or *Tabor Wye* (SO092530). Although none of the cartographic sources marks an early building at this spot, an enclosed triangular block of land may represent the site of some sort of habitation, the surprisingly fertile nature of the soil in the enclosure being typical of that found on upland sites where cattle have been regularly corralled over many years. From *Tabor Wye* it was but a brief journey across the hill to join Hungry Green and the lane for Cregrina.

Beyond Cregrina was a choice of routes to the border. The first of these, taken by drovers moving into northern Herefordshire, ran along the valley of the Clas Brook before joining the road to Glascwm and Colva described in an earlier chapter. Both these villages boasted drovers' inns in the years immediately preceding World War I. The second trail, towards the Wye crossing at Rhydspence, initially involved crossing Llanbedr Hill for Painscastle. Leaving Cregrina, the drove plodded through Rhulen, where a route to Newchurch along the green lane above Bryngwyn headed north east. Thence it went along the side of the hill to the south of the ruins of Ireland Farm and through deserted country before descending to Painscastle along an enclosed way entering the village by the Maesllwch Arms. The tiny hamlet of Rhulen, with its peculiar little church, seems to have lain at the beginning of a series of trackways ascending Llanbedr Hill, many of these still leaving great swathes of greensward through the pernicious bracken (SO138499). Conveniently for the present-day traveller to Painscastle the main drove road has been recently metalled. Driving along this road as it snakes its way over the hill one is still intensely aware of the sense of loneliness and melancholy which the surrounding countryside might have induced in the more sensitive drovers.

Opposite the impressive remains of the Norman castle, a lane leaves Painscastle in the direction of Francis Kilvert's beloved Clyro Hill (SO168462). This lane, leaving Wern Fawr to the south, runs across the top of the hill and then, by way of Penycae and Penyrheol, steadily curls towards Rhydspence, some four miles from Painscastle (SO243473). Kilvert himself spent many hours attempting to locate the sites of the 'Coldbrook' and the 'Black Ox', two inns reputed to have been used by drovers following this route. The Clyro Tithe Map shows the 'Coldbrook' to have been close to the present Whitehall Cottage, and though there is no reference to the 'Black Ox' there remains a strong local tradition of a drovers' tavern of this name somewhere on Clyro Hill. Rhydspence itself, on the English border in the exquisite vale of the Wye, also had two inns, the one standing today having its origins in the mid-fourteenth century.

TAFARN TALGARTH TO PAINSCASTLE

Drovers converging on Painscastle from the north were probably careful to avoid arriving at the village at the same time as one of the many droves from North Carmarthenshire approaching from the Wye crossing at Erwood. To trace the route followed by the latter we must make our way to the village of Llanfair-ar-y-bryn in the Brân valley to the north-east of Llandovery. Here, at Tafarn Talgarth, (now the Glanbrane Arms), animals from Cilycwm in the north and from Llandovery itself were prepared for the ascent of the Mynydd Epynt. The route from the inn followed the existing road to Tirabad and provides fine views of the rainswept hills to the west of the Brân valley and of the impressive railway viaduct carrying the line down to Pembrokeshire. The latter may well have been an object of wonder to the last of the drovers. Tirabad is an unprepossessing modern village that has grown up around Llanddulas Farm and would scarcely have been recognizable to drovers of the nineteenth century (SN879414). The old whitewashed church, however, would be familiar to them,

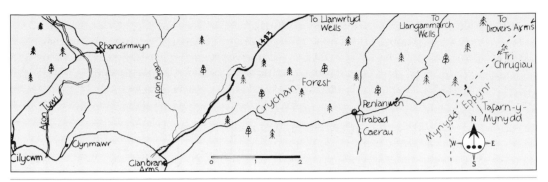

Drovers' road from Mynydd Epynt to Erwood

though they would have some difficulty in locating the celebrated Cross Inn near Penlanwen, as this is now submerged beneath coniferous forest (SN898419). A second drovers' inn, The Spite, stood on the roadside on the approach to Tirabad. It is widely believed that this hostelry was opened to 'spite' Cross Inn, but it more likely represents the site of an ancient monastic *hospitium* since Tirabad and Ystrad-ffin to the north were part of the property of the monks of Strata Florida. At Penlanwen, approximately a mile beyond Tirabad, the drovers deviated from the lane to Llangammarch Wells to join the Tricrugiau trail at Tafarn-y-Mynydd (now a ruin on the edge of a block of forestry) and to ascend Mynydd Epynt (SN918422).

The great upland tract of the Epynt, in the past a formidable and inhospitable place, is now positively dangerous for the traveller because the Army uses much of the plateau for manoeuvres and target practice. Despite the panoramic views it offers, the Epynt is a dull, treeless and gloomy place brightened only by sinister red warning flags and enlivened by the occasional rattle of gunfire. Here, even the sheep bear a frightened and hunted look which the author came to share after a nerve-racking (and unsuccessful) attempt to isolate the old drovers' track from the network of military roads. Walkers, therefore, follow the trail at some considerable risk, especially when the red warning flags are hoisted! By the early 1800s the Epynt was a celebrated breeding ground for Brecknockshire cattle and sheep and the drovers, while not having to worry themselves about stray bullets and flying shells, would have had some difficulty in keeping their animals separated from the herds and flocks grazing on the open mountain. On their way to the Drovers Arms to the east they might have purchased stockings and other knitwear from one of the many (now abandoned) sheep farms on the Epynt where weaving and knitting were important means of supplementing a living from the farm. The Drovers Arms itself, approached by today's traveller on the B4519 road between Llangammarch Wells and Upper Chapel, was a notable port of call on the journey to the east (SN986451). Today, one suspects, even the shades of the old drovers would avoid this rather melancholy building, its shored-up windows and corrugated iron roof lending it a distinctly uninviting air.

Eastwards of the inn the military authorities have recently constructed a concrete road linking with the B4520 Builth Wells-Upper Chapel road near the Griffin Inn, a pleasant little pub also well-known to the drovers (SO022433). Between it and the Drovers Arms is open mountain and no clearly identifiable drove trail remains. However, slightly to the north of the Griffin a distinct track, reputed to be that taken by the drovers to the Wye crossing, runs to the south of Pwll-du and across the bleak hillside towards Cwmgwenddwr Farm. From here it was a matter of driving the animals through more gentle countryside along the lanes linking the farm with Cefn Hirwaun, approximately a mile to the south-east (SO066441). Cefn Hirwaun stands at the head of a steep and circuitous road descending to the peaceful, tree-lined

Drovers' road from Mynydd Epynt to Erwood

banks of the Wye north of Erwood. Over the centuries thousands, if not millions, of livestock were jostled down here towards the river crossing. A local historian writing two generations ago recalled the condition of the road before the council surfaced it with tarmac: 'The track was ploughed by the hoofs of the cattle in the damp weather, and manured by the cattle as they passed over it. In the dry weather it would be harrowed by the hoofs of the cattle again. No bracken or fern has grown on it since and it is still today a green sward which has not been used since the black cattle went over it'. Known locally as the 'Twmpath' the lane joins the nineteenth-century turnpike road opposite the modern bridge across the Wye, the latter having been constructed slightly to the north of the original ford over the river (SO089438). Below the bridge, on the eastern bank stands *Glanyrafon*, a fine villa whose name in the early years of the present century was *Cafn Twm Bach*. Although the term is rarely used today, the Welsh *cafn* originally referred to a small boat, so the name lends credibility to the tradition that cattle and sheep were ferried across the river at times when high water flooded the ford. Twm Bach (Little Tom), the last of the ferrymen, apparently loaded the animals into a box-like boat which he then winched across the water by means of a heavy chain. Since he ran *Cafn Twm Bach* as an inn, the little man would have relished the prospect of rain so that the drovers obliged to use the ferry would seek consolation in the temptations of his bar parlour. Twm Bach, it seems, died rather romantically when, together with his son, he tried to recover his boat after an accident on the river. The flood proved too much for them and the unfortunate pair were swept away to a watery grave further downstream. This sad event must have taken place before the 1860s when an iron bridge was thrown over the river on the site of the present one.

After safely negotiating the ford or the rigours of Twm Bach's ferry, the drovers could breathe a collective sigh of relief for the most arduous part of the journey was over. Behind them lay the drama of the mountains, the western rains and treacherous fords; ahead was the gentle, easy countryside of England. They pushed on along the eastern bank of the Wye before taking the narrow lane for Llandeilo Graban passing between the medieval church and what is now a deserted farmyard. The next stage took them along the south-eastern flank of Llandeilo Hill towards Llwetrog, leaving Llan-Bwlch-llyn lake to the south (SO120464). After a mile through open moorland beyond Llwetrog, a deep lane carried them past Llanbedr Church and onto the Painscastle road, entering that village to the north of the castle mound.

LAMPETER TO TAFARN TALGARTH

Drovers arriving at Painscastle by the well-trodden route from Tafarn Talgarth normally had with them livestock purchased from the Lampeter area or from further west at one or more of the many country fairs around Newcastle-Emlyn in Carmarthenshire. Lampeter, in particular, enjoyed a strong connexion with the livestock trade. The town is mentioned regularly in drovers' account books while references in the Tithe Apportionments to the Drovers' lane and Drovers' Arms Fields on the banks of the Teifi are further reminders of the importance of

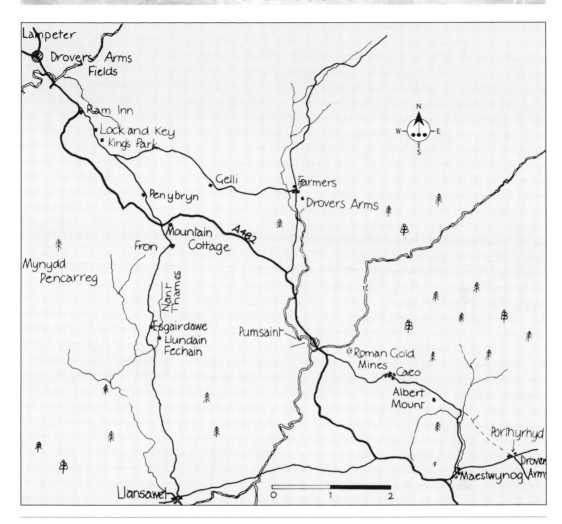

Drovers' roads from Lampeter to Caeo

the trade to the little town. Several routes between Lampeter and Tafarn Talgarth were available to the drovers and among these one of the most important was that leaving Lampeter by Cwmann and heading for Pumsaint past the Ram, and Lock and Key taverns (SN583473). 'Lock and Key' incidentally, is a common name for old inns close to established drovers' roads and seems to have derived from the inn of the same name in London's Smithfield Market where many Welsh drovers were accommodated in the early nineteenth century. By the 1850s, when the Smithfield tavern had also become the venue for harp and singing concerts for homesick Welshmen, it was under the proprietorship of a Mr Robertson who seems to have specialized in executing the wills of drovers unfortunate enough to die before their return to Wales. Among several wills executed by Robertson was that of John Walters of Llancrwys in Carmarthenshire who died at Hyde in Middlesex in 1859 leaving a modest fortune of some £1,500.

Passing through the Cwmann tollgate the drovers pressed on to Treherbert, and then took the narrow lane past King's Park and Pen-y-bryn to rejoin the Lampeter to Llanwrda turnpike (the present A482) a mile or so later near Mountain Cottage (SN613437). At this spot there

Caeo Village

was reputedly a shoeing forge although there appear to be no remains of the enclosures normally associated with cattle shoeing forges nor do any of the cartographic sources indicate a smithy in the immediate locality. Entries in several account books recording tollgate payments suggest that at least some of the drovers followed the turnpike road to Pumsaint. On the other hand, those with an eye to reducing overhead costs may well have made use of the old drift road at Brynmanhalog approximately 1³/₄ miles to the south of Cwmann. This lane, having all the characteristics of a drovers' road, leaves the parish road to head towards Fron to the south-east, where it linked with another parish road joining the turnpike *below* the Pentre-Davies tollgate at Pumsaint. It is difficult to trace the lane along the whole of its course past Caer Pencarreg to Fron but it can be picked up between the latter and Esgair Farm.

To the south of Fron, on the outskirts of Esgerdawe, the maps of both Emmanuel Bowen and Thomas Kitchin locate the farm of *Llundain Fechain* (Little London) and the stream of *Nant Thames* running through it (SN614407). *London* type elements are relatively common in place names adjacent to drove routes. There is, for example, a *Glan Thames* near Talyllychau in Carmarthenshire and a *Llundain Fach* at Brechfa in the same county, while Montgomeryshire boasts a *Little London* near Llandinam and Cardiganshire a *Llundain Fach* near Talsarn. Similarly *Picadilly*, *Holborn*, *Victoria* and *Smithfield* names frequently occur in association with drove routes. However, the *Llundain Fechain* near Esgerdawe is of particular interest as this was the first overnight resting-place for Cardiganshire drovers en route to the Epynt crossing. The claim that the drover/hymnologist Dafydd Jones of Caeo settled and named the farm cannot be upheld since an indenture of 1708 (three years before Jones was born) relating to turf cutting on nearby Panaugleision mentions the farm by its present name. Jones, nevertheless, may well have occupied the place at some time or other during his career and if so he would have been acquainted with *Cwm y Gof* (Smith's hollow) on nearby Pwllau Farm where, local lore has it, cattle from Cardiganshire were regularly shod. He would also have been wary, as he took his cattle or sheep down the road to Pumsaint, of animals from the north joining the route by way of the old Roman road from Ffarmers a mile or so above the village, their owners perhaps less than sober after an hour or so in Ffarmers' celebrated *Drovers Arms*.

Making their way from Pumsaint the drovers passed the remains of the Roman gold mines at Ogofau as they trudged the parish road to Caeo. In their company, one day in the early 1850s, walked a nervous young girl, wide-eyed with excitement at the prospect of going to work in London. This was Jane Evans of Ty'nywaun, who, as a commemorative plaque in the vestry of Pumsaint Church tells us, eventually found her way to the Crimea where she joined Florence Nightingale in her efforts to alleviate the sorry lot of the soldiers wounded in that tragic and pointless war.

Caeo was one of the largest cattle trading centres in this part of Wales and great fairs were held on 30 May and 6 October to coincide with the seasonal movements of the drovers to England. As usual, facilities were available for shoeing, either at Gornoethle or in the paddocks behind the church while at Blaendyffryn, a long two miles to the east of the village, the farmer's wife offered both food and ale to drovers as they awaited the shoeing of their animals (SN714403). From Caeo the eastwards route pursued the present parish road to Albert Mount before turning on to one of the several lanes and trackways to Blaendyffryn and thence over Pen Lifau and past Cwmfranfawr to Cilycwm (SN753400). The great expanse of Caeo Forest bedevils the tracing of the precise route beyond Blaendyffryn. However, the Cilycwm Tithe Map records *Holborn Fields* alongside the lane from Cwmfranfawr (SN736397). *Holborn* is a name element often associated with a drove route while the *Drovers Arms* in Cilycwm itself, together with the open drain previously used for watering livestock, recalls the presence of the drovers in the village.

The hamlet of Porthyrhyd lay on a second route from Albert Mount to Cilycwm. At Aberbowlan, approximately a quarter of a mile beyond Albert Mount, where the present road deviates towards Maestwynog, drovers en route for Llandovery forded the Dulais stream and followed the old Roman road across the hills to pass by Llynglas and into Porthyrhyd opposite the former Drovers' Arms (SN711378). Many drovers, including Roderick Roderick and David Jonathan came this way, the latter in particular being a regular visitor to the Drovers' Arms. In the accounts of both men reference is made to the toll payments at the Dolauhirion gate above Llandovery. This would suggest that these drovers, at least, used the turnpike road between Porthyrhyd and Llandovery and so crossed the Tywi by William Edwards's splendid single-arched Dolauhirion Bridge, completed in 1773. Neither set of accounts indicate payments at the Porthyrhyd gate, and so they probably managed to find some means of getting

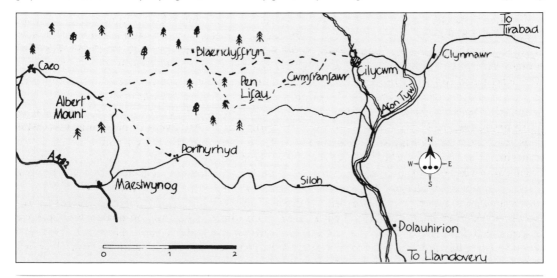

Drovers' routes from Caeo towards Llandovery

through the village without dispensing coin to the gate keeper.

Llandovery, considered by Benjamin Malkin to be one of the worst towns in Wales, '......its buildings mean, irregular and unconnected; its streets filthy and disgusting', was nevertheless, a flourishing centre for the cattle trade. Here a host of saddlers, carriers, glovers and leather sellers waxed prosperous on the by-products of the trade and relaxed in the town's numerous taverns so deplored by Vicar Rhys Prichard in the seventeenth century. The denizens of Llandovery were seemingly much addicted to beer which, after the Beer Saloons Act of 1830, could be sold in shops and other places of work as well as at established taverns. The 1830 Act enabled the number of registered beer houses in Llandovery to rise from twenty-one in 1811 to more than fifty in 1840. Visually depressing the town may have been, but it was a beer-drinker's paradise, with each little shop and tavern selling its own peculiar brew and providing the discriminating drinker with the variety of tastes so lamentably absent nowadays.

LLANDYSUL TO PORTHYRHYD

Another drove route, connecting the Epynt with South Cardiganshire and North Pembrokeshire, ran from Llandysul in the west towards Porthyrhyd and Cilycwm. Leaving the steep streets of the little town of Llandysul along the course of the present B4336, this route crossed the B4559 at Bryn Teifi southwards of Llanfihangel-ar-arth where an inn, Pwll Dwr, was a frequent port of call (SN458393). Further east, at the junction of the B4336 and A485 (the Llanybydder to Carmarthen turnpike) lay yet another inn, the Drovers' Arms, mentioned by name in the mid-nineteenth-century Tithe Apportionment. From the Drovers' Arms, the last inn for some miles, the route traversed the Mynydd Llanllwni and Mynydd Llanybydder along what is now the road to Rhydcymerau, a journey originally taking the drovers over open mountain. Today's metalled road, known locally along the latter part to-wards Rhydcymerau as *Heol Lloegr* (England road), passes for much of the way through the northern reaches of the Forest of Brechfa. Rhydcymerau itself apparently offered a cattle shoeing smithy at Efail Fach and the Cart and Horses tavern, a house well-known to the drovers but now reduced to a farm barn (SN578388). Instead of following the line of the B4337, the onward route to Llansawel turned left at the Cart and Horses towards Post Carreg where it joined the drift road above Cwmcoedifor and Cwm Hywel before merging with the B4337 at Sunnybank Farm, half-a-mile to the west of Llansawel (SN612364). Once again there is no ground evidence or references on the early maps, but local people talk of the one-time existence of a shoeing enclosure at *Cwm yr efail bach* on this old road as it passes above Cwmcoedifor (SN588384). As recently as the mid- 1880s, however, cattle were certainly

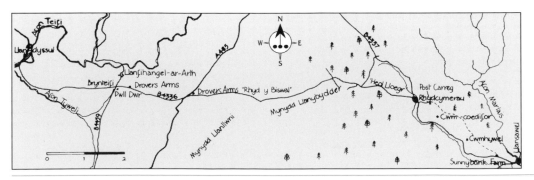

Heol Lloegr ('England Road') across Mynydd Llanybydder

shod at Llwyn Felfryn field in Llansawel while both Sunnybank Farm and Rhydyglyn Farm to the south provided overnight accommodation for men and animals. Onwards from Llansawel, the drovers crossed the Cothi above Glanrannell Park and worked their way towards Porthyrhyd along today's road connecting Llansawel and Porthyrhyd by way of Maestwynog.

MACHYNLLETH TO WELSHPOOL

Many of the long-distance drove routes across Wales, last used in the nineteenth century, must have been as old as the livestock trade itself. Making his way across windswept hilltops and avoiding where possible the vales of the lowland, the early drover sought a route which reduced to a minimum the number of rivers to be forded and which allowed him an extensive view of the surrounding terrain and ample warning of would-be marauders. By the late eighteenth century, however, when some semblance of law and order had settled on the countryside and the need for security had become less critical, the most direct routes to England were provided by the turnpike system and the more enterprising dealers and drovers abandoned the older routes in favour of the turnpikes as the network developed. Others used both the turnpikes and the old drift roads, as was the case with some of the routes described earlier.

Typical among the larger drovers, David Jonathan and members of his family regularly followed the turnpike between Machynlleth and Shrewsbury with droves of cattle purchased around Dinas Mawddwy and Mallwyd. The Jonathan papers contain references to toll payments at Welshpool and Llanfair Caereinion in Montgomeryshire, while an account of the county in the 1830s draws attention to 'great herds of cattle' being shod in the Wynnstay Fields near the latter town. Alternatively, drovers intending to circumvent the toll bars on the Welshpool to Shrewsbury turnpike crossed the meadowlands to the east of Welshpool before fording the Severn and climbing up to the Welsh Harp Inn on the Long Mountain. Here they joined the Roman road linking Forden and Shrewsbury by way of Westbury. The importance of this route was emphasized in 1853 by witnesses before a Parliamentary Select Committee discussing the establishment of the Montgomeryshire railway, when they pointed out that the great majority of the cattle being driven through Welshpool reached Shrewsbury via the Long Mountain and Westbury.

At the little village of Forden, south of Welshpool, the route across the Long Mountain was joined by an important long-distance trail used for centuries by both cattle drovers from north west Wales and fish traders from the Dyfi Valley and the villages on the coast of Cardigan Bay. Throughout the droving era Machynlleth was the principal town in this part of the country (SN745006). Served by the port of nearby Derwenlas it was an important centre for the weaving, lead and timber trades besides having featured as an administrative base in the ill-fated Owain Glyndŵr's dreams for an independent Welsh nation. Drovers converging on the town from Gwynedd and north Ceredigion may have known of the Roman auxiliary fort at nearby Pennal, of Cromwell's reputed battle with Royalist supporters on the banks of the Dyfi in 1644 and of Royal House, the old town gaol, where Charles I was reputedly held prisoner. Since the late thirteenth century, when Edward I granted a market and fair charter to the town, Machynlleth had been a venue for generations of drovers. By the 1800s the roads leaving the town had been incorporated into the turnpike system and drovers moving eastwards had no option but to pay tolls on their stock as they made for Penegoes, the first convenient point for leaving the turnpike (SN776006). From Penegoes, birthplace in 1714 of the celebrated landscape painter Richard Wilson, drovers could travel for virtually the whole way to Welshpool without the inconvenience of further tolls. Keeping the valley of the Crewi to the right they journeyed towards Rhiwfelen Farm along the present metalled lane. Approximately

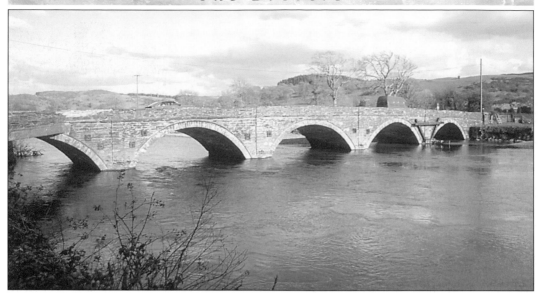

The bridge at Machynlleth

a mile beyond the farm, the metalled road curves southwards towards Penybryn, the original roadline continuing as a hedged farm track across Ffridd Uchaf. This, the drovers' trail, eventually meets the Talywern-Melinbyrhedin road at the guest house of Rhiwgoch on top of the hill above Talywern (SN825999). After the steep and winding descent to Talywern the drovers and others now joined the old Newtown-Machynlleth road, which steadily ascended through the valley to the pass of Bwlchglynmynydd and then, by way of Dolgadfan Farm, to Bontdolgadfan on the River Twymyn (SN886002).

The replacement of this road by the new turnpike through Cemmaes Road and Llanbrynmair in 1821 effected a minor revolution in local communications. Farmers, previously obliged to carry their lime and manure from the port of Derwenlas along the tortuous upland trackways, now had a graded road and were thus able to replace the packhorse with the cart. Similarly, cottagers making a slender living from flannel weaving could now reach the markets of

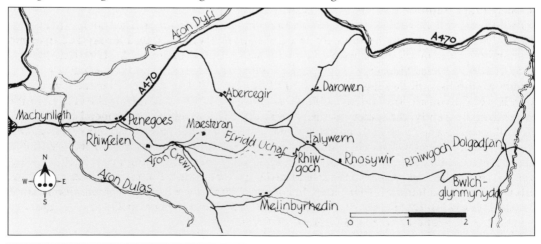

Drovers' road from Machynlleth to Dolgadfan

This toll house survives to the north of Machynlleth on the road to Corris at the junction of the road to Cemmaes

Welshpool and Newtown with comparative ease, either on foot or by courtesy of some obliging long-distance carter. The flannel industry was vital to the economy of this part of Wales. For centuries the vast majority of farmers carded and spun their wool at home and although several factories with carding engines and spinning-jennies had sprung up by the early nineteenth century, the weaving process remained essentially a cottage industry. A weaving factory built by John Howell at Bontdolgadfan around 1800 supplemented the efforts of the cottage weavers for half a century until competition from the large-scale operators in Yorkshire and Lancashire forced it to close, along with many other small factories. The growth of efficient, mechanised factories in the north of England also sounded the death knell for the cottage weavers and the click of the shuttle was finally hushed in hundreds of cottages in west Montgomeryshire. In 1850, flannel to the value of £8,000 was produced by 500 people in the parish of Llanbrynmair alone. By the 1890s this cottage industry had virtually disappeared; like so many other traditional crafts it was destroyed by the Industrial Revolution.

Eighteenth and early nineteenth-century travellers coming down from the Bwlchglynmynydd pass to Bontdolgadfan on the River Twymyn found a busy and dynamic community, most of its members being employed in the weaving trade. Like that famous fictional weaver, Silas Marner, the people in the village and from the countryside around were mainly Methodists. Following the visit in 1739 of Howell Harries of Trefecca, one of the founders of Calvinistic Methodism, a Methodist Society had been formed in the village. In the early days, apparently, the society was beset with difficulties and one of the members, Richard Howell, planted a sprig of holly in a hedgerow, declaring as he did so that God's intercession in the growth of the bush would reflect the future prosperity or otherwise of the Methodist cause. Howell's action indicates a belief in a superstition predating Christianity itself, yet God was clearly on the side of the Methodists, for the sprig became a flourishing bush which was still thriving over a hundred years later. In common with others of their communion in rural Wales, the early Bontdolgadfan Methodists met at each other's homes until the first chapel was built in 1767 on land belonging to Dolgadfan Farm.

After resting at Bontdolgadfan the drovers, by now perhaps in company with groups of weavers on the way to Newtown, pressed on past Werngerhynt on the old road to the south of Newydd Fynyddog across poor, wet country for Talerddig which lay on the 1821 turnpike

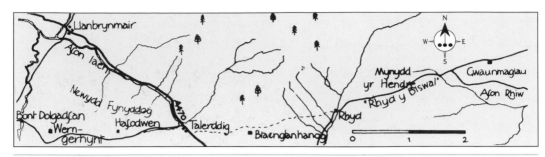

Drovers' road from Dolgadfan towards Welshpool

(SO931001). Even if it was a small village, early nineteenth-century Talerddig boasted a woollen mill, an inn and a thriving Sunday school. Again reflecting a practice common throughout the Welsh countryside, the school was originally held in a Talerddig farmhouse. When this could no longer hold the congregation, people crammed themselves into the house for the introductory part of the service before dispersing to their cottages for private Bible study and returning later for a concluding session of hymn-singing and prayers. The very fact that a school room for 247 people built in 1812 proved to be too small, speaks volumes for the enthusiasm with which Welsh country people espoused the Methodist cause.

Walking for a short while along the turnpike road to the south of Talerddig, the drovers and their fellow travellers turned in an easterly direction along the old green road running past Caeauduon and Blaenglanhanog to the hamlet of Rhyd. This road, delineated on the first Ordnance Survey map published in the 1830s, can still be traced for part of its course. After almost two hundred yards out of the village along the turnpike (the present A470) a gate on the left leads to a recently-constructed set of farm buildings from which the old drovers' road runs in an easterly direction across the hills towards Rhyd (SO934998). Initially it takes the form of a somewhat overgrown green lane, varying between fifteen and forty yards in width, in part enclosed by hedgebanks and in part forming a hollow way across the fields. After about a mile the course of the road has been obscured by modern agricultural activities. Towards Rhyd, though, it becomes an overgrown track joining the metalled road for Llanllugan behind the modern telephone kiosk and tiny deserted chapel (SO975005). The track, ascending Llanllugan Mountain, is dignified with the name *Rhyd y Biswal* on the early Ordnance Survey map, a name shared with the track across Mynydd Llanllwni, described earlier in the chapter. The standard Welsh dictionaries translate *Biswal* as 'dung' and it might be argued that 'dung' in relation to a road might merely imply a muddy track. However, since the name is associated with known cattle trade routes it seems that, in these two cases, it may derive from the droppings of livestock passing along the road.

The *Rhyd y Biswal* ascends steeply from Rhyd along a recently-metalled course across the windy, treeless moorland of Mynydd yr Hendre. After almost two miles a relatively new road branches south for Adfa, the *Rhyd* continuing past Gwaunmaglau to the Cefn Coch Inn where the drovers left their weaver friends who normally approached Welshpool by Gibbet Hill and Castle Caereinion (SO048028). The drovers are likely to have visited the isolated Cefn Coch Inn and, if one subscribes to the traditional belief that farmers prepared to accommodate cattle and sheep drovers planted pine trees outside their houses, Gwaunmaglau may also have been a port of call. It has to be borne in mind, though, that there remains an equally strong legend that Scots Pine trees were planted by Welsh Jacobite sympathisers as a secret means of identifying 'safe houses' to those of their cause on the run from the authorities.

Beyond Cefn Coch the drovers' route turned south-eastwards along a narrow lane to ford the River Rhiw at Llanllugan before turning left at the crossroads west of Adfa to take the road

Stocking knitter; late nineteenth century

for Llanwyddelan and New Mills (SO056010). The onward route to the banks of the Severn below Welshpool cannot be made out in detail. Many old lanes wind through the undulating countryside beyond New Mills, eventually converging on Berriew and the Severn Vale. Some of these may have been used by drovers, although the most logical route to Berriew would seem to have been by way of Manafan and the valley of the River Rhiw.

As the first steam trains chugged into the valleys of east Wales the more perceptive drovers must have realised that the advent of the railway spelt the beginning of the end of long-distance movement of livestock on the hoof. But they had little to fear for some time, since the evolution of the Welsh railway system took place over a long period, with almost fifty years separating the completion of the Llanelli railway in 1839 and that of the Whitland-Crymych branch-line, one of the last lines to be constructed. The great droves continued throughout this period to be taken across the mountains into England, though it seems that once the railhead had reached a convenient point the bigger drovers and dealers were not slow to exploit the new system.

By the mid-1850s Shrewsbury was linked by rail to the major towns of the Midland plain and ten years later, to Machynlleth, Aberystwyth and other towns on the coast of west Wales. The Jonathan family papers show that these dealers responded to the situation by abandoning the old Tregaron-Abergwesyn drove route in favour of the turnpike to Shrewsbury and the new railhead. By the sixties even this journey was no longer necessary and from then on 'droving' merely involved assembling animals and driving them to the new station at Aberystwyth. Exploiting the railway facilities meant that henceforth the Welsh livestock dealer would be spared the problem of obtaining forage for his animals on the way to England – a problem made particularly acute in the wake of the Cattle Plague epidemic of 1865-6, when farmers and innkeepers were less willing than before to provide overnight accommodation to drovers of animals of diverse origins. Also, the railway offered benefits in terms of timeliness of marketing and a real reduction in the cost of conveying animals to the fairs of the Midland grazing counties. To take just one example from the Jonathan papers: in the period 1840-9 the average cost per head of taking a drove from west Cardiganshire to Northampton amounted to 12s. By 1865, when the same journey was being undertaken by rail, the cost had declined to 9s 9d.

But the old drover still had his uses. Livestock fairs and markets had by now become concentrated around the railway stations, and yet dealers still needed to employ the skills of the drover to ensure that animals were carefully conveyed to the sidings and loaded into the carriages. Moreover, droving of sheep in particular, continued within Wales until quite recently, and one of the last of the long-distance drovers, Dafydd Isaac of Trefenter in Cardiganshire, regularly took flocks of 3-400 sheep on the ninety mile journey from Machynlleth to Brecon Fair in the early years of the present century. Of Dafydd's fellow drovers, those who had prospered at their trade often settled on farms in Wales, others taking holdings in the English Midlands. Indeed, many of the Lewises, Evanses and Williamses currently enjoying a good living as graziers in the Shires owe their prosperity to drover ancestors with the good sense to establish a foothold in these lush pasture lands. These were the fortunate ones and for each of them there must have been dozens who sank without trace into that saddest of nineteenth century social groups, the unskilled labourers.

Yet their shades remain. In his mind's eye the sensitive traveller might see them; smoking noonday pipes under a nearby tree and casting wistful looks down the long and empty road as they exchange ancient yarns in an ancient language.

5 THE TURNPIKE ERA

The route was not along one continuous trust,
but here over a bit of turnpike and there
over a bit of turnpike, with ever and anon long
interregnums of township roads, repaired in the
usual primitive style with mud and soft fieldstone,
that turned up like flitches of bacon.

R. S. Surtees
Mr Sponge's Sporting Tour, 1852

Regardless of the efforts of a few enlightened landowners to renovate them, most Welsh roads in the eighteenth century remained in a deplorable condition, their maintenance quite beyond the meagre resources of most parishes. The indifference and ineptitude of other parishes was of grave concern to the postal authorities who were often in the habit of applying to the local Quarter Sessions for the imposition of collective fines, these to be appropriated towards the hire of professional road repairers. As late as 1820, for example, long after the establishment of the turnpike system, we find the Post Office writing to the Trustees of the Brecknockshire Turnpike Trust warning them that unless the roads in the county were improved, the Office would apply to the magistrates for a fine to be levied and equally apportioned between the Trust and local parishes. Unfortunately efforts of this sort met with little success since the magistracy comprised local landowners and professional people who were far from enthusiastic about imposing fines which in the main would be met from their own pockets.

Gradually, however, landed proprietors throughout Britain as a whole began to realize that the development of trade and their own social aspirations urgently demanded that measures be taken to improve communications. In 1663, under the first Turnpike Act, the Justices of Hertfordshire, Huntingdonshire and Cambridgeshire had been empowered to raise tolls for the maintenance of the Great North Road from London. This was soon followed by other Acts and after 1700, the powers of erecting barriers and levying tolls were vested in local bodies termed 'Turnpike Trustees'.

The development of turnpiking reflected a growing awareness that the provision of a network of highways was a matter of national as well as local importance. Although there was often lack of co-operation between Trusts, cases of corruption at the tollgates and acute financial difficulties, the Trusts gradually improved the road system, and turnpikes began to multiply rapidly, embracing some 20,000 miles of road by 1830.

To qualify as a Turnpike Trustee, a man had to enjoy a yearly income of £80 from rents, or be the owner of real estate to the value of £2,000. In association with like-minded fellows he would advertise in the local press his intention to establish a turnpike, at the same time inviting interested parties to a meeting to discuss the matter. If they managed to agree among themselves the group would now arrange to subscribe to the cost of securing the passage of the necessary private Act through Parliament. By the time the lawyers, surveyors, clerks and a multitude of others had been paid, this could often amount to more than £500, particularly where the Act was opposed by local vested interests. Having obtained their Act (normally renewable every 21 years) the trustees now addressed themselves to the business of purchasing

NOTICE
IS HEREBY GIVEN,
THAT THE
TOLLS

Arising at the **TOLL GATES** upon the Turnpike Roads in the First District of the *Montgomeryshire* Roads, called or known by the names undermentioned,

Will be Let by Auction,

To the best Bidder, at the **PUBLIC ROOMS**, situate in the Town of *Newtown*, in the said County of *Montgomery*, on the fifth Day of March next, between the Hours of Eleven and Two, in the Manner directed by the Act passed in the third Year of the Reign of his Majesty King GEORGE the Fourth, " For regulating Turnpike Roads," which Tolls produced the last Year the several following Sums, above the Expenses of collecting them, and will be put up at those Sums respectively, (viz.)

St. Giles' and Pwllybidron Gates	£520	Clatter Gate	£190
Park and Scafell Gates	850	Manafon Gate	125
Berthllwyd Gate	340	Cross Lane Gate	134
Glandulas Gate	220	Llivior Gate	67
Tynycwm Gate	163	Abermule Gate	117
Bryndu Gate	49	Kerry Gate	176
Felindre Gate	62	Dolvor Gate	170
Botalog Gate	19	Upper Dolvor and Bwlch Gates	85
Dolhafren, Frankwell, and Weeg Gates	190	Bronywood Gate	35

Whoever happens to be the best Bidder, must, at the same time pay one month in advance (if required) of the Rent at which such Tolls may be let, and give security, with sufficient Sureties to the satisfaction of the Trustees of the said Turnpike Roads, for Payment of the rest of the money monthly.

All Persons wishing to bid for any of the above-named Gates, are requested to take Notice, that they will be put up to Auction

Precisely at 12 o'Clock

On the above Day; and all Persons bidding must be prepared with Sureties, either to be present, or in writing under their hands, agreeing to be Sureties; and the highest Bidder for each Gate will be required immediately to pay down one month's Rent in advance.

Notice is also hereby given, that the Trustees of the said Roads will, at the above time and place, proceed to the Election of new Trustees, in the room of those who are dead or refuse to act.

WM. HUMPHREYS,
Clerk to the Trustees of the said Turnpike Roads.

DATED FEBRUARY 5th, 1841.

J. AND E. SALTER, PRINTERS, NEWTOWN.

Toll auction notice; 1841

Toll Tickets

land, building tollhouses and appointing surveyors and toll collectors, all of which involved borrowing large sums of money. The problem of financing these initial capital developments was a major one for the trustees. Many people who had promised financial support failed to deliver, while the business ability of the trustees themselves often left much to be desired, so that many Trusts soon got into difficulty. Indeed, by the mid 1840s, thirteen of the twenty-nine Trusts in South Wales were bankrupt, some of them irretrievably so. The situation was not helped by the fact that among those trustees public spirited enough to attend meetings, local political intrigue often came to the fore, so that gatherings came to be held in an atmosphere of bickering and frustration.

Nevertheless, once conceived, the project rapidly forged ahead and roads were surveyed and tolls collected. In the earlier years the trustees themselves arranged for the collection of toll money, but as time passed there arose the practice of leasing gates or groups of gates by auction, for periods of up to three years. By so doing the trustees knew their annual income in advance while the lessees, a growing class of professional 'toll farmers', were enabled to pocket any income from tolls in excess of the rent of the gates payable to the trustees. Toll farmers like Richard Morgan, also surveyor of the roads for the Radnorshire Turnpike Trust, were asked to provide security for their lease. If they failed to do so the trustees acted quickly, as in the case of John and Stephen Owens, who rented the Walton and New Radnor gates in 1801. At a meeting of the trustees shortly after the Owens had taken the gates, it was ordered that men be employed 'to turn them out of possession of the tolls and gates and appoint other persons to collect the tolls, they having neglected to give security for payment of the rent according to their agreement'.

For obvious reasons the toll collectors were an unpopular and often despised group of people, subject to the vilification of some travellers and readily tempted by 'backhanders' from others. Rather like today's traffic wardens, they did an unpopular job in difficult conditions. In the early days their tollhouses by no means approximated to the delightful Georgian and Victorian structures still to be seen today, the originals being flimsy affairs, often of wood and from time to time mounted on wheels. Gradually things improved and more permanent houses were erected, typically of the design recorded in the minutes of the Radnorshire Turnpike Trustees in 1768:

Ordered that Edward Breese build a Turnpike House at the Turnpike Gate at New Radnor, twelve foot in length and ten foot in breadth in the clear within the walls and to erect a chimney at the end and to top the same with brick. To erect a stone wall six foot and an half in height all round the Building and to fix a partition within across the Building and also another partition to divide the pantry from the bedchamber and to compleat the whole including glazing, thatching, carriage etc. in a workmanlike manner at the sum of Ten Guineas on or before the twenty second day of October instant.

From houses such as this the tollkeeper operated his gate or bar, the tolls he collected varying from Trust to Trust according to the extent to which trustees believed a particular conveyance would damage the road surface.

In theory the trustees were supposed to maintain the road surface, but in reality legislation over the years seems to have been designed to make vehicles conform to the requirements of the road rather than to enforce the improvement of the road to facilitate the passage of traffic. On the grounds that they did excessive damage to the road surface (if, in the eighteenth century it could be dignified by such a term) discrimination was particularly severe against narrow-wheeled vehicles. Shortly after the Restoration, wheels of less than 4in wide were prohibited from the roads and from that time onwards the authorities persistently strove to increase wheel width and to reduce the weight of waggons and coaches. This led to surcharges being levied on overweight vehicles while, after 1773, traffic on wheels of more than 16in wide was relieved from toll. It is not surprising that the narrow-wheeled mail coaches, increasingly common after 1780 and exempt from toll, hardly endeared themselves to turnpike trustees the length and breadth of the land. Exempt too were all military horses, waggons and coaches, travellers to and from church or chapel, funeral cortèges, horses going to be shod, livestock moving to water, vagrants with passes and citizens travelling to vote at Parliamentary elections. Similarly exempt were vehicles concerned with the carriage of dung, timber and lime for farming purposes.

To the disgust of the agricultural interest, above all in Wales where large quantities of lime were required to neutralise the acid soils, the lime exemption was discontinued in the first decade of the nineteenth century. Typically, the Brecknockshire Turnpike Trust imposed tolls in 1809 with the concession that a lime cart would pay toll at a gate only once during the day, and thus would be freed from toll if the return journey from the limekiln was completed within a 24-hour period. This meant that the roads were crowded with scores of farmers setting out for the kilns at the break of day in the hope that they could get to the head of the queue, purchase their lime, and be home by midnight. Little wonder that tempers became frayed and fists and knives flashed as they jostled for position. Little wonder too that resentment came to a head with such violence during the Rebecca Riots of the early 1840s when many gates were destroyed, when tollkeepers were assaulted and when the arsonist stalked the countryside. Even before that, the appearance of a tollgate or tollbar provoked local rioting, particularly when people believed, with some justification, that the amount of toll collected was usually out of all proportion to the rate of road improvement. Thus, on 10 November 1780, John Lukes of New Radnor was gaoled for attacking the Stanner Gate near Kington with a hedge bill and thirty years later, Charles Lawrence of Llanelwedd was summoned for wilfully breaking the lock on the Builth Wells gate. These men and many others held that tolls were only justified if they were used effectively to improve road surfaces.

The minute books of some Trusts reveal that great care was taken in the selection of competent surveyors and clerks who discharged their duties diligently. Others, however, suggest that many surveyors were quite useless, being ignorant of the techniques of road maintenance and, in some cases, not even knowing which roads belonged to the particular Trust by which they were employed. In the case of the surveyor to the Carmarthen Trust this was understandable since he was illiterate! His colleague in the Llandeilo and Llandybie Trust was rarely sober, while the clerk to the Main Trust was both sober and cunning enough to abscond to America in 1823 with £650 of trust funds. Hardly the sort of men to inspire public confidence!

Gentlemen, farmers, drovers and others resorted to all manner of ruses to avoid toll payments. These ranged from the use of the dog-drawn (and thus toll-free) cart to the rather ingenious idea, successfully adopted by one man, of constructing a cart to be pushed by a horse thereby circumventing the regulation that tolls be payable on horse-drawn vehicles. Others might unhitch an extra horse from their cart and lead it through the gate, and so pay less toll, while farmers were often in the habit of hiding loads of corn beneath a covering of manure or straw, both of which travelled free of toll. Drovers, in particular, would often attempt to pass round a gate, a relatively easy matter when the road traversed unfenced common land. The Trusts attempted, usually unsuccessfully, to counter this by cutting long, wide trenches at appropriate points on the roadside to prevent people from leaving the highway. Alternatively, where side roads could be used to avoid a gate, they placed heavy chains across them. This was of questionable legality as was the practice of many toll farmers, keen to maximise their income, of setting up extra gates on fair days. The tenant of the New Radnor gate did this on the occasion of St Luke's Fair in 1771, and, to the credit of the Radnorshire Turnpike Trustees, he was fined fifteen shillings for his trouble.

How far the turnpike trustees put their tolls or gate rents to good use varied enormously. Some Trusts improved gradients, forged 'cross roads' and renovated surfaces, while others, less enlightened, were rather more concerned with income than expenditure, so that surfaces tended to remain unimproved. This was gall and wormwood to travellers by coach or post-chaise in the early years of the nineteenth century, as the antiquary Henry Skrine bore witness after a liver-jolting journey through Radnorshire: 'Their turnpike roads may rank among the worst in the kingdom for, notwithstanding the frequency of their tolls and the abundance of good materials in the country, they are generally suffered to languish in a shameful state of neglect for want of a little public spirit'. To the traveller on horseback, poor road surfaces were a minor inconvenience and one would expect criticism to be at its most astringent from those who travelled in some form of wheeled vehicle. Moreover, the nature of the countryside and state of mind of the traveller was bound to influence his attitude towards the condition of the roads. Barber's bitter tirade against the dangers of fords in Wales may not have been entirely unconnected with the fact that he, together with his books, papers and drawings, received a thorough soaking when he forded the upper reaches of the River Loughor. In other words, some of the complaints of contemporary diarists and journalists should be taken with a pinch of salt.

In the eighteenth century commentators had persistently agitated for a system enabling the

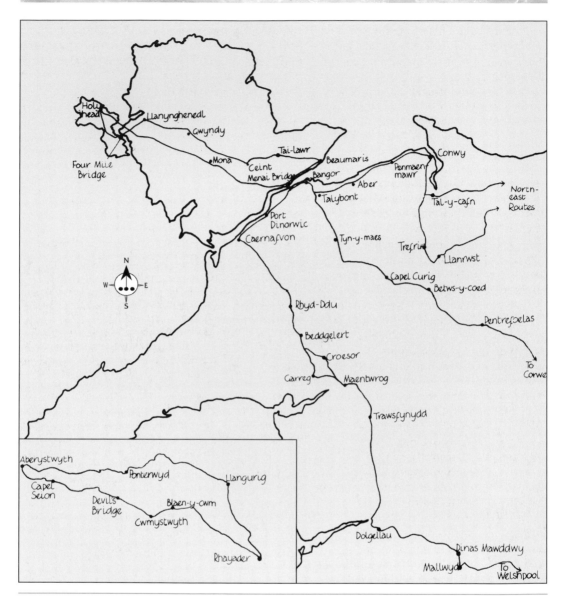

Some turnpike roads in North Wales

more rapid and effective exchange of mail. This applied especially to North Wales where, in the 1750s, a package destined for Ireland by way of Holyhead could find a waggon as far as Chester, but no further. Twenty years later traffic capable of safely carrying bulky mails between Shrewsbury and Bangor was limited to a single privately-owned cart travelling twice weekly. The poorly-paid, letter-carrying postboys mounted (often inadequately) on horseback were readily susceptible to bribes and being unarmed were easy prey for wayside vagabonds. So acute, in fact, were the dangers of highway robbery that the Post Office advised its clients who proposed to mail money to cut their banknotes in two and to despatch each half separately. Besides the poor quality of the mail service, the inadequacy of the roads between Wales and England made life difficult for the growing number of Irishmen wishing to come to Britain after the Act of Union. Also, growing numbers of Englishmen, stimulated by the writing of Walpole and Gray and with their senses heightened by the 'Gothick' splendours of Alpine scenery, were keen to explore the romantic scenery of Wales with its druidic associations and picturesque legends.

Regular coach travel through North Wales to Holyhead did not come until 1776 when the enterprising landlord of the White Lion in Chester, showing entrepreneurial spirit typical of the times, started a daily 'flying post chaise' service to Holyhead, charging 2 guineas per passenger. Three years later another innkeeper, Robert Lawrence of the Raven and Bell in Shrewsbury, became the first man to link Holyhead and London by a coach system, thereby siphoning off much of the traffic from Chester and laying the basis to his subsequent fortune. These various developments provided food for thought for John Palmer, a West Country merchant. Protégé of Ralph Allen of Bath, the model for Squire Allworthy in Fielding's *Tom Jones*, Palmer believed he had the answer to the problem of the posts. In 1783 he presented Prime Minister Pitt with a plan for running the mail system on the basis, not of solitary postboys, but of special coaches running according to strict schedules. These would also carry parcels and a limited number of paying passengers where appropriate. Seeing the obvious benefits of Palmer's proposals, Pitt over-ruled the objections of the conservative Post Office and the stage was set for the glamorous era of the mail coach. So successful was the system, with its carefully-scheduled horse changes and well-planned routes supplied with excellently appointed inns, that by 1830 mail coaches nightly covered more than 12,000 miles of road and represented the most efficient system of land transport in the world. Initially they rarely travelled at speeds in excess of 7-8mph and yet they were widely recognized as a major step forward and it was not long before the English mail coach became synonymous with speed and efficiency.

Advances in coach design and the replacement of wooden benches with sprung cushion seats helped considerably, yet the lot of the passenger in the early mail coaches could be less than pleasant, especially before the widespread adoption of Telford and Macadam's methods of road surface improvement. Lurching along on a winter's night, swathed in blankets or straw and peeping nervously at the driver as he pulled at his flask, the traveller may well have wondered whether it was worth travelling at all. His safety was very much dependent upon the reliability and sobriety of the coach drivers, of whom many seem to have taken perverse pleasure in terrifying the wits out of their passengers. Howell Rees, for example, mail coach driver on the Brecon to Llandovery stretch of the turnpike to Haverfordwest, allowed his enthusiasm for keeping to a strict schedule to override any concern for his fellow road users. On one occasion, when Rees had sent a cart from Cardiganshire rolling down the hillside, its red ochre-painted woodwork and gearing smashed to pieces, he responded to the unprintable invective of the carter with a casual wave and the promise of a glass of brandy at their next meeting! In 1827 Thomas Morgan was gaoled for 'furiously driving the Milford and Carmarthen day coach', while Enoch Hughes, a private coach owner, was fined £5 for drunken driving and the use of abusive language as he drove passengers between Shrewsbury and Aberystwyth. Another driver, Edward Jenkins, drunkenly careering along the road to Llandovery, managed to overturn the Gloucester to Carmarthen mail coach outside the town. On this occasion a rather shaken local squire emerged from the coach and administered immediate rough justice by, as the local paper picturesquely put it, 'kicking the coachman's posterior down the road' (see page 140). After such harrowing escapades passengers were able to enjoy a brief period of respite while the horses were being changed, perhaps ruminating on the remark of a traveller in 1815: 'Once you crawled and were overset gently; now you gallop and are bashed to atoms'.

Alongside the mail coaches ran a growing number of conveyances operated by private individuals and by the 1820s villages throughout North Wales, hitherto experiencing little

Above: Rescuing the Gloucester and Aberystwyth Mail Coach from the River Frome

LONDON
AND
ABERYSTWITH
Old Coaches.

The Public are respectfully informed that a Coach will start

On Wednesday the Twelfth day of June instant,

FROM THE

KINGS HEAD INN, KINGTON,

At Five o'Clock in the Morning, and arrive at ABE-RYSTWITH at Seven o'Clock the same Evening.

Also, a Coach will leave ABERYSTWITH the same Morning at Six o'Clock, and arrive at KINGTON at Eight o'Clock the same Evening.

After the *Eighteenth* instant, the above Coaches will continue to run Twice a Week, viz. every Wednesday and Sunday Mornings, from Kingtou and Aberystwith at the hours above-mentioned.

At Kington it will meet with the LONDON COACH, which leaves that place at Four o'Clock every Monday and Thursday Mornings, for Leominster, Worcester and Oxford, and arrives at the BULL AND MOUTH, LONDON, on the following Mornings by Eight o'Clock; leaves the Bull and Mouth every Monday and Friday at Three o'Clock in the Afternoon, and arrives at Kington on the following Night by Nine o'Clock.

As Worcester it will meet with Coaches for Bristol, Bath, Cheltenham, Birmingham, Manchester, Liverpool, &c. &c.

FARES.

	£.	s.	D.
Inside to Aberystwith	1	2	0
Outside	0	16	0

Performed by JAMES HAYWARD, *and Co.*

Who will not be accountable for any Goods lost or damaged above the value of Five Pounds, unless regularly booked and paid for accordingly.

4th. June, 1816.

Printed at the Office of J. Bartoll, Kington

Left: Coaching advertisement; 1816

more than the ponderous waggons of local carters, were now regularly visited by gaily-painted stage coaches. Together with the Irish Mail to Holyhead, stage and mail coaches plied between Shrewsbury and Aberystwyth via Welshpool and Newtown, while towns in Merioneth and Llŷn and Denbighshire and Flintshire were provided with coach services linking with these major routes. Also, stage waggon services to deal with heavy freight began to radiate from Chester and Shrewsbury into North Wales, to the great benefit of the wool and flannel trades.

Despite the numerous waggons, mail and stage coaches and the atmosphere of cut-throat competition in the transport business, travel and the despatch of mails remained a very costly affair. To send a letter from Wales to London around 1800 cost more or less twice a labourer's daily wage and it was not until the introduction of the fourpenny and penny posts in 1839 and 1840 that correspondence came within the range of most people's pockets. Expensive though it was, transmission of letters between the major post towns was now very fast and efficient, the journey from London to Holyhead being shortened in stages from forty-eight to twenty-seven hours between 1784 and 1836. As early as 1790 a letter posted in London would arrive in Dublin three days later – Irish sea conditions permitting. The letter would be carried in the mail coach leaving the 'Swan with Two Necks' in Gresham Street, London and be deposited at the 'Eagle and Child' in Holyhead. Irish travellers alighting from the Dublin packet normally proceeded to the 'Eagle and Child' to pick up their coaches for Shrewsbury, London or Chester. These, in the first decade of the nineteenth century, would convey them to their destinations at the following rates:

	Inside			Outside		
Royal Mail to London	£6	5s	0d	£3	0s	0d
Royal Mail to Chester	£2	5s	0d	£1	5s	0d
Ancient Briton to London	£4	4s	0d	£2	10s	0d
Ancient Briton to Shrewsbury	£1	15s	0d	£1	5s	0d
Prince of Wales to Shrewsbury	£1	15s	0d	£1	5s	0d

Swift and safe communication with Holyhead was a major objective of the promoters of road improvements in North Wales in the eighteenth and nineteenth centuries. Important too, for local gentlemen with social aspirations, was the need to forge good road links between north-west Wales and the Llŷn Peninsula and the English turnpike system leading to London. By 1752 the road from Shrewsbury to Wrexham had been turnpiked, followed, four years later by the Chester to Conwy route through Rhuddlan, a road line taken by John Taylor ('The Water Poet') on his journey to Beaumaris as far back as 1653. This particular turnpike, however, was soon modified to pass through St Asaph from Holywell thereby avoiding the marshy land around Rhuddlan. 1759 witnessed the opening of yet another turnpike from Chester to reach Conwy by way of Denbigh, Llansannan, Llangernyw and Tal-y-cafn, thus linking, like the other roads, with the crossing of the Lavan Sands to Beaumaris and thence to Holyhead.

The problem with these roads, (and one which was to remain until the construction of Telford's remarkable bridges) lay in crossing the River Conwy and subsequently the Menai Straits. The Conwy boasted two ferries, one located at Tal-y-cafn and a second lower down the river near Conwy itself. Besides the nuisance of having one's journey interrupted, the crossing of the Conwy was not without its dangers and there are numerous accounts of instances of loss of life and property during the crossing. In the mid-seventeenth century, for example, the ferryboat sank with the loss of all passengers save for one fortunate young woman, who was to live with her memories until the age of 116 and be laid to rest in Llanfairfechan in 1744. In the early nineteenth century the danger may have been less, yet the 'shameful impositions' of the ferrymen who charged half a guinea for the carriage of a gig, '.... and after that importune for liquor', remained prejudicial to the blood pressure of the traveller. The Reverend Mr

The Llandovery Mail Coach Pillar

Situated on the A40, some 2½ miles from Llandovery on the Brecon Road is the Mail Coach Pillar. The inscription tells its own story and on a side panel, it states that the pillar was erected by J Bull, inspector of mail coaches, in 1841. It cost £13.16.6d, subscribed by 41 people and was restored in 1930 by postal officials.

The inscription reads:

This pillar is called Mail Coach Pillar and erected as a caution to mailcoach drivers to keep from intoxication and in memory of the Gloucester and Carmarthen mailcoach which was driven by Edward Jenkins on the 19th day of December in the year 1835, who was intoxicated at the time and drove the mail on the wrong side of the road and going at a full speed or gallop met a cart and permitted the leader to turn short pound (sic) to the righthand and went down over the precipice 121 feet where at the bottom near the river it came against an ash tree when the coach was dashed into several pieces. Colonel Gwynn of Glan Brian Park, Daniel Jones Esq of Penybont and a person of the name of Edwards were outside and David Lloyd Harris Esq of Llandovery solicitor and a lad of the name Kernick were inside passengers by the mail at the time and John Compton Guard.

Bingley, who wrote of these 'shameful impositions', was not alone in his condemnation of the ferrymen. Some years previously Richard Fenton and his friends managed to get safely across the river, '.... after having our patience tried to the utmost by waiting for above 2 hours at the ferry and experiencing the most unexampled and savage insolence from the ferrymen'. By 1808 the opening of the Capel Curig Road to Bangor and the Menai meant that the ferry could now be avoided, while the completion of Telford's bridge over the Conwy in 1826 freed travellers on the northern route from the inconvenience of the Conwy Ferry. It is worth recording, though, that before the bridge was opened Hugh Evans and five other ferrymen managed to petition successfully for compensation for loss of livelihood.

CONWY TO BEAUMARIS AND MENAI BRIDGE

From Conwy there were several routes to the Menai crossing. One of these was by the old Roman road directly opposite Tal-y-cafn, which ran to Aber via Bwlch-y-ddeufan and Bont Newydd (SH787718). Described as 'an exceedingly bad mountainous road' this was previously used by the Parliamentary army during its conquest of Caernarfonshire. In the 1750s the possibility of turnpiking this road was mooted as a means of reducing the length of the journey to the Menai Straits. However, the nature of the terrain made this rather impractical and the Turnpike Acts of 1777 and 1780 took in the road between Tal-y-cafn and Conwy, which then headed for Dwygyfylchi and Penmaenmawr through the rocky defile of the Sychnant Pass.

The old road bridge at Aber

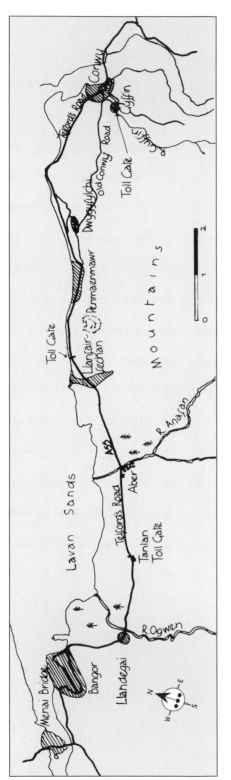

Telford's road across Penmaenmawr, running above the present A55

Turnpike road from Conwy to Menai Bridge

The onward traveller from Conwy, having refreshed himself at one of the many inns of the ancient borough and perhaps, like Henry Skrine, been 'regaled with the strains of a blind harper', said a short prayer, crossed his fingers and advanced on the next stage of his journey to Holyhead – the awesome crossing of Penmaenmawr. For centuries the short stretch of the journey around Penmaenmawr had struck terror into the hearts of all but the most hardened travellers and as their coaches, gigs or chaises clattered up the Sychnant Pass and along the Old Conwy Road, hearts would begin to beat just a little faster. In 1631 Sir John Braunston had to 'lift his wife over the back of the saddle for her fright', while Dr Johnson was quite terrified by this stage of the journey. Thinking, as ever, of his creature comforts, the doctor was greatly relieved to reach Bangor in safety, only to discover that the accommodation available was limited to '... a mean Inn and in a room where the other bed had two men'. In 1762, a Mr Jones, Rector of Llaneilian, riding on horseback with a lady on the saddle behind him, fell with horse and lady down the steepest part of the rock. 'The divine,' Pennant tells us, 'with great philosophy, unsaddled the steed and marched off with the trappings, exulting at his preservation'. The fact that his passenger had been killed in the accident seems to have been of little concern to the reverend gentleman.

Originally the crossing of Penmaenmawr was by way of a road running above the present A55. In the 1700s a succession of roads had been built, but none of these seems to have improved greatly upon its forerunners. Consequently travellers continued to peer nervously out of their carriages at the sea pounding the shore far below and to run the risk of rock falls from above due, according to the Reverend John Evans, to, '.... the goats, skipping from crag to crag to browse the alpine shrub'. So bad was the road – in 1770 a mere 7ft wide – that the nerves of Irish travellers could stand it no more and the city of Dublin subscribed to the cost of building a breast-high wall on the seaward side. Two years later a Parliamentary grant enabled improvements to be made by the engineer John Sylvester whose efforts sufficed until Telford's restructuring of much of the course of this, and other North Wales roads, several decades later. Henry Skrine was lavish in his praise of Sylvester's work, writing of 'An excellent and almost level road, well protected with walls... cut for above a mile on the shelf of this mountain and the traveller passes on in the utmost security in spite of the impending horror of the rocks above and the tremendous precipice beat by the roaring billows below'.

Today's motorist on the Old Conwy Road joins the seemingly endless flow of traffic on the A55 as it runs through the long, straggling village of Penmaenmawr towards the notorious rock. Until it reaches a point on the outskirts of the village where a brilliantly-conceived diversion, completed in the 1930s, carries it on a series of arches around the steepest part of Penmaenmawr, the A55 follows roughly the course of Telford's road. Above this diversion, however, a short stretch of Telford's original may be seen, a low wall on the seaward side giving protection for the whole length of the road until it once again merges with the A55 on the outskirts of Llanfairfechan (SH692758).

Since the sixteenth century Holyhead had replaced Chester as the principal point of departure for royal couriers and the Royal Mail to Ireland. The route to Holyhead crossed Anglesey from Beaumaris, the latter being approached from Caernarfonshire by a ferry which had been in existence since the reign of Edward II. Passengers embarked from Aber, a village on the turnpike currently occupied by the line of the present A55 trunk road (SH655727). Like other ferries in North Wales, that to Beaumaris exposed the traveller to a considerable element of danger as it was necessary for passengers and their coaches to traverse the shifting Lavan Sands before reaching the channel where the little boat plied. The danger was such that in 1623 the postmaster of Beaumaris had asked that posts might be fixed in the sands to mark out the track for, '.... many times when sudden mistes and foggs do fall the danger is very great upon the sandes so that the Kinges packetts and subjects are like to perish'.

Beaumaris had thrived under the Tudors to become an important port for the receipt and

The Telford road (left) approaches the suspension bridge at Conwy, with the modern replacement to the right

The Sychnant pass

The Tanlan tollhouse, near Llandegai

despatch of all manner of merchandise besides developing into a shipbuilding centre of some significance. In earlier times Edward I's fine castle had served as a deterrent to the marauders and pirates haunting the coastline of this part of Wales. However, by the seventeenth and eighteenth centuries Beaumaris, and the coves and inlets around the Anglesey coast, had become a haven for pirates and smugglers and Revenue cutters frequently fought running battles with those engaged in illegitimate trading in tea, tobacco, rum and other highly-taxed commodities.

In 1718 Beaumaris yielded its position as a post town to Bangor and even if some wealthy travellers continued to use the Lavan Sands crossing, most began to show a preference for the way through Bangor, by this time 'on the great road from London to Holyhead'. After clearing the Penmaenmawr tollgate, this road, turnpiked in the 1760s, ran through Llanfairfechan and Aber to reach Bangor by way of Llandegai, passing en route the Tanlan tollhouse westwards of which the castle of Penrhyn rose majestically above the surrounding trees.

To the west of Bangor a road branched from the turnpike to the Menai Straits and the Porthaethwy ferry to Anglesey. By the 1780s the ferry was served by an excellent (if overpriced) inn, where travellers could look out over Anglesey as they quaffed their wine and listened to the beguiling strains of the harp. To late-eighteenth century gentlemen, with an interest in the 'Sublime and Picturesque', this was the perfect way to spend a warm summer's evening. 'I listened,' wrote Bingley, wrapped in a pleasing melancholy, 'to the sweetly flowing tones.' Had he arrived on a cattle fair day, Bingley's finer feelings might have been shocked by the sight of huge droves of cattle being swum across the Straits by their drovers. This was a subject which moved Richard Llwyd to verse and numerous travellers to incredulous comments. As one wrote, 'The people tie ropes to the horns of five or six bullocks at once, get into a boat and drag as hard as they can while others on shore beat them cruelly to force them into the water and when they have plunged in, it seems impossible they should not be drowned as their heads often get under the boat's bottom'.

Like other ferries, Porthaethwy was not without its dangers, nor were travellers any less subject to the rapacity and rudeness of the 'rugged Welsh ferrymen' who rarely stood on ceremony. At 2s 0d per wheel, together with 'a liberal remuneration for the ferryman', charges were very high, but at least the ferry was available at all stages of the tide and remained the most effective means of crossing the Menai until the opening of Telford's remarkable bridge in 1826. This wrought iron masterpiece wherein Telford applied the suspension principle on such a vast scale, was opened on 3 January. The same day the owner of the ferry, Miss Jane Williams, received £26,557 in compensation, a vast sum considering that the bridge itself cost a mere £123,000. The opening, the culmination of eight years work, was a very splendid affair. The London and Chester coaches passed grandly over the bridge at the head of thousands of people; flags were waved, bands played and cannon fired, while the redundant ferrymen looked on, perhaps thinking of the £26,557. At last a safe passage to Anglesey was open to all who could pay the modest tolls: 1d for a pedestrian, 1s for a four-wheeled waggon, 2s 6d for a stage coach and 3s for a post-chaise or private four-wheeled carriage.

ROADS ACROSS ANGLESEY

The establishment of Bangor as a post town heralded the gradual decline of the Lavan Sands crossing and consequently of the original post road. Leaving Beaumaris along what is now the B5109 this road passed the fine set of seventeenth-century almshouses on the Baron Hill estate and ran on through delightful rolling country to a junction with the modern A5025 beyond which it took a narrow lane to the little village of Ceint (SH490750) before following a route to Holyhead taken by later roads as described below.

The 'George' Inn, overlooking the Porthaethwy Ferry and the Menai Bridge; 1844

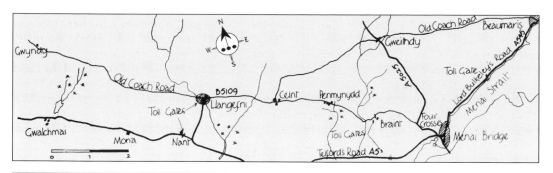

Turnpike roads in southern Anglesey

Menai Bridge

Robert Morden's 1704 map shows this road as the sole route from the Menai crossing, but later maps such as those of Thomas Taylor (1718) and Thomas Kitchin (1755) indicate the road connecting Porthaethwy and Ceint as the principal highway. This passed Four Crosses and along the lane to Braint before making a right turn for Penmynydd (leaving the almshouses on the left) and thence past Pen-yr-allt for Ceint. As they rode through Penmynydd (SH510745), eighteenth-century travellers might have paused to think of Owain Tudor, grandfather of Henry VII who was born in 1400 and raised in the village, only to meet his end at the hands of the hangman for having the temerity to marry Henry V's widow, Catherine de Valois.

Proceeding into rather featureless country, the traveller now passed through Llangefni and along the course of the present B5109 to Llanynghenedl before turning southwesterly towards Holy Island, to which he gained access across the sands close to Four Mile Bridge (SH280784).

The importance of this line of road in the early eighteenth century is emphasized by the fact that the erection of milestones (long since disappeared) along its length was sponsored by the

The ruins of Gwyndy

proprietors of the Dublin packet. William Morris of Holyhead spoke well of the road's condition or rather, of its condition in parts. Writing from Holyhead to his brother Richard in 1753 he observed, 'We can boast of having four miles of as compleat a road as any in His Majesties Dominions whatever may be the condition of the rest of it to Borth [Porthaethwy]'. His concern with the state of the eastern stretch of the road prompted Morris to combine with other local gentlemen to arrange for it to be turnpiked. An appropriate Act reached the Statute Book in 1765 (being subsequently renewed by Acts of 1775 and 1807) and gates were erected at Braint, Llanynghenedl and Holyhead.

Returning from Holyhead to Bangor in the 1770s, Thomas Pennant drew the attention of his readers to 'the comfortable inn called "Gwindy"'. Gwyndy, located between Trefor and Llynfaes, was a substantial inn which had for many years also served as a post office (SH395794). Unusually for a Welsh inn, most travellers praised its accommodation and its table. Henry Skrine's remarks are typical '.... every accommodation was admirably supplied and much enhanced by the attention of our worthy old landlady who had been fixed on the spot for about forty years'. This stalwart matron was probably the wife of Hugh Evans of Gwyndy who regularly carried the mail between the inn and Holyhead from 1745 until the arrival of the first mail coach in 1785. Thomas Telford himself was mindful of the excellent service provided by Gwyndy and when he completed his new road through Anglesey in the 1820s he recommended that Eliza Jones, widow of the Gwyndy postmaster, receive a pension by way of compensation for lost trade. Today Gwyndy is a gaunt, ivy-clad ruin.

Like many turnpike roads of the time, the Porthaethwy-Holyhead highway served its purpose as long as the traffic loading remained modest. However, following the Act of Union with Ireland in 1800 the road came into heavy use and before long the competence of the turnpike authorities to maintain it in a safe condition was called into question. Finally, in 1819, a Parliamentary Select Committee was set up to investigate the present condition and future role of the road and as it collected evidence some horrific stories came to light. Coaches had been overturned, coachmen's legs had been broken and horses had died of exhaustion. An angry Lord Jocelyn explained to the committee that as far as he was concerned travelling along this particular road in a mail coach could not be undertaken without risk to life and limb. Thomas Telford, appointed by the committee to survey the road, had no doubt as to its

inadequacies. Citing its narrowness, awkward bends, poor surface and numerous hills he recommended that the existing road be abandoned and replaced by a completely new highway. Subsequent pressure from Irish parliamentarians and others prompted the authorities to adopt Telford's proposals and the construction of a new road across Anglesey, along with the building of the Menai Bridge, was sanctioned by Act of Parliament in 1819. The bulk of the new road, the present A5, was in use by 1822, the project being completed the following year when an embankment was built to carry the highway from the Anglesey mainland to Holy Island and Holyhead. Five gates were positioned: at Stanley (on the end of the causeway to Holyhead), Cae'r Ceiliog, Gwalchmai (on the right of the junction with the road to Bodwina), Nant (on the junction of the road crossing to Llangefni) and Llanfair. Of the handsome octagonal tollhouses controlling these gates, those at Cae'r Ceiliog, Llanfair and Gwalchmai still remain in much their original condition, as do the elegant milestones placed at intervals along the highway. Motorbound travellers along the busy A5, provided their nerves allow their attention to stray momentarily from the traffic stream, will also notice Mona, the fine two-storied house put up by Telford between

An A5 turnpike milestone at Bethesda

1819 and 1821 (SH424750). Built to replace

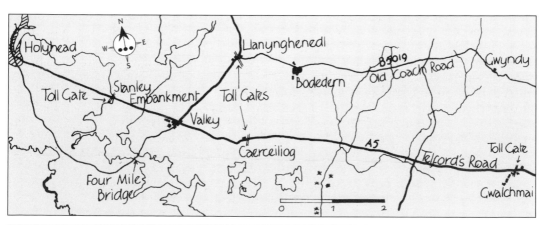

The old coach road and Telford's road to Holyhead

The toll house at Llanfair

Gwyndy as a post house, Mona remained an important pull-in for stage coaches until the arrival of the railway in 1848. The tradition of hospitality is still maintained by the present owners of the house who provide bed and breakfast for jaded and car-sick travellers en route for Ireland.

Whichever route he took, the earlier traveller's usual destination was Holyhead and the sea passage to Ireland. Few people were impressed with the run across Anglesey which lacked the scenic splendours of Caernarfonshire and failed to kindle the sense of awesome grandeur so dear to the heart of the early nineteenth-century 'man of taste'. George Borrow, blunt as ever, echoed the majority view when he spoke scathingly of Anglesey in general and the landscape around Holyhead in particular: 'The country looked poor and mean – on my right was a field of oats, on my left a Methodist chapel – oats and Methodism! What better symbols of poverty and meanness!'.

Arriving at the rather shabby town of Holyhead the traveller could now look forward to the prospect of a sixty-mile boat journey across the Irish Sea, lasting for six to nine hours depending on the direction and force of the winds. In pre-steam days tides and winds determined times of departure and it was quite usual for passengers to have to kick their heels in the town for several days as they awaited the right conditions. On other occasions they were obliged to wait until the captain was sober enough to set sail or until the boat was filled with sufficient people to make the journey worthwhile. More than once this happened to the

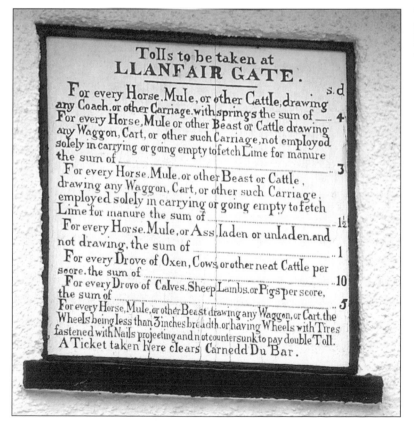

The Llanfair sign affixed to the toll house with its list of charges

unhappy Dean Swift. Advancing in years, deprived of the wit of his friends and stranded among people whose language he did not understand, he sat in a smoky inn early in 1727 and penned the following lines:

Lo, here I sit at holy head,
With muddy ale and mouldy bread;
I'm fastened both by wind and tide,
I see the ships at anchor ride.
All Christian vittals stink of fish,
I'm where my enemyes would wish.
Convict of lies is every sign,
The Inn has not one drop of wine;
The Captain swears the sea's too rough –
(He has not passengers enough)
And thus the Dean is forc'd to stay,
Till others come to help the pay.

Now (presumably) among more convivial company and in a rather happier place, the Dean will derive a crumb of comfort from the knowledge that his name is commemorated in the 'Swift' Service Station on the outskirts of the port of Holyhead!

BEAUMARIS TO MENAI BRIDGE

With the decline in importance of the Lavan Sands crossing, Lord Bulkeley of Baron Hill constructed a fine road from Beaumaris to Porthaethwy and the site of the Menai Bridge. Built in 1804-5 at a cost of £3,000 the road served Bulkeley's own use and the convenience of travellers to Beaumaris. The latter were enabled to enjoy the facilities of, '.... a house in castellated style for the resort of passengers in case of inclemency of the weather', built by Bulkeley at Garth, half way to Beaumaris (SH575736). By the time the Menai Bridge had opened, the road had deteriorated considerably and since no funds were available for its renovation a Turnpike Act was successfully secured and the Beaumaris-Menai Bridge Turnpike Trust created in 1828. The trustees provided milestones, some of which may still be seen set into the containing wall, and took their tolls at a gate located approximately a hundred yards west of the path from Garth ferry to Llandegdan. This road carried a great deal of traffic, from both the bridge and the ferry, a hackney coach service to Beaumaris being operated by the ferry proprietors. It continued to run until the Trust was wound up in 1885.

TURNPIKE ROADS THROUGH CAERNARFONSHIRE

In the late 1770s the attention of travellers was being drawn to a new route from Shrewsbury through Oswestry, Llangollen and Corwen to Llanrwst and thence to Conwy. This was turnpiked in 1777 so that Conwy, by way of its link with Bangor through Penmaenmawr, became part of the great coach road between Holyhead and London, a journey that could be accomplished in three days by 1780.

Until the completion of the highway through Betws-y-coed and Capel Curig in 1804-5, Llanrwst was an important town on the Holyhead road (SH800620). The original turnpike approach left the line of Telford's A5 at Pentrevoelas (SH873514) and took the old road across the Denbighshire moors currently marked by the B5113 and B5427. This was an exhausting journey, initially through enclosed farmland, and then across high open moorland before a steep and (for coaches at least) difficult descent through woodland into Llanrwst itself. Besides being celebrated for the manufacture of fine harps, Llanrwst had long been the principal wool and hide market for North Wales and the town continually thronged with merchants and farmers from the adjoining countryside. The River Conwy, tidal to nearby Trefriw, carried sloops and cutters laden with wool down to the bay and incoming boats supplied the town with the coal, lime and cast iron vital for agricultural and commercial development. Llanrwst's main claim to fame lies in the tradition that Inigo Jones hailed from the area and that he was responsible for building Gwydir Chapel and designing the bridge across the Conwy, completed in 1636. While the attribution is spurious, this splendid structure, described by the chronicler of the Duke of Beaufort's travels through Wales in 1684 as 'a fair new bridge consisting of three arches of stone, the middle one being 26 foot wide and that on each side 16', has earned the admiration of travellers over the centuries. It remained the only bridge across the river until the construction of Waterloo Bridge at Betws-y-Coed and the Conwy suspension bridge two hundred years later. At the western end of Llanrwst bridge lies *Ty Hwnt i'r Bont* (The house beyond the bridge), a charming, if modest building which, from humble beginnings as a farmhouse, rose to become the local Court of Sessions when the Wynnes of nearby Gwydir Castle held sway in the area.

An important consequence of the construction of the turnpike from Llangollen through Pentrevoelas to Llanrwst was that travellers were now spared the inconvenience of the Conwy or Tal-y-cafn ferries, a thought which may have gladdened their hearts as their carriages, post-chaises and gigs lurched across the seventeenth-century bridge and through the Gwydir tollgate. With the Conwy valley on their right and the great block of the Snowdonia massif on their left, they pressed on for Conwy along the course of the present B5106. This was a glorious journey in late summer when, as Bingley put it, 'the gay tints of cultivation once more

Tal-y-cafn Ferry; late nineteenth century

beautified the landscape, for the fields were coloured with the richest hues that ripened corn and green meadows could impart'. Though their reveries may have been rudely disturbed at the Gyffin (Sarnymynech) tollgate (SH778768), such a drive ensured that most travellers who sat down to dinner in Conwy did so in good spirits. Refreshed with mutton chops and porter, they normally set off for Bangor the following morning. Before 1828 their route would have taken them through the Sychnant Pass and the dreaded Penmaenmawr crossing, though this was finally rendered obsolete by Telford's coastal turnpike round Penmaenbach and Penmaenmawr joining the old Bangor turnpike near Llanfairfechan.

BANGOR TO PENTREVOELAS

To late eighteenth and nineteenth century travellers, Snowdonia was a magical place, mysterious, difficult of access and shrouded in the mists of Celtic legend. Its very mention evoked among them a sense of awe similar to that prompted by Timbuctoo or Samarkand to wanderers of a later age. Poets and painters strove in their works to capture something of the 'sublime' qualities of the rugged landscape, while the ordinary genteel traveller, keen to impress his friends with his well-honed sensitivity, struggled manfully to do so in his diaries, letters and sketch-pads. Naturalists too, impressed by the wide variety of habitats – rock faces, moorland, lakes, rapidly-flowing rivers and coastal sand-dunes – flocked to Snowdonia from their rooms in Oxford and rectories in the Shires.

The possibility of opening up a road through the mountains of Snowdonia to serve the growing needs of these people and to avoid the circuitous journey to Bangor via Conwy had long been pondered by the postal authorities and the gentry of Caernarfonshire. The most obvious route was from Pentrevoelas, at the end of the turnpike from Llangollen to Betws-y-coed and from there up the Llugwy valley to Capel Curig and along the Nant Ffrancon Pass to

Lord Penrhyn's road and Telford's road to Capel Curig

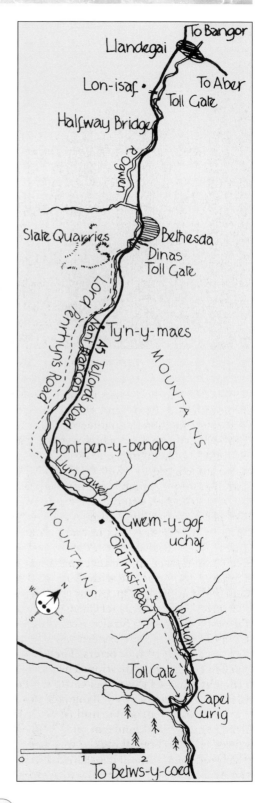

Looking up the old turnpike road towards Llyn Ogwen

Bangor. The earlier stages presented few problems, but the steep inclines and rugged terrain between Capel Curig and the great slate quarries at Bethesda would prove to be a major headache for highway engineers. Apart from two horse paths described by Pennant, no attempt had been made to drive a highway through the Nant Ffrancon Pass until Lord Penrhyn, owner of the Bethesda quarries, took a road up the western side of the valley in 1791-2, extending it to Capel Curig by 1800 (SH720581). Here he built a sixty-roomed inn where horses and carriages were available for hire to travellers. The inn, now Plas-y-Brenin, the Snowdonia recreation centre, offered dried goat as its speciality, a delicacy refused by Bingley when he visited the place, only to dine instead on bacon and eggs and 'dreadfully bad new ale'. Several decades later Penrhyn's inn had become celebrated and the staunch Borrow dined, '.....in a grand saloon amidst a great deal of fashionable company, who, probably conceiving from my heated and dusty appearance that I was some poor fellow travelling on foot from motives of economy, surveyed me with looks of the most supercilious disdain, which, however, neither deprived me of my appetite nor operated uncomfortably on my feelings'.

Penrhyn's road to Capel Curig was the first real step towards opening up a new gateway from the east to the Menai Straits. Accordingly when he proposed seeking a Turnpike Act for a road from Llandegai up the eastern side of Nant Ffrancon and on to Capel Curig and Pentrevoelas he found plenty of supporters. The Act was passed in 1802 and six years later the new road was opened amid due celebration. The same year, 1808, the Post Office, acting on Telford's advice, officially adopted this Capel Curig road for the mail coach service to Holyhead with the result that the Llanrwst-Conwy-Bangor highway was relieved of much of its traffic.

The Capel Curig Turnpike Trust road left the Caernarfonshire Trust road from Penmaenmawr at Llandegai and followed the course of the A5 to the River Ogwen where it turned right and ran along the west bank of the river to Pont Twr and the Dinas tollgate. Here it crossed the river and proceeded along the eastern side of the Nant Ffrancon Pass following the A5 as far as Llyn Ogwen, with Lord Penrhyn's older road running roughly parallel to it on

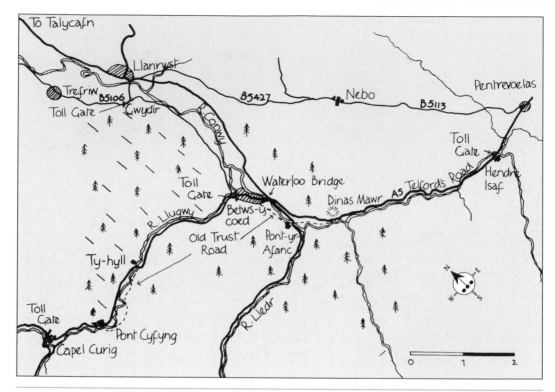

Turnpike roads near Betws-y-coed

the opposite side of the valley (SH650604). Passing over the outflow of the lake by a new bridge and thence along its southern shore, the road deviated from the course of the A5 at the far end of the lake to run past Gwernygof Uchaf and over the moorland to Capel Curig and the Ty'n Lôn tollgate (SH672605-722581). This road, now a rough track overlooked by the massive pile of Tryfan, may still be seen several hundred yards to the south of the main A5 and parallel to it. After rejoining the A5 at Capel Curig, the trust road once again left the later highway at Pont Cyfyng and proceeded south of the River Llugwy on a lovely tree-lined lane, to pass the site of the Roman fort at Caer Llugwy, and to merge again with the A5 opposite the fifteenth-century cottage of Ty-hyll outside Betws-y-coed (SH734572-756575). At Pont Cyfyng, incidentally, the remains of Lord Penrhyn's road to the old quarries on Moel Siabod are still visible. Clearing the Betws-y-coed tollgate, those journeying along the trust road passed behind the Waterloo Hotel and along the lane to Pont-yr-Afanc, where they crossed the Conwy and skirted the Fairy Glen along what is now an unmetalled lane enclosed between walls and flanked by tree-lined hills. This romantic stretch of road, with splendid views of the Conwy and Llugwy rivers, rejoined the onward road to Pentrevoelas opposite Dinas Mawr, whence one could travel free of toll until reaching the Capel Curig Trust's final gate at Hendre Isaf, a mile-and-a-half out of Pentrevoelas (SH855512).

Between 1810 and 1811 a Parliamentary Committee investigating the condition of the mail roads received clear evidence that the local turnpike trusts between Bangor and Shrewsbury had neither the finances nor the expertise adequately to maintain a satisfactory road. Telford, as usual, was commissioned to review the situation and his report, published late in 1811, condemned the Capel Curig Trust road's narrowness (in some places no more than 9ft wide) and poor surfaces. Parliament's reaction, after four years of apparent deliberation, was to vote

Betws-y-coed, early in the 20th century

Waterloo Bridge and the turnpike road at Betws-y-coed

a grant of £20,000 in 1815 and further sums of £30,000 in 1817 and 1818 towards the improvement of the road, thereby creating employment for many people suffering the adverse effects of local land enclosures and the post-Napoleonic War slump. By 1818 the work had begun and a new body, the Shrewsbury-Bangor Ferry Turnpike Trust, was created to supercede existing Trusts and was provided with Government funds to maintain the whole Welsh section of the mail road. Thus the Capel Curig Trust came to the end of its seventeen years' life, its relative success compared with other trusts indicated by a positive balance of £251 0s 0d in its favour in 1819. The following extract from the Capel Curig Trust surveyor's accounts typifies the sort of expenditure incurred by a conscientious surveyor employed by a competent group of trustees:

	£	s	d
Jan. 1806 By a dinner provided at Capel Curig for a Turnpike meeting the day so bad nobody attended but myself and surveyor	1	5	0
Feb. 1806 Finger Post at Llandegai	0	7	0
July. 1807 By Printer's bill for Notices to the different parishes to perform Statute work etc	2	3	6
Dec. 1807 Thomas Griffith & Co. for clearing snow	29	5	0
Mar. 1808 Thomas Griffith & Co. for clearing snow in Feb	6	12	2
July. 1809 By expenses at Capel Curig letting the tolls viz Ale at Auctions, Dinner for Commissioners when only one attended	2	10	0
Feb. 1811 Lewis Hughes a Quarter's expenses and cutting snow and repairing a bridge broke by flood	104	8	6
Nov. 1811 Wm. Edwards Esq., for trespass and gravel for the making of the road	5	0	0
Feb. 1813 Mr. Worthington 4 lamps for Tollhouses	3	2	10
Mar. 1814 My son's expenses in taking 3 journeys along the road to settle with workmen before appointment of new surveyor - out 5 days	3	0	0
July. 1814 Ale at Letting and Dinner Bill	4	19	3
Aug. 1817 Ale at Letting and Dinner Bill	8	10	6
Sep. 1818 Ale at Letting and Dinner Bill	10	10	6
Aug. 1819 Paid Mr. Richard Jones of the House of Commons for his trouble respecting the Holyhead Road Bill	1	0	0

Thomas Telford, the son of an Eskdale shepherd, had already become famous with his celebrated Pontcysyllte viaduct over the River Dee, completed in 1805. His remarkable 'Irish Road', 109 miles of it between Shrewsbury and Holyhead, represents an outstanding achievement and established once and for all that road building was now a matter for professionals. Telford's standards were extremely high and he expected the contractors whom he employed to live up to the exacting requirements. John Jones of Bangor had cause to remember this when Telford had him re-make the Llandegai section of the road, his first efforts being considered slipshod by the master. On the other hand, men like John Staphen of Shrewsbury and Thomas Stanton, who had both worked with Telford on the Ellesmere Canal, applied themselves diligently to the task of constructing their sections of the road according to Telford's detailed instructions.

Apart from its narrowness, the old Capel Curig Turnpike Trust road, and, for that matter, its eastern extension through Denbighshire to Shrewsbury, suffered from inadequate foundations so that its gravel surface tended to sink into the underlying soil after a period of heavy rain. Telford therefore insisted that his contractors lay a solid foundation of handset stones before surfacing the road. As far as the overall road line was concerned, his basic strategy was to keep as closely as possible to the old trust road, and while he had encountered few major problems on the Denbighshire stretch through Corwen and Llangollen, the steep gradients of the Caernarfonshire section presented some formidable engineering challenges. This was particularly so in the Nant Ffrancon Pass where the old trust road negotiated a gradient of 1:6 in parts. It is a tribute to Telford's engineering genius that the steepest gradient on his road up the eastern side of the Nant Ffrancon does not exceed 1:22.

Opposite Lôn Isaf, approximately one mile south of Llandegai, Telford's road ran to the River Ogwen where he raised the Halfway Bridge, so called because it lay halfway between the George Hotel, Bangor Ferry and Ty'n-y-maes Inn at the head of the Nant Ffrancon Pass where the horses were changed on the first stage of the mail to Shrewsbury (SH608690). From Halfway Bridge (dated 1819) a new road was driven through Bethesda and the trust road between Pont Twr and Y Benglog at the western end of Llyn Ogwen, was completely renovated.

Snowdon Ranger Youth Hostel, once an hotel beside the turnpike road between Caernarfon and Beddgelert

New tollhouses were erected at Ty'n Twr, overlooking Pont Twr and at Lôn Isaf, while the Dinas gate was discontinued. Beyond Llyn Ogwen, the old road past Gwernygof Uchaf was abandoned in favour of a new line to Capel Curig, as was the Pont Cyfyng to Ty-hyll road to the south of the Llugwy. Instead, Telford constructed a new highway to the north of the river which rejoined the renovated Capel Curig Trust road at Ty-hyll for Betws-y-coed. Here he built the Waterloo Bridge, a fine example of his use of cast iron, together with a new road along Dinas Mawr connecting the bridge with Rhydlanfair and Pentrevoelas. This completed the great road through Caernarfonshire, which still serves as the principal route to Ireland.

BANGOR TO MAENTWROG

Travellers from Bangor intending to journey through Dolgellau into Cardiganshire and south Wales usually made Caernarfon their first port of call. In 1837 the Caernarfonshire Turnpike Trust built a new road (the present A499) leaving Bangor by Glanadda and passing through Port Dinorwic to the ancient town of Caernarfon. Previously the turnpike ran through Penycwintan and Penrhosgarnedd on the outskirts of Bangor and thence along the periphery of Vaynol Park to the tollgate at Tafarn-y-Grisiau, near St Mary's church, Port Dinorwic (SH522671). From here it followed the A499 into Caernarfon. Along with the Caernarfon-Llanberis road and several of the roads linking with the Llŷn Peninsula, the original Bangor-Caernarfon turnpike was extensively repaired under the 1810 extension of the Caernarfonshire Turnpike Act. Even before this it had been considered an excellent road, as the Honourable John Byng bore witness in the 1780s. 'In the evening,' he wrote, 'we left Caernarfon and rode to Bangor, but not at our usual rate for we went these nine miles in an hour and 20 minutes; owing I suppose to the novelty of a good road.'

The condition of this road, with its tollgates at Vaynol and Pont Seiont, may reflect the fact that Caernarfon lay on an alternative route to Holyhead for travellers from mid-Wales who would cross to Anglesey on the ferry plying between Caernarfon and Newborough. This route, however, never rivalled the one through Beaumaris, and later Bangor. Yet, late eighteenth-century Caernarfon was an important outlet for the export of slate from the mines around Llanberis and for flannels, webs and stockings for which there was a heavy demand in the industrial towns of the north-west. By 1800 it had even become a fashionable resort where assemblies were regularly held and a company of actors from Chester performed three times weekly throughout the summer season. The cheapness of provisions, with salmon at 2d per pound and a pair of soles selling for 6d, may have been one of the factors attracting 'genteel families' to the town, while Lord Uxbridge's recently-completed hot and cold baths may have tempted those with a taste for the exotic.

The turnpike road from Caernarfon to Beddgelert and Maentwrog, constructed in 1801, took the route of the A487 past the ruins of the Roman fort of *Segontium* and through the Glangwna gate to head once again towards the high crags of Snowdon by way of Llyn Cwellyn where the enthusiast could pick up a guide for the ascent of Snowdonia. South of the lake the road negotiated the River Gwyrfai by a fine bridge of three arches, and a mile further on the Rhyd-Ddu gate keeper exacted his toll before the traveller could press on for Beddgelert past Llyn-y-Gadair and Lion Rock (SH575500).

Beddgelert was a much-celebrated port of call for eighteenth- and nineteenth-century tourists who admired both its romantic scenery and the sentimental tale of the dog Gelert, a gift to Prince Llewelyn the Great from his father-in-law, King John. Apparently, they learned, the prince had left the dog to guard his young son while he went out hunting. Returning, Llewelyn found the animal with blood dripping from its jaws and assuming that it had attacked the child, immediately slew it – only to discover that the wretched creature had, in fact, killed

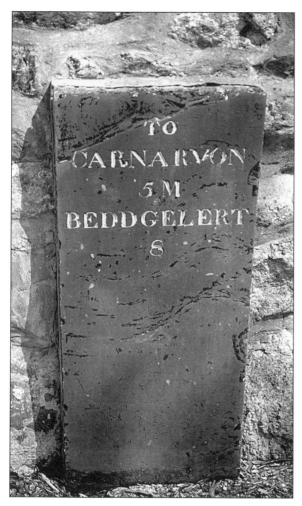

Milepost at Bettws Garmon

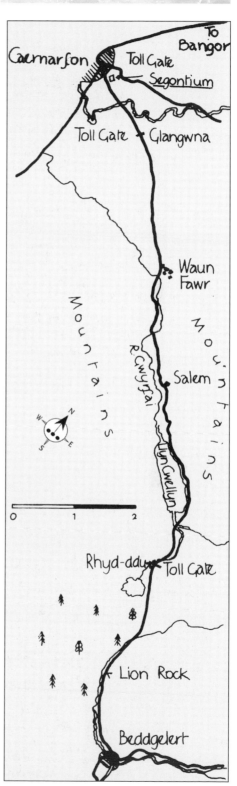

Turnpike road from Caernarfon to Beddgelert

Pont Glaslyn at Beddgelert (above) and Pont Aberglaslyn (below)

a wolf which had attempted to carry off the boy. Overcome with remorse, he buried Gelert with great ceremony and the place thereafter became known as Beddgelert (Gelert's Grave). The story, of course, is apocryphal, having its origins in a tale put about in the 1790s by one David Prichard, landlord of the Royal Goat Inn. In league with the parish clerk, Prichard concocted the tale and built 'Gelert's Grave' in the meadow beside the church, hoping that the romantic 'legend' would persuade travellers to pause at the village and sample the fare offered by the Royal Goat. The growing importance of Beddgelert and of the road passing through it is reflected in its increasingly salubrious inn. In the 1780s and 1790s the local hostelry was barely distinguishable from the rest of the poor houses in the village. Even so, its charges were excessively high, the walls of its rooms full of holes and its fleas unusually voracious. Complaining to one of the servants after a particularly flea-ridden night, Bingley received the splendidly blasé retort that, '…. if we were to kill one of them ten would come to its burying'. Things were very different by 1810 when a new and comfortable inn was opened, complete with the blind harper, by now virtually *de rigueur* in a Welsh tourist hotel. Three years later we find

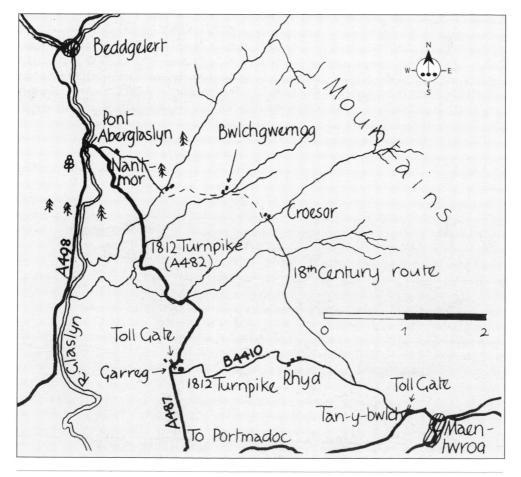

Turnpike routes from Beddgelert

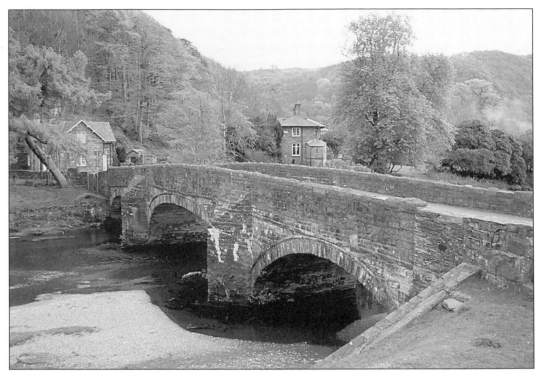

The turnpike trust bridge at Maentwrog

an enterprising local entrepreneur, who also served as the village schoolmaster, advertising his several services on the new inn door: 'William Lloyd, conductor to Snowdon, Moel Hebog, Dinas Emrys, Llanberis Pass, the lakes, waterfalls etc. etc. Collector of fossils and all natural curiosities in these regions. Dealer in superfine woollen hose, socks, gloves etc.'. Today's Beddgelert attracts tourists in their thousands and apart from the inevitable mushrooming of gift shops selling their tawdry trinkets, the little town, at the confluence of the Glaslyn and Cwelyn rivers has changed little since the early years of the nineteenth century.

Onward travellers to Maentwrog were now obliged to negotiate the rocky defile of the Aberglaslyn Pass, which, until the first decade of the nineteenth century, was a narrow track carried over the tree-lined chasm by Pont Aberglaslyn and able to accommodate horses and foot travellers only (SH595462). Beyond the present bridge, the eighteenth century traveller deviated from today's road to take a lane running towards Bwlchgwernog (SH612452), where, at a 'T' junction, the continuation of the old turnpike can be followed on foot in an easterly direction along a rough track through heather and bracken. Rarely more than 10ft wide, this track forges through mountainous country above the hamlet of Croesor before picking up a narrow winding lane to join the later turnpike (the B4410) near Llyn Mair (SH649415). Described by the Reverend John Evans as '... eight miles of the worst road in the Principality', this old route was abandoned in 1812 following the opening of the Caernarfonshire Turnpike Trust's new highway round the foot of the mountain. This followed the later A487 as far as the tollgate at Garreg and then turned eastwards to pass through Rhyd to the Tanybwlch gate and on to Maentwrog along the present B4410.

The massively-built stone village of Maentwrog, many of its houses graced with finely-ornamented slate roofs, is at present by-passed on a modern highway across the Vale of Ffestiniog, which, for the onward journey to Dolgellau, more or less follows the earlier turnpike. However, just below the bridge carrying the highway around the outskirts of the village lies an older bridge on a short stretch of the original turnpike road. In the wall of this bridge is set a tall narrow stone on which is roughly engraved, along with other distances, the comforting fact that London lies a mere 226 miles away.

During the early decades of the nineteenth century, the Caernarfonshire Turnpike Trust created a number of other roads. Caernarfon, Tremadoc and Pwllheli were linked by a turnpike system joining with the Porthdinllaen Trust and thereby opening up the remoter regions of the Llŷn Peninsula. The latter Trust also joined the Capel Curig Trust by way of a road from Tremadoc to Beddgelert through Nant Gwynant and on to Capel Curig via Penygwryd. Llanrwst and the slate mining centre of Blaenau Ffestiniog, meanwhile, were connected through Dolwyddelan. These and other roads dramatically improved local communications to the benefit of both agriculture and commerce and allowed tourists fascinated by the scenery of North Wales to see more of it in convenience and relative safety.

MAENTWROG TO WELSHPOOL

People travelling from Caernarfonshire into mid-Wales had a tough route ahead of them. The turnpike from Maentwrog to Dolgellau made, like many other Merionethshire roads, under the Merioneth Turnpike Act of 1777, was simply appalling. As late as 1834 its condition was being condemned by a correspondent to the *Caernarvonshire and Denbighshire Herald* and even allowing for the hyperbole of the times, his description suggests that the surface was less

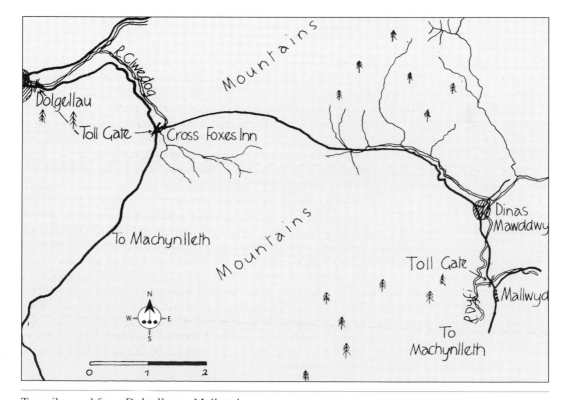

Turnpike road from Dolgellau to Mallwyd

than ideal: 'In every yard of it there is a rut deep enough for the grave of a child, and to ensure breakdowns the space between is filled up with lumps of stones each as large as cannonballs or Swedish turnips'. If he survived these hazards the traveller passed through Llanelltyd, with its limekilns and ships' chandlers, into Dolgellau, the principal market town of Merionethshire (SH729178).

Dominated by the glowering pile of Cadair Idris on one side and the gentler slopes of Foel Faner on the other, Dolgellau lies in a narrow valley at the junction of no fewer than three Roman roads. Today it is a quiet, rather handsome place of massively-built stone houses and crooked streets whose basic layout has changed little since Glyndŵr held the last Welsh Parliament in the town in 1404. Later, Dolgellau became an assize town and an important centre for the manufacture of flannel, which may explain why it was well-served by tollgates in Georgian times. Our traveller, weary and thirsty after his journey from Maentwrog, paid his toll and made a bee-line for the Golden Lion and after jostling with coach passengers awaiting a change of horses, he was able to eat and drink to his fill.

During much of the eighteenth century, individuals travelling for pleasure through this part of the country were few and far between, perhaps no more than a dozen or so annually. By 1800, however, a general improvement in the availability of accommodation, coupled with a growing interest in Wales as a whole fostered by the published descriptions of tourists, encouraged increasing numbers of visitors on foot or on horseback. Some may have been deterred by the tradition, still strong in the late eighteenth century, that the unwary could fall prey to the *Gwylliaid Cochion Mawddwy,* the red-haired bandits apparently descended from outlaws settling in the countryside between Dolgellau and Dinas Mawddwy after the Wars of the Roses. According to several contemporary observers, travellers often forsook the turnpike road in favour of a hike across the mountains in order to avoid the banditti, while nervous local residents placed scythes in their chimneys to dissuade them from attempting an unorthodox entry!

Stout-hearted tourists, however, pushed on along the turnpike, pausing from time to time to view the large flocks of sheep and cattle on the surrounding mountains or to watch a farmer and his horse as they struggled across a hill face with a sledge laden with peat from the mountain turbaries. Initially their journey from Dolgellau took them through lightly-wooded country, but this soon gave way to a steep climb into rock-strewn mountains before the descent to Dinas Mawddwy through a lovely pass dominated by mixed woodland (SH859148). Originally a medieval administrative centre of some importance, Dinas Mawddwy was little more than a post-town on the turnpike by the 1780s. Here travellers were confronted by 'a miserable collection of mean houses' occupied principally by lead and stone miners whose intemperate habits were criticized by many a passing reverend gentleman. The English could never quite get the hang of Dinas Mawddwy and they rarely remained in the place for very long. 'Altho' in England I appeared like other men,' wrote Mr Hutton in the opening years of the nineteenth century, 'yet at Dinas Mawddwy I stood single. The people eyed me as a phenomenon, with countenances mixed with fear and enquiry. Perhaps they took me for an inspector of Taxes; they could not take me for a window-peeper, for there were scarcely any to peep at and the few I saw were in that shattered state which proved there was no glazier in the place.'

A run-down place indeed! Not so, however, Mallwyd the next port of call where the traveller arrived after a journey of a mile or so (SH863125). Here visitors were able to forget the dreariness of Dinas Mawddwy in the company of David Lloyd, keeper of the inn for the first three decades of the nineteenth century. A man of considerable enterprise, Lloyd ran a large farm to supply the local inn with fresh produce, besides operating a thriving post chaise business between Mallwyd, Machynlleth and Dolgellau. He was also blessed with several tall and comely daughters who gladdened the hearts of the most jaded traveller. The Reverend Mr Warner, a man much given to the pleasures of the table, was entranced by the Cross Foxes. 'Mr.

Tanybwlch inn and the old bridge at Maentwrog

The Cross Foxes Inn, on the Machynlleth to Dolgellau road

The Cann Office Hotel dates from 1310

Lloyd,' he wrote, 'had provided for us a most substantial meal of mutton chops, bacon and plumb-pye [sic], beans and peas, at which his daughters, two girls of pleasing person, formed manners and good education, did us the honour of attending.' Lloyd and his daughters now slumber in the peaceful churchyard of St Tydecho not far from the resting place of the Reverend John Davies who assisted with the production of the Revised Translation of the Welsh Bible of 1620. The present church at Mallwyd dates from the mid-1300s and has many interesting features including a barrow-vaulted sanctuary roof, eighteenth-century tiered pews to the rear of the nave and a seventeenth-century porch over which are suspended two great, mouldering prehistoric animal bones allegedly unearthed in the nearby fields.

The Mallwyd-Welshpool turnpike had its origins in the comprehensive Montgomeryshire Turnpikes Act of 1769 which brought the main routes across the county into one highway system administered by trustees presiding over four turnpike districts. As the powers of the trustees were extended by amendments to the Act over the years, more stretches of highway were taken over and by 1810 there were 260 miles of turnpike road in the county. In spite of the prosperity of the area and the efforts of the trustees, the inadequacy of local road-building materials meant that the standard of surfaces in Montgomeryshire fell below that of much of the rest of North Wales until the widespread adoption of Macadam's methods of surfacing.

Leaving Mallwyd for Welshpool along the course of the present main road, the tourist went through thinly-inhabited countryside to the tollgate at Garthbebio and thence to Cann Office. This was an inn founded in the fourteenth century and by now served as receiving house for letters from a widespread area of the surrounding uplands (SH012108). Apparently the whitewashed tavern was far from salubrious and '..... the filth within by no means corresponded with the cleanliness without'. To make matters worse the wind was kept out of the broken windows by 'the refuse of the family wardrobe'. The Reverend John Evans, vexed author of these comments, followed his usual practice of protecting himself against nocturnal visitors by fixing his bedroom door to its lintel with two large screws! This certainly deterred intruders although it did little to soften the commotion made by the drunken revellers below who disturbed the old parson's slumbers. Today, though, Cann Office is a fine and well-appointed pub, its ample outhouses and stabling facilities testifying to its important role as a posting-house in those far-off coaching days.

From Cann Office the turnpike progressed to Llanfair Caerneinion and the Milford tollgate and then on to Welshpool, the last significant town before Shrewsbury. Today's motorist, following the turnpike along the main road towards Welshpool will notice that as the hills yield to rolling pastureland, and the stone walls to straggling hedgerows, so does the domestic architecture change with fine half-timbered farmhouses beginning to come into prominence as the English border draws closer. This part of Wales, with its favourable soil and weather conditions and access by land to the rich markets and towns of England has always enjoyed a higher standard of material culture than the hills and vales of the west. Agrarian prosperity, coupled with the fact that this is excellent oak-growing country, laid the basis for the development of the half-timbered house from a simple medieval open-hearthed structure to the sophisticated and often highly-ornate buildings of later times.

Welshpool itself has several handsome half-timbered houses dating in the main from the years before the town achieved prominence as an important market for the sale of flannel. Established in 1782, the fortnightly market drew its trade from a wide area and Sunday afternoons witnessed the arrival of packhorse trains and heavily-loaded waggons from all corners of Montgomeryshire, their owners keen to be ready to start trading as early as possible the following morning. Some sellers arrived even earlier, especially those from the countryside around Llanbrynmair, who, '.... since they were very religious men and having conscientious scruples against Sunday travelling, made the journey on the preceding Saturday'. Cloth buyers from the English border counties and as far north as Cheshire and Lancashire flocked to Welshpool and the little town flourished as never before, with sales exceeding £65,000 in the peak year of 1816. It was only with the commercial development of Newtown and the establishment there of a flannel market in 1832 that Welshpool's years of boom drew to a close. Thereafter it was Newtown, with its warehouses, commercial offices and elegant public rooms that became, '..... the principal seat of the flannel manufacturing in the Principality [and] has acquired a appellation of the Leeds of Wales'.

PRESTEIGNE TO ABERYSTWYTH

Not all tourists made North Wales their destination, many preferring the softer contours of the central counties or the coastal resorts of the west, in particular the expanding town of Aberystwyth. Described by Defoe in 1725 as 'a populous but very dirty, black, smoaky place', Aberystwyth had become a bustling commercial centre for ship building, fishing, the lead trade and agriculture by 1800. More importantly for the man in pursuit of pleasure, the town was beginning to enjoy some reputation as a tourist centre with its Assembly Rooms, walks and bathing facilities. To a great extent Aberystwyth's popularity resulted from the successful attempt of a local landowner, Thomas Johnes, to advertise the place. It was he who persuaded Uvedale Price, the authority on the 'Picturesque', to build Castle House (on the site of the splended neo-Gothic extravaganza occupied by the University of Wales) and to encourage wealthy English gentlemen to brave the roads of mid-Wales in order to visit the little seaside town and enjoy the delights of its hinterland. By 1800 weekly mail coaches were leaving the Gogerddan Arms (later the Lion Royal) for Presteigne or Kington, while the Aberystwyth to Ludlow mail coach would set out from the Talbot Inn at 4.00am for Ludlow, returning to Aberystwyth the same evening.

The principal road into mid-Wales at this time ran into Presteigne and thence along the road (described in an earlier chapter) through Beggars Bush and Kinnerton to New Radnor. It was on this road that Lipscomb met some of the hundreds of Cardiganshire migrant labourers who, 'quitting their native retirement, the peaceful retreat of innocence and penury', trekked east each year to seek employment in the harvest fields of Hereford or Shropshire or even in the Deptford dockyards. Sparing a casual thought for these unfortunates, coach-bound travellers sped through Llanfihangel Nantmelan and Llandegley towards Penybont along what is now the A44 trunk road, the more carefree pedestrian or horseman taking time off to view 'Water-break-its-neck', the waterfall near New Radnor. Even for the traveller by coach there was plenty to see, with fine views across pastoral country on either side of the road. Watching the 'innocent' peasantry at work was a diversion dear to the hearts of devotees of the concept of the 'Picturesque' and Lipscomb rhapsodised on the peasant women in Radnorshire 'who are in general very robust and well calculated to endure fatigue' as they ploughed and harrowed the fields alongside the turnpike. Their pleasantness and hospitality too gave pleasure to many tourists, and Benjamin Malkin would quite happily have lingered in Llandegley had it not been for the poor accommodation offered by the local inn. He was nevertheless distressed by the practice here, and elsewhere in Radnorshire, of dancing and the pursuit of other 'sports' in the churchyard and he commented sombrely: 'It is rather singular... that the association of the place, surrounded by memorials of mortality, should not deaden the impulses of joy in minds in other respects not insensible to the suggestions of vulgar superstition'.

At Penybont, a bustling little place made prosperous by generations of cattle and sheep fairs and John Price's Radnorshire Bank, coaches passed through the tollgate and pulled into the Fleece Inn where horses were changed in preparation for the next stage of the journey. The Fleece, an ancient inn on the banks of the river, was re-built in 1777 only to be replaced in 1814 by the present Severn Arms. Leaving Penybont the turnpike passed through Nantmel, Dolau and Hendre Fach before reaching Rhayader where travellers could hire post chaises at the Red Lion Inn for journeys north and south of the town. In the early years of the nineteenth century the Red Lion was kept by a Mr Evans, to whose civility, hospitality and knowledge of Welsh orthography several tourists paid tribute. Above all, Evans provided a fine table at reasonable prices. Lipscomb praised one particular meal which must have wrought havoc with the digestion of passengers on a mail coach: 'A couple of very fine roasted fowls, a hare, a dish of veal cutlets, a piece of cold roast beef and excellent tarts; for all of which, including about a quart of strong beer per man, we paid only one shilling each'.

Rhayader was virtually encircled by tollgates, and as each of the six roads entering the town was barred, considerable resentment arose on the part of local people and passing travellers. In the 1830s and early 1840s dissatisfaction with the general running of the turnpike system and the frequency of tolls was widespread throughout much of central and south-west Wales, especially among the farming community who had experienced a series of bad harvests combined with low prices for their products. Together with the influence of Chartism, the effects of the New Poor Law and Tithe Commutation, these elements were instrumental in sparking off the Rebecca Riots, wherein a frustrated and embittered rural population vented their wrath on the hated tollgates, regarded by many of them as potent symbols of repression. Though rioting was at its most intense in Cardiganshire and Carmarthenshire, Rhayader was troubled with several outbreaks in 1843. On 2 September, for example, two gates, placed at a point where a lane branched off the road to Aberystwyth beyond the bridge over the Wye, were destroyed and a month later rioters pulled down the Bodtalog gate further along this road. Attacks on the gates were often very violent and when the Bodtalog gate was stormed, its keeper, an elderly woman, was virtually blinded by a shot from a powder-loaded gun (SO867747).

The Main and Whitland Trusts in Carmarthenshire were the epicentres of the riots and the majority of their gates and toll houses were either attacked or destroyed in 1843 and 1844 only

LLYTHYR.

"At y Cyhoedd yn gyffredinol, ac at ein Cymmydogion yn neillduol.

"NYNI, *John Hughes, David Jones,* a *John Hugh,* ag sydd yn awr yn gyfyngedig yn ngharchar Caerdydd, gwedi ein heuogfarnu am yr ymosodiad a wnawd ar glwyd ffordd-fawr Pontardulais, ac ar y personau a sefydlwyd i'w hamddiffyn—ac wedi ein dedfrydu i alltudiaeth—a ddymunwn, ac a n'wn yn ddifrifol ar ereill i gymmeryd rhybydd oddi-wrthym, ac i ymattal yn eu gweithredoedd gwallgofus, cyn y cwympont i ein con-demniaeth.

"Yr ydym yn euog, ac wedi ein barnu i ddyoddef, pan y mae cannoedd wedi dihengyd—bydded iddynt hwy, a phawb, gymmeryd gofal na byddo iddynt gymmeryd eu har-wain etto i ddifrodi meddiannau gwladwriaethol neu bersonol, a gwrthwynebu gallu y gyfraith, oblegid bydd yn sicr o'u dal gyda dialedd, ac a'u tyn i ddystryw.

"Nid ydym yn awr ond mewn carchar, ond mewn wythnos neu ddwy ni a fyddwn wedi ein trosglwyddo megys anfad-ddynion—i fod yn gaethion i ddyeithriaid mewn gwlad ddyeithyr. Rhaid i ni fyned yn moreuddydd ein bywyd o'n cartref-leoedd hyfryd, i fyw a llafurio gyda caethion o'r radd waethaf, ac edrych arnom megys lladron.

"Gyfeillion—gymmydogion—pawb—ond yn neillduol dynion ieuainc—cedweh rhag cyfar-fodydd nosol! Gocheiwch wneuthur ar gam, ac ofwch ddychryniadau y barnwr.

"Meddyliwch am beth a *raid* i ni, a pheth a *ddichon* i chwi *ddyoddef*, cyn ag y byddo i chwi wneyd fel y gwneisom ni.

"Os bydd i chwi fod yn heddychlon, a byw etto fel dynion gonest, trwy fendith Duw gell-weh erfyn llwyddiant; a nyni, ddihirod ysgymunedig a thruenus, a ddichon ddiolch i chwi am drugaredd y goron—oblegid nid ar un telerau ereill ond eich ymddygiad da chwi y dangosir tosturi i ni, neu ereill, pa rai a ddichon gwympo i ein sefyllfa braidd anobeithiol.

(Arwyddnodwyd)

"JOHN HUGHES,
"DAVID JONES,
"Marc ✗ JOHN HUGH.

"Carchar Caerdydd, Tachwedd 1faf, 1843.
"Tyst, JOHN B. WOODS, Llywodraethydd.'

ISAAC THOMAS, PRINTER, ST. MARY-STREET, CARDIGAN.

200 Copies for Mr Geo. Griffiths, Aber...

A LETTER.

"To the Public generally, and to our Neighbours in particular.

"WE, *John Hughes, David Jones,* and *John Hugh,* now lying in Cardiff gaol, convicted of the attack on Pontardulais turnpike gate, and the police stationed there to protect it—being now sentenced to transportation, beg, and earnestly call on others to take warning by our fate, and to stop in their mad course, before they fall into our condemnation.

"*We are guilty, and doomed to suffer,* while hundreds have escaped. Let them, and every one, take care not to be deluded again to attack public or private property, and resist the power of the law, for it will overtake them with vengeance, and bring them down to destruction.

"We are only in prison now, but in a week or two shall be banished as rogues—to be slaves to strangers, in a strange land. We must go, in the prime of life, from our dear homes, to live and labour with the worst of villains—looked upon as thieves.

"Friends—neighbours—all—but especially young men—keep from night meetings! Fear to do wrong, and dread the terrors of the judge.

"Think of what we *must,* and you *may suffer,* before you *dare* to do as we have done.

"If you will be peaceable, and live again like honest men, by the blessing of God, you may expect to prosper; and we, poor outcast wretches, may have to thank you for the mercy of the Crown—for on no other terms than your good conduct will any pity be shewn to us, or others, who may fall into our almost hopeless situation.

(Signed)

"JOHN HUGHES,
"DAVID JONES,
"The ✗ mark of JOHN HUGH.

"Cardiff Gaol, Nov. 1st, 1843.
"Witness, JOHN B. WOODS, Governor."

'A Letter', from contrite Rebeccaites

The former turnpike road north of Rhayader

to be replaced by the authorities and visited by the rioters once more. Eventually, after the intervention of the Yeomanry and a body of Home Office constables the rioting died away; a few ringleaders were transported, others fined and the countryside returned more or less to normality. But it had been more than a storm in a teacup and the Government, recognizing the seriousness of the grievances, set up a Commission of Inquiry under the chairmanship of the distinguished civil servant Thomas Frankland Lewis of Harpton Court in Radnorshire. Concluding that the rioters' only remedy had been to take the law into their own hands, Lewis considered the whole episode to have been 'a very creditable portion of Welsh history'. The final Report of the Commission recommended the consolidation of the South Wales Turnpike Trusts and the establishment of uniform tolls at gates which would be at least seven miles apart. This was enshrined in law at the end of 1844 and County Road Boards were established to manage the roads of South Wales on an equitable basis, and to discharge (with a Government grant of £225,000) the liabilities of the old Trusts.

Around 1800, however, these distressing events lay far in the future and most genteel travellers in mail or private coach would rarely concern themselves with the grievances of the countryfolk, even if they noticed their existence. To the majority the peasant was a shadowy figure in the landscape, briefly to be pitied and then conveniently put out of mind. Uppermost in our travellers' minds as they feasted in Rhayader's Red Lion were the rigours of the next stage of their journey: the old coach road to Devil's Bridge and on to Aberystwyth. This was a gruelling course for both man and beast once they crossed the single span bridge over the Wye at Rhayader. Henry Skrine wrote of his state of 'perpetual alarm' as he ascended the rocky road out of the town and subsequently lamented the dreary, treeless expanse of open hill which he traversed 'in mournful silence'. Michael Faraday was hardly less gloomy. 'After a while we got among more mountains and nothing but large concave forms met the eye for a long time. Lively little cattle with myriads of sheep now and then diversified the general monotony and a turfcutter or a peat digger here and there drew the eye for want of a better object.' Other tourists who negotiated the 'dreadful steep pitches and frightful precipices' were relieved to reach the single arch of Blaenycwm bridge, built across the River Ystwyth by Baldwin of Bath in 1783 (SO826755). The blessings of tarmac have made the journey along the old turnpike rather less eventful for the modern traveller. Yet the steep climb from Rhayader by way of Cwmdauddwr is still there and the treeless countryside of peat bog and cotton grass is still capable of inducing the same melancholy as it did in the past. In summer, sheep and horses graze these uplands and the occasional skylark soars joyously towards the sun, but in winter the landscape is deserted save for the ever-watchful carrion crows seeking what pickings they can. Beyond Blaenycwm bridge it was a short run to Cwmystwyth (or Pentrebrunant as it was known to early nineteenth-century travellers) and the Fountain Inn where horses were changed and restorative liquors were available (SO789740).

Left: Today, the "squalid garb and savage manners of the male and female miners" are recalled in the ruined buildings and waste heaps of the Cwmystwyth Lead Mines

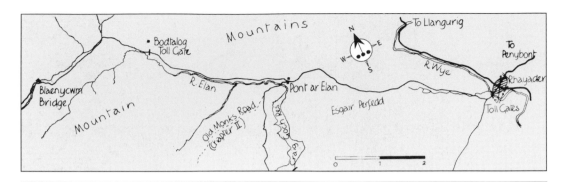

Turnpike road from Rhayader towards Aberystwyth

This was lead mining country and held little appeal for visitors in search of romantic scenery. As one put it: '...the dingy and unsightly piles of dross and sifted refuse, with the squalid garb and savage manners of the male and female miners, was hardly a welcome sight'. Today's natives are rather more prepossessing although the 'dross' of centuries of lead mining scars the landscape; great banks of shale loom out of the mist to dominate the ruins of early miners' cottages and their associated enclosures while scrub hawthorn bushes represent the remains of once-luxuriant woodland.

The present minor road to Devil's Bridge now marks the continuation of the turnpike and passes close to Pwllpeiran Experimental Husbandry Farm where officers of the Ministry of Agriculture endeavour to follow in the footsteps of Thomas Johnes of nearby Hafod who began improvement of hill land in the locality two hundred years ago. Collector, scholar, antiquary and farmer, Johnes represented the ideal of the eighteenth-century 'rounded' man. Like so many such men, however, his rather grandiose aspirations outstretched the depth of his pocket and he ended his days in frustration and relative poverty. His activities as a land improver and forester may still be seen in the surrounding countryside, although his marvellous fairy-tale home, to which both John Nash and Baldwin of Bath contributed, is now reduced to rubble. For the enthusiastic seeker after the 'picturesque', though, there are still monuments of Johnes's endeavours to be found, including the elegant ice-house to the south of the ruins of the mansion, and the overgrown remnants of his crippled daughter's garden, close to which stands a rather delicately constructed obelisk placed there by the squire to commemorate his friend Francis, 4th Duke of Bedford. A staunch patriot, Johnes celebrated the jubilee of George III by building a stone arch over the turnpike as it passed the outskirts of the Hafod demesne (SO765756). Modern travellers on the turnpike pass beneath the arch as they drive through the coniferous uniformity of the Ystwyth-Myherin Forest and thence to the Hafod Arms at Devil's Bridge, yet another Johnes foundation largely rebuilt by the fourth Duke of Newcastle in the 1840s. For the remainder of the journey to Aberystwyth the turnpike pursued the modern A4120 road above the glorious Rheidol Valley to enter the town at the site of the 'Picadilly' tollgate on the junction of this road with the turnpike to Cardigan (SN593798).

Whether real or imagined, the risk to life and limb apparently presented by the old Rhayader to Aberystwyth turnpike seemed great enough to persuade the Aberystwyth Turnpike Trustees to find an alternative route for mail and private coaches. This took the form, in 1812, of a new road from Aberystwyth to Ponterwyd and the base of Pumlumon where it joined the old parish road from Devil's Bridge to Llangurig at the ford over the River Castell. As the latter road was progressively being improved, the Llangurig Turnpike Trust was building a new highway up the valley of the Wye between Rhayader and Llangurig so that by 1829 a complete turnpike link had evolved and the line of the modern A44 trunk road had been laid. Shortly afterwards

Two views of Devils Bridge. It consists of three bridges, two of them built above a predecessor

One of five toll houses in the Kington area, this one is in the middle of town

Kington came to replace Presteigne as the principal 'gateway' to Wales from Herefordshire and a turnpike, with new gates at Walton and Stanner, was established between Kington and New Radnor. Once work on this road had been completed, the Postmaster-General sanctioned a mail coach service between Kington and Aberystwyth, the first coach leaving Kington early in 1835 following a celebration dinner in the Commercial Inn when 'the wines were of a superior

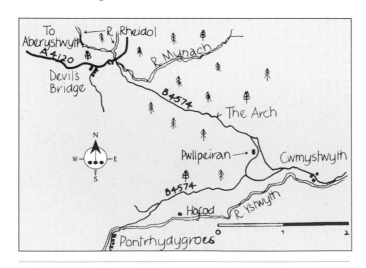

Rhayader-Aberystwyth turnpike near Devil's Bridge

vintage and mirth and harmony prevailed till a late hour'. Thus was abandoned the Presteigne-New Radnor route and the old Rhayader-Aberystwyth road in favour of that 'by way of Pont Erwydd and Llangerrig, thereby avoiding those dangerous precipices on the old road, which deterred many visiting a bathing place so improving and healthful'. A traveller by coach could now leave london at 8.00pm and arrive at Aberystwyth at 8.15pm the following day after a journey only slightly more tiring than that experienced by one undertaking the same journey by British Rail in the 1980s.

Until the advent of the railways, the turnpike roads were the major thoroughfares in England and Wales. Following the General Highway Act of 1835, finally abolishing Statute Labour and giving parishes the right to combine into Highway Boards, an Act of 1841 empowered justices to levy rates to relieve the by now impoverished Turnpike Trusts. Effectively this meant the end of the tollgates which gradually disappeared over the next fifty years, the tollhouses being converted to other purposes when the County Councils took over responsibility for the roads in the late 1880s. The last turnpike gate in Britain was removed in 1895 and the turnpike era came to a close after two hundred and thirty two years.

In its later stages, in particular, it had been a stormy era. The conclusion of the Napoleonic Wars had heralded the onset of a lengthy period of agrarian depression bringing with it social unrest and an acceleration in the flow of people from the countryside to the rapidly-growing industrial towns. The old, seemingly immutable, order of the mid-eighteenth century was doomed. Radical demagogues from both Britain and Europe challenged the very structure of rural and market-town society, based essentially on enlightened paternalism. With agriculture giving way to manufacture as the major source of the country's wealth, large numbers of working people gathered in the towns and there developed an undercurrent of protest with an increasingly vocal demand for social, economic and political reform. As Jill and Hodge

The now abandoned turnpike bridge at Ponterwyd

wandered home from church along the turnpike in the 1840s they were just as likely to be discussing that strange new movement called Chartism as more homely matters like the prospect of the harvest or the price of wool. Others of the congregation, their thoughts on the eternal round of agricultural drudgery which Monday would bring, might have paused for a while to watch the dusty turnpike curving away from the village towards a distant town. At moments like this, perhaps, they came to see the turnpike as a means of liberation, whose course, if they had the courage to take it, would lead them to all manner of delights and prospects.

Roads as yet untrodden can have this unsettling effect on people. No doubt the same sort of feelings arose in the mind of the medieval Welsh peasant as he contemplated the rocky track leading to the next valley, or to his seventeeth century counterpart as he watched a packhorse train struggle through the mire towards some far-off destination. Few of these people risked the perils of a journey far from home, yet their nineteenth-century descendants had little hesitation about doing so. Demand from the industrial towns of South Wales and the harvest fields of the Midlands tempted thousands of footsore Welshmen and women to trudge down the turnpikes in the hope of securing a job. Many returned later in the year to their little farmsteads while others, seduced by prospects of the New World, left Wales by way of one of the southern ports. Migrations of this sort were at their height in the 1830s and 1840s. Within twenty years, however, the turnpike was no longer the principal means of communication and migrant Welshmen had available a new and remarkably efficient railway system which opened up previously undreamt-of vistas.

Less than a hundred and twenty years later, matters have come full circle. Of those few Welsh railway lines remaining many can only be travelled upon with inconvenience and discomfort. Whether they like it or not, most country people in Wales are now forced to rely on their motor cars for both long and short journeys. In the sense that virtually all the major roads in Wales lie on the course of a turnpike (which itself may represent the line of a much older road), we might be said to have entered the second turnpike age. Like readers of *Punch* in 1856 we must, for the foreseeable future, grin and bear, 'the 'ammer, 'ammer, 'ammer along the 'ard 'igh road'.

Since this book was completed, the study of Welsh history and historical geography has

proceeded at a dizzy pace. Indeed, it may not be too far-fetched to suggest that the past twenty years have witnessed a greater rate of knowledge accumulation in this field than the previous fifty years. The old maxim 'for Wales, see England' has itself been finally consigned to the dustbin of history as historians from both sides of Offa's Dyke have repeatedly emphasized the differences between the neighbouring countries in terms of their social, cultural, economic and, of course, linguistic development. The scope and depth of the outpouring of learned publications in both book form and in the periodical literature is a testament to the assiduousness of scholars and the preparedness of publishers to take on manuscripts which, at first sight at least, are hardly likely to reach best-seller status. Alongside the more 'general' historical and historical geography texts have appeared studies of urban and rural social and economic history, industrial and agricultural history, social anthropology, the history of vernacular architecture and of tools and trades and a variety of distinguished works concerned with the development of the Welsh language. Meanwhile, archaeology, aided by developments in the physical and biological sciences, has progressed to such a degree that much of the prehistory of Wales is currently being rewritten.

My book was originally compiled for the 'general' reader in the hope that he or she would find it of some help in enjoying the Welsh countryside. In the years that have elapsed since publication of the first edition numerous correspondents have suggested that any future edition contain some general references to the history of Wales as a whole. Accordingly, besides fleshing out the original bibliography to include recently published books and articles specific to each chapter, I submit a brief list of more general texts. Scholars will doubtless quibble about my selection but will concurrently agree that choosing a dozen or so works from a corpus of such distinction is no mean task.

Most of these books are to be found in any decent local library or, of course, the National Library of Wales, where the bulk of the manuscript and cartographic material used in the preparation of *Roads and Trackways of Wales* is located. Local historians and other readers wishing to pursue the subject in further detail will also find a wealth of material among the files and archives of the Royal Commission on the Ancient and Historical Monuments of Wales in Aberystwyth.

General Texts

Briggs, C.S. (ed), *Welsh Industrial Heritage: a review*, Council for British Archaeology, 1992.

Burnham, B., and Burnham H. 'Recent Survey on the Fort and ruins at Pumsaint', *Carmarthenshire Antiquary*, 22, 1986.

Davies, J., *A History of Wales*, London, 1993.

Davies, J., *The Making of Wales*, John Sutton, 1996.

Davies, J. L., 'Coinage and Settlement in Roman Wales and the Marches: some observations', Archaeologia Cambrensis, 122, 1983.

Davies, J. L., 'Excavations at Trawscoed Roman Fort, Dyfed', *Bulletin of the Board of Celtic Studies*, 31, 1984.

Davies, J. L., 'Excavations at Pen Llwyn Roman Fort, Capel Bangor, Dyfed', *Bulletin of the Board of Celtic Studies*, 33, 1986.

Davies, R. R., *The Age of Conquest: Wales 1063 — 1415*, Oxford, 1987.

James, H. and James, T., 'Aerial Survey and the Roman Road from Carmarthen to Llandovery'. *Carmrthenshire Antiquary*, 20, 1984.

Howell, D. W., *The Rural Poor in Eighteenth Century Wales*, Cardiff, 2000.

Jenkins, G. H., *The Foundations of Modern Wales, 1642 — 1780*, Oxford, 1987.
Jenkins, J. G., *Life and Traditions in Rural Wales*, London, 1976.
Moore-Colyer, R. J., *Wales* in E. J. T. Collins (ed.), *The Agrarian History of England and Wales. VII. 1830-1914*, Cambridge, 2000.
Morgan, K. 0., *Rebirth of a Nation: Wales 1880-1980*, Oxford, 1981.
Rees, D., 'The Northern Approaches to Carmarthenshire', *Carmarthenshire Antiquary*, 33, 1997.
Waddelove, E., 'The Roman Road between *Varis* and *Canovium*', *Archaeologia Cambrensis*, 132, 1989.

Chapter 1

Alcock, L., 'The defenses and gates of Castell Collen Auxiliary Fort', *Archaeologia Cambrensis*, 1964.
Anon, 'Roman Britain in 1965', *Journal of Roman Studies* 156, 1966.
Arber-Cooke, A. T., *Pages from the History of Llandovery*, Llandovery, 1975.
Boon, G. C. and Brewer, R. J. 'Two Central Gaullish Bottles from Pennal, Merioneth and early Roman Movement in Cardigan Bay,' *Bulletin of the Board of Celtic Studies*, 29, 1981.
Codrington, T., *Roman Roads in Britain*, 2nd edn. London, 1905.
Davies, J. L., *The Roman Period, Ceredigion County History* (Vol I), Cardiff, 1984.
Davies, J. L., 'A Roman Fortlet at Erglodd, Talybont, Dyfed,' *Bulletin of the Board of Celtic Studies* 28, 1980.
Davies, R.W., 'Roman Wales and Roman Military Practice Camps', *Archaeologia Cambrensis*, 117, 1968.
Dilke, O. A. W., *The Roman Land Surveyors, An Introduction to the Agrimensores*, Newton Abbot, 1971.
Evans, J., 'Derwenlas', *Montgomeryshire Collections*, 51, 1949.
Fenton, R., *Tours in Wales, 1804-13*, J. Fisher (ed), London, 1917.
Houlder, C. H., *Wales, an Archaeological Guide*, London, 1974.
Hughes, S., 'The Mines of Talybont; AD70-1800', *Industrial Archaeology*, 16 (3), 1981.
Jones, G. D. B., 'The Roman Camps at Y Pigwn', *Bulletin of the Board of Celtic Studies*, 23, 1970.
Jones, G. D. B., 'Fieldwork and Aerial Photography in Carmarthenshire', *Carmarthenshire Antiquary*, 7, 1971.
Jones, G.D.B., 'The Towy Valley Roman Road', *Carmarthenshire Antiquary*, 8, 1972.
Jones, G. D. B. and Thomson, R. W., 'Caerau; A Roman Site in North Breconshire', *Bulletin of the Board of Celtic Studies*, 17, 1958.
Lewin, J., Hughes, D. and Blacknell, C., 'Incidence of River Erosion', *Transactions of the Institute of British Geographers*, 9 (3), 1977
Littler, J., in Barnes, T. and Yates, N. (eds), *Carmarthenshire Studies*, Carmarthen, 1974.
Livens, R.G., 'The Roman Army in Wales' AD120-220', *Welsh History Review*, 7, 1974.
Liversidge, J., *Britain in the Roman Empire*, London, 1973.
Lloyd, J.E., *A History of Carmarthenshire*, Cardiff, 1935.
Lloyd, J.E., *The Story of Ceredigion*, London, 1937.
Lodwick, M. and E., *The Story of Carmarthen*, Carmarthen, 1972.
Malkin, B., *The Scenery, Antiquities and Biography of South Wales*, London, 1804.
Margary, I.D., *Roman Roads in Britain*, London, 1957.
Nash-Williams, V. E., 'The Roman Goldmines at Dolaucothi', *Bulletin of the Board of Celtic Studies*, 14,1950-2.
Nash-Williams, V. E., *The Roman Frontier in Wales*, Cardiff, 1954 and 1969 eds.
O'Dwyer, S., *The Roman Roads of Cardiganshire and Radnorshire*, Newtown, 1936.
O'Dwyer, S., *The Roman Roads of Brecknock and Glamorgan*, Newtown, 1937.
Richmond, I. A., 'Roman Britain in 1957', *Journal of Roman Studies*, 48, 1958.
Richmond, I. A., *Roman Britain*, Penguin Books, 1963.
St. Joseph, J. K, 'Air Reconnaissance in Roman Britain', 1973-6, *Journal of Roman Studies*, 1977.
St. Joseph, J.K 'Air Reconnaissance in Britain, 1955-7', *Journal of Roman Studies*, 48, 1958.
Taylor, C., *Roads and Tracks in Britain*, London, 1979.
Wilson, R., *A guide to the Roman Remains in Britain*, London, 1975.

Chapter 2

Bromwich, R., *Dafydd ap Gwilym: Poems*, Gomer Press, 1982.
Cunliffe, B., *Iron Age Communities in Britain*, London, 1974.
Davies, D., *Brecknock Historian*, Aberystwth, 1977.

Davies, E., *A Gazetteer of Welsh Place-Names*, Cardiff, 1975.

Davies, W., *Wales in the Early Middle Ages*, Leicester, 1982.

Finberg, H.P.R. (ed), *The Agrarian History of England and Wales, AD., 43-1042*, Cambridge, 1972.

Fraser, M., *West of Offa's Dyke*, London, 1958.

Hawkes, J., *A Guide to Prehistoric and Roman Monuments in England and Wales*, Sphere Books, 1973.

Hindle, B., 'The Road Network of Medieval England and Wales', *Journal of Historical Geography*, 2,1975.

Jones, J. E. J., 'Fairs in Cardiganshire', *Cardiganshire Antiquarian Society Transactions*, VII, 1930.

Jones, P., *Welsh Border Country*, London, 1938.

Leland, J., *Itinerary in Wales*, L. T. Smith (ed), London, 1906.

Lewis, W. J., *Leadmining in Wales*, Cardiff, 1967.

Linnard, W., *Welsh Woods and Forests, History and Utilization*, Cardiff, 1982.

Mercer, R. (ed.), *Farming Practice in British Prehistory*, Edinburgh, 1982.

National Library of Wales, *The Crosswood Deeds*, Aberystwth, 1927.

Owen, A., *Ancient Laws and Institutes of Wales*, London, 1841.

Perkins, A., 'Some Maps of Wales and in particular of the counties of Pembrokeshire, Cardiganshire and Carmarthenshire,' *Carmarthenshire Antiquary* 5,1964.

Pierce, T. Jones, 'Strata Florida Abbey', *Ceredigion*,1,1950.

Powell, S.M., 'Pilgrim Routes to Strata Florida', *Cardiganshire Antiquarian Society Transactions*, 8,1931.

Stenton, F.M., 'The Road System of Medieval England', *Economic History Review*, 7,1936.

Thorpe, L (ed), *Gerald of Wales; the Journey through Wales*, Penguin Books, 1978.

Tomos, D., *Michael Faraday in Wales*, London, 1980.

Turner, E. Horsfall, *Walks and Wanderings in County Cardigan*, 1901.

Chapter 3

Dineley, T., *An account of the Progress of His Grace, Henry, first Duke of Beaufort through Wales in 1684*, C. Baker (ed), London, 1864.

Howse, W., *Radnorshire*, Hereford, 1949.

Kilvert, F., *Diaries*, William Plomer (ed), London.

Kissack, K., *The River Wye*, Lavenham, 1978.

Lawteree, B., 'Llaithddn, Davids well and New Well', Radnorshire Society Transactions, LXXII, 1992.

Lewis, M. G., 'The Printed Maps of Breconshire, 1578-1900,' *Brycheiniog*, 16, 1972.

Lewis, M. G., 'The Printed Maps of Cardiganshire, 1578-1900', *Ceredigion*, 2, 1955.

Symonds, R., *Diary of the Marches of the Royal Army during the great Civil War*, C.E. Long (ed), Camden Society, 1859.

Taylor J., *A short Relation of a long journey... encompassing the Principality of Wales*, London, 1653.

Toynbee, M. R., 'A Royal journey through Breconshire and Radnorshire in 1645', *Radnorshire Society Transactions*, XX, 1950.

Williams, D., *A History of Modern Wales*, London, 1969.

Chapter 4

For reference to the primary and secondary sources used in this chapter and a full bibliography of the droving trade see: Moore-Colyer, R. J., *The Welsh Cattle Drovers*, Cardiff, 1976. Although many of the roads to which they refer were not connected with the droving trade, Godwin, F. and Toulson, S., *The Drovers Roads of Wales*, London, 1977, is a useful work especially for walkers. Bonser, K. J., *The Drovers*, London 1970, has a chapter on drove roads from the Welsh border into England.

Since the appearance of these volumes several works dealing *inter alia* with drovers have been published in the Welsh periodical literature. These include:

Barnes, T., 'Derry Ormond; some new evidence', *National Library of Wales Journal*,

Moore-Colyer, R.J., 'Further references to the Welsh cattle trade', *National Library of Wales Journal, 25, 1987-8*.

Richards, E., 'Yng Nghwmni'r Porthmyn', *Anglesey Antiquarian Society and Field Club Transactions, 1996*.

Thomas, S P., 'Twelve miles a day: some thoughts on the drovers', *Radnorshire Society Transaction, LIV, 1984*.

Watson, R., 'Droving and the Farm Economy in 18th Century Wales: some documents from the Allt-y-Cadno papers', *Carmarthenshire Antiquary XVII. 1981*

Chapter 5

Atikin, A., *Journal of a Tour through North Wales*, London, 1797.

Archer, M.S., *The Welsh Post Towns*, Phillimore, 1970.

Archer, M.S., 'The Postal History of Wales with particular reference to Merioneth', *Journal of the Merionethshire Historical and Records Society*, 6, 1971.

Baker, J., *A Picturesque guide through Wales and the Marches*, London, 1795.

Bingley, W., *A Tour round North Wales in 1798*, London, 1800.

Borrow, G., *Wild Wales*, 1963 edn.

Bradley, A.G., *Highways and Byways in North Wales*, London, 1898.

Bright, G.A., 'Tour in Central Wales in 1805', *Radnorshire Society Transactions*, xxvii, 1958.

Byng, J., *The Torrington Diaries*, C. Bruyn Andrews (ed), London, 1936.

Cary, J., *Traveller's Companion*, London, 1806.

Moore-Colyer, R.J., 'The Hafod Estate under Thomas Johnes and the Fourth Duke of Newcastle', *Welsh History Review*, 8, 1978.

Moore-Colyer, R.J., *A Land of Pure Delight: selections from correspondence of Thomas Johnes of Hafod, 1748-1816*, Gomer Press, 1992.

Davies, H.R., 'The Conway and Menai Ferries', *Bulletin of the Board of Celtic Studies*, 8, 1948.

Davies, W., *General View of the Agriculture of North Wales*, London, 1810.

Dodd, A.H., 'The Roads of North Wales, 1750-1850', *Archaeologia Cambrensis*, 5, 1925.

Evans, J., *A Tour through part of North Wales in 1798*, London, 1800.

Fenton, R., *Tours in Wales, 1804-13*, J. Fisher (ed), London, 1917.

Hughes, M., 'Thomas Telford in North Wales, 1815-1830', in D Moore (ed), *Wales in the Eighteenth Century*, Swansea, 1976.

Hughes, D., and Williams, D., *Holyhead, the Story of a Port*, Denbigh, 1967.

Howell, A., 'Roads and Canals of Montgomeryshire', *Montgomeryshire Collections*, 9, 1876

Howse, W., 'The Turnpike System', *Radnorshire Society Transactions,* xxii. 1952.

Hyde-Hall, E., *A Description of Caernarvonshire*, E. Gwynne-Jones (ed), Caernarvon, 1952.

Jenkins, J.G., *The Welsh Woollen Industry*, Cardiff, 1968.

Jones, E., Inglis, *Peacocks in Paradise*, London, 1950.

Jones, R., 'The Post Roads in Anglesey and Caernarvonshire', *Postal History International*, 2. 1973.

Lipscombe, R., *Journey into South Wales*, London, 1802.

Pennant, T., Tours in Wales (3 vols), London, 1810.

Pritchard, R., 'The Capel Curig Turnpike Trust', *Caernarvonshire Historical Society Transactions*, 1958.

Pritchard, R., 'The History of the Post Road in Anglesey', *Anglesey Antiquarian Society and Field Club Transactions*, 1954.

Pritchard, R., 'The Beaumaris-Menai Bridge Turnpike Trust', *Anglesey Antiquarian Society and Field Club Transactions*, 1959.

Pritchard, R., 'Denbighshire Road and Turnpike Trusts'. *Transactions of the Denbighshire Historical Society*, 12, 1963.

Roscoe, T., *Wanderings and Excursions in North Wales*, London, 1853.

Senior, M., *The Crossing of the Conway*, Llanrwst, 1991.

Smith, P., *Houses of the Welsh Countryside*, HMSO, 1975.

Sylvester, D., *A History of Gwynedd*, Phillimore, 1963.

Tomas, D., *Micheal Faraday in Wales*, London, 1980.

Warner, R., *A Second Walk through Wales*, London, 1800.

Williams, D., *The Rebecca Riots*, Cardiff, 1971.

Williams, R., *The History of Llanbrynmair*, 1889.

GLOSSARY OF WELSH WORDS AND TERMS

This brief glossary of some of the more common terms frequently appearing as elements in place-names in rural Wales may be of help to English readers of this book, while those interested in more detail will find Elwyn Davies's *A Gazetteer of Welsh Place-names*, Cardiff, 1975, and Dewi Davies, *Welsh Place-names and their meanings*, Aberystwyth (nd) particularly informative. The former provides an outline of the principles of Welsh pronounciation.

aber: mouth of (a river or stream)
afon: river
allt: hillside or wood
bach: small
banc: mound, bank or hillock
bedd: grave
berth: hedge
blaen: source of river; valley head
bont: bridge
brain: crows
bron: hillside
bryn: hill
buarth: farmyard, enclosure
bwthyn: cottage
cae: field
calch: lime
capel: chapel
carn: cairn; stone-pile
carreg: rock
castell: castle
cefn: ridge
cerrig: stones (as of walls)
craig: rock
cribyn: crest
croes: cross (roads)
crug: mound, cairn, stone-pile
cwm: valley
cwrt: mansion, court
dafad: sheep
dan: under, below
derw: oak
dôl: meadow
du: black
dwr: water
eglwys: church
eithin: gorse
erw: acre
esgair: mountain ridge
fan: peak
felin: mill
ffald: pound; enclosure
ffordd: road
ffos: ditch, brook
ffridd: hill pasture
ffynnon: spring, well
foel: bare hill
fron: hillside
gaer: camp; fort
garth: enclosure
garreg: rock

glan: riverbank
gors: marsh; bog
gwaun: meadow
Gwyddel: Irish
gwyn: white
hafod: summer dwelling
hendre: winter dwelling
heol: road
hir: long
lan: climb; ascent
llan: enclosure; church
llawr: low ground
Lloegr: England
lluest: upland farm
llwyn: grove
llys: mansion
maen: rock
maes: field
mawn: peat
mawr: big
mynydd: mountain
nant: stream
neuadd: mansion, hall
newydd: new
pandy: fulling mill
pant: valley; hollow
parc: park
pentre: village
plas: mansion
pont: bridge
pwll: pond; pool
rhiw: slope; hillside
rhos: moorland
rhyd: ford; stream; brook
saeson, saesneg: English
sarn: paved way; causeway
tal: end
tomen: mound
tre: town
ty: house
tyn, tyddyn: cottage, small house
van: peak
vron: hillside
waun: meadow, moor
y: the
ychen: oxen
ynys: island, water meadow
ysgubor: barn
ystrad: valley; wide vale

INDEX

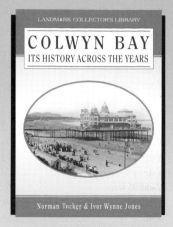
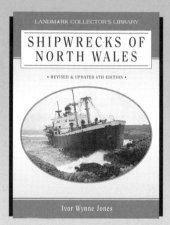
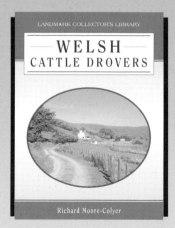
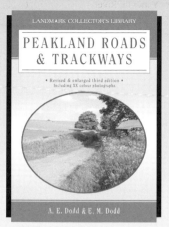
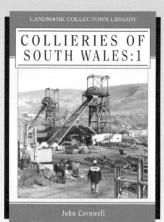
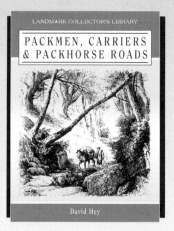